You might not remem
but you'll always re
made you feel.

Poets on Teaching

A SOURCEBOOK

edited by

Joshua Marie Wilkinson

University of Iowa Press IOWA CITY

University of Iowa Press, Iowa City 52242
Copyright © 2010 by the University of Iowa Press
www.uiowapress.org
Printed in the United States of America

Design by Richard Hendel

The University of Iowa Press is a member of Green Press
Initiative and is committed to preserving natural resources.

Printed on acid-free paper

Library of Congress Cataloging-in-Publication Data
Poets on teaching: a sourcebook / edited by Joshua Marie Wilkinson.
p.   cm.
Includes bibliographical references.
ISBN-13: 978-1-58729-904-9 (pbk.)
ISBN-10: 1-58729-904-6 (pbk.)
1. Poetry—Study and teaching.   2. Poetry—Authorship.
I. Wilkinson, Joshua Marie, 1977–
PN1101.P578 2010
808.1′07—dc22   2010002366

For

J. W. Marshall and

Christine Deavel,

in whose bookstore

I found a kind of

classroom

Contents

TALKS / DIRECTIVES

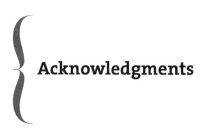 **Acknowledgments**

Linh Dinh's essay "What I Usually Say to My Students" first appeared on the Poetry Foundation's Harriet Blog.

Kent Johnson's essay "Thirty-three Rules of Poetry for Poets Twenty-three and Under" first appeared in *Almost Island*.

Ada Limón's essay "Mystery and Birds: Five Ways to Practice Poetry" first appeared on the Poetry Foundation's Harriet Blog.

Michael Theune's essay "Trust the Turn: Focusing the Revision Process in Poetry" was previously published in *The Best of the AWP Pedagogy Papers 2009*.

Teachers are the majority
by far of those who bring
the young to poetry.
—Robert Creeley

Introduction

Suffice it to say, assorted critiques of poetry's presence in academia abound. I need not rehearse them here. To take a poetry course (in literature or creative writing), I think, is only an indication that it is a subject worthy of one's attention and time, like philosophy, microbiology, or the history of, say, Italian cinema. Of course, you needn't go to school to become a poet or even to learn about poetry, though studying it with a dedicated teacher might allow for discoveries in reading and practice more difficult to come by on one's own at the library.

Tenney Nathanson, whose class I took as a graduate student at the University of Arizona, was one of the most memorable teachers of poetry I've had. Tenney arrived with a load of books—usually an extra duffel bag full of secondary texts, like Hugh Kenner's works and beat up anthologies he'd apparently had for decades—and then he would talk us through a close reading of a single Emily Dickinson poem for two hours or more. (I remember one night dedicated entirely to "She sweeps with many-colored Brooms.") He didn't touch the other books he lugged to class. They just sat there on the desk. When I told my friends what the class was like, they'd invariably say, "One poem for the whole class? Didn't he at least give you a break?!" He would. And after about ten minutes, we'd sit back down in our semicircle only to re-enter the same Dickinson poem, and we'd pick up our reading at the third or fourth stanza until we finished it or ran out of time, usually the latter.

I'm exaggerating here, but only slightly. I don't remember a class where we'd get through more than two or three poems. Tenney's passionate concentration, his visceral allegiance to the possible specific meanings a poem might accommodate—coupled with his stories about reading the *Cantos* on the subway in New York and sitting in on Kenneth Koch's undergrad courses at Columbia—all haunted the landscape of poetry for me. When you tendered a suggestion about a possible reading of a word or a line that seemed useful or new to the discussion, Tenney would sort of nod and shake and say, "yeah yeah yeah" very quietly, over and over—while you were talking—in rising excitement, signaling not that you'd gotten the answer right, but that you were actively altering, even deepening, the world that the poem was opening up.

As an MFA student in Tucson, I was reading and writing poems, working as an editor, a teaching assistant, and an archivist of a special poetry collection (while going to readings and talks, preparing for classes and writing essays)—and all these activities got tangled into a single practice that seemed to border on nothing less than embodiment. This energy and the classes I was teaching as a grad student led me to trust that my chosen vocations of teacher and poet weren't the default resignation of a hapless humanities major. Teaching, too, was bound up in the work of becoming a poet, as the classroom itself became a proving ground.

Some years prior to Tucson, having just completed my AA from a local community college in Seattle, I found myself in a poetry writing course taught by Bruce Beasley. Bruce was provocative enough to teach Susan Howe's *The Nonconformist Memorial* alongside Billy Collins's *Picnic, Lightning*. Whatever you think of either book, the discord on the syllabus was palpable. The class discussion—featuring exclamations of indignation, awe, humor, annoyance, and elation—was electric. I remember Bruce playing us a recording of Howe reading from her book, whispering the lines that were printed upside down, and I became enthralled by what a poem could be and do. Suddenly, I no longer cared that I didn't know what the poem was *about*. The experience of the poem's language and its arrangement glowed otherwise. Bruce knew to trust that the class's agitation and exuberance was, in part, a measure of how the poetry was beginning to change our ideas of what language might be made to do.

I find that the common assertion that poetry has no significant audience is merely the uncritical sentiment of its sad detractors, eager to persuade us that what they don't care to understand doesn't actually exist. In my teaching and poetics, I am sustained by two remarks on poetry's so-called difficulty and supposed inaccessibility. The first is when John Yau notes, "Saying that poetry is inaccessible is just a comment on your own laziness." The second is from Susan Howe herself:

> Why should things please a large audience? And isn't claiming that the work is too intellectually demanding also saying a majority of people are stupid? Different poets will always have different audiences. Some poets appeal to younger people, some to thousands, one or two to millions, some to older people, etc. If you have four readers who you truly

touch and maybe even influence, well then that's fine. Poetry is a calling. You are called to write and you follow.

Teaching, too, is a calling. No doubt, many of us have had teachers who would've rather been elsewhere, but the more I talk to poets the more I hear about how much they thrive in the work of teaching and how it feeds into their own poetics, their own thinking, and, often enough, into their own poetry. In my own courses, I've drawn for years on various anthologies, poetics collections, activities from my own past teachers and classes, cribbed syllabi, comments on my teaching evaluations, students' suggestions, and overheard stories. My own haphazard, ever-changing methodology was what led me, finally, to want to create a new resource for teachers of poetry.

I didn't have an exact picture of what this book would look like before I began to accumulate the essays that now comprise it. In fact, I was conducting an interview for the *Denver Quarterly* with poet Tyrone Williams when I was compelled by the following exchange, which sparked this project. In my initial letter of invitation to over two hundred poets, I included the following excerpt of the interview:

> JMW: What's your response to folks who say that experimental poetry
> . . . doesn't relate to "the average reader," that it's too caught up in
> self-referentiality to be meaningful to the uninitiated?
> TW: First, there is no "average reader"; even less probable is the
> "average reader" of poetry. Since I just finished teaching some
> experimental poets the subject/issue is very much on my mind.
> . . . What's really behind those kinds of statements is not anti-
> experimental poetry or even anti-poetry per se but a residual anti-
> intellectualism in general which, contrary to popular opinion, is
> not an after-effect of the rise of television, cinema, popular music,
> etc.
>   As for my students, the process of acculturation—and it is
> that—depends on their suspension of disbelief. I tell them the
> bad news first: learning to read poetry—any kind of poetry—is
> like learning to spell: there are no shortcuts. It is very much akin
> to learning to swim; you have to learn to trust your body in the
> water, so to speak. The first thing most people want to do—given
> the way we are trained in our educational system—is to figure out
> a poem's "meaning." I tell them to look for patterns, for forms, for
> the internal logic of the poem. Those old standbys—alliteration,

assonance, rhythm, etc.—come in handy. Pedagogically, I'm trying to do a kind of regression, to get them to shed years of reading habits, to return to a kind of play and wonder, not in order to romanticize poetry but in order to re-open those alternative ways of engaging language closed off by public and/or private education.

In my letter, I followed this excerpt from the interview by asking for strategies and techniques in the classroom, methods or exercises that have worked best. Basically, I wanted a new set of approaches to teaching poetry—strategies for reading it and new tricks for writing it—from a broad swath of teaching poets. What I received from the more than one hundred poets who contributed was broader than I could have planned or imagined.

The essays included here are arranged in four rather broad sections, but hopefully this division of the contents aids in the book's usefulness. The first section, entitled "Reflections / Poetics," encompasses the most expansive approaches to teaching poetry, where poets reflect variously on what teachers can bring about and cultivate in their classrooms. In Dan Beachy-Quick's words, "contradictions abound, and the teacher is devoted to them." On "wildness" in the poetry course, Sarah Gridley writes: "I feel the same is true in *teaching* poetry: the best class is one that is weirded out—punctured—made eccentric—by the creeping, crawling, flashing, or thundering in of something that is *not* in the classroom."

"Exercises / Praxis," the book's second section, is comprised of hands-on approaches to reading and, especially, writing poems. From Jen Hofer's two-dozen English-to-English translation techniques to Laynie Browne's sonnet experiments, this section collects new ideas for generating poems. In an exercise drawing on Francis Ponge, Rae Armantrout asks: "What happens when markedly different kinds of subjects/tones/discourses come into contact? Sparks may fly."

The third section, "New Approaches to Poetry Courses and Methodology," features essays on rethinking specific courses, offering new ideas for course design and pedagogy: from Arielle Greenberg's "The Contract Model of Workshop" to Hoa Nguyen's groundwork for backyard community workshops. Jennifer Moxley's "Poundian Poetic Ambition on the Semester System" (linking students with potentially transformative poets) is here beside Lisa Jarnot's alternate curriculum for three years of study in poetry under the auspices of abolishing the traditional MFA program.

"Talks / Directives," the fourth and final section, is a series of more informal and conversational discussions geared toward becoming a stronger reader, writer, teacher, and student of poetry. A wide range of guidance is here, from Ada Limón's suggestion to "cultivate silence" to Linh Dinh's exhortation to "Be as crazy and as perverse as possible, be inspired to the point of madness, but don't be glib." Indeed, for Terrance Hayes, "The pursuit of something that cannot be caught or mastered can be a source of deep despair and frustration. But doesn't it keep you dancing on your toes? doesn't it keep you open and surprised?"

Determined to mitigate the lack of resources for more wide-ranging approaches to teaching poetry, I worked to gather these essays for poets, critics, and scholars who teach, and for students themselves wishing to learn about the disparate ways poets think about how a poem comes alive, from within—and beyond—a classroom. My hope is that this book provides a new assemblage of ideas, exercises, methods, and questions to expand one's approaches to teaching poetry.

This project owes a debt to my poetry teachers: Tom Williams at Roosevelt High School in Seattle; Carol Hamilton at North Seattle Community College; Bruce Beasley, Pam Hardman, James Bertolino, and Nicholas Margaritis at Western Washington University; Colleen McElroy and Mark Doty in Prague; Yusef Komunyakaa, W. D. Snodgrass, Robert Phillips, and Marie Howe in San Miguel de Allende; Carolyn Forché in Key West; Jane Miller, Jon Anderson, Allison Hawthorne Deming, Tenney Nathanson, Eric Hayot, Boyer Rickel, and Charlie Bertsch at the University of Arizona; and Bin Ramke, Eleni Sikelianos, Selah Saterstrom, Eleanor McNees, and Clark Davis at the University of Denver. This book would not have been realized without its forbears: Joan Retallack and Juliana Spahr's *Poetry and Pedagogy*, Robin Behn and Chase Twitchell's *The Practice of Poetry*, and Kenneth Koch's books on teaching poetry. I thank my students past and present for their continued insights and curiosity, and I'm indebted to my colleagues in the English Department at Loyola University Chicago who supported the idea of this project from the beginning by offering valuable suggestions, especially Joyce Wexler, David Michael Kaplan, Paul Jay, Jeffrey Glover, and Victoria Anderson. I am grateful to all the contributors for their essays, their enthusiasm and vigilance, and their belief in the value of this book. I thank Joseph Parsons, Holly Carver, Charlotte Wright, and Allison Thomas Means at the University of Iowa Press along with the rest of the Press's excellent staff, with whom I have had the unlikely opportunity of being able to work on a number of projects. I was offered helpful suggestions by anonymous outside readers, and for their time and energies I remain grateful. I am indebted in these pages and beyond to Lily Brown, Noah Eli Gordon, David Rubin, and Solan Jensen for their dedication, critique, and support—without which, nothing would follow.

Reflections / Poetics

March Hares and Wild Trout Against the Domestication of Poetry

SARAH GRIDLEY

Teaching, the eccentric art.
Teaching the eccentric art.

Poet. Teacher. Do I contradict myself?

I contradict myself. I tend practical skills and reckless fancies. I know and have no clue. I am full of worry and surety, shy and open to encounter. I am put together and pixilated. I orbit and am orbited. My trees clap their hands and weep.

Here we are in our partialities. Embodied minds, disputed souls, wobbly selves. Where is a body of knowledge between us. A circumference. A flower. An abundant radius.

We have felt that effortful form of facing each other, singing to and with each other.

Without the world (at large) for their convergence, our senses should be senseless.

Thus the mind is made up. Like the expression, "a mountain pass."

Dylan Thomas said: "The best craftsmanship always leaves holes or gaps . . . so that something that is *not* in the poem can creep, crawl, flash, or thunder in" (190).

I feel the same is true in *teaching* poetry: the best class is one that is weirded out—punctured—made eccentric—by the creeping, crawling, flashing, or thundering in of something that is *not* in the classroom.

QueeQueg was a native of Kokovoko, an island far away to the West and South. It is not down in any map; true places never are (Melville 70).

■

One day I take a pragmatist's approach to teaching poetry. I call myself neither materialist nor idealist. I call myself "a meliorist." I tie my shoes. I go to work. I open the windows to the rain and bells.

One day I take a Tarot card approach to teaching poetry. I am the Fool at Zero. I tie my worldly belongings to the end of a staff, I put my

{3

blindfold on, I call my barking dog to heel, I step off from a cliff. To my students I say: Do as I do, not as I say.

One day I take a Taoist approach to teaching poetry. I stay at home. I read A. R. Ammons to my overweight cat: "Poetry is a verbal means to a non-verbal source. It is a motion to no-motion, the still point of contemplation and deep realization. Its knowledges are all negative and, therefore, more positive than any knowledge. Nothing that can be said about it in words is worth saying" (8).

Hey Educator, Hey Agent of Clarity, where are you leading them?

From a dictionary of anecdotes: When Chester Harding painted Daniel Boone's portrait, the painter asked the frontiersman, who was then in his eighties, if he had ever been lost. Boone replied, "No I can't say I was ever lost, but I was bewildered once for three days." (Faragher 65).

In a chapter of *Exuberance* devoted to the topic of play, Kay Redfield Jamison notes that trout raised in hatcheries are known to have smaller brains than those born in the wild. She also quotes Darwin, who found that the brains of domestic rabbits were "considerably reduced in bulk in comparison with those of the wild rabbit or hare" (59).

Poet. Teacher. What species is it? Does it *educate*? Or point the ways toward wilderness?

When the students are themselves poets, are they not pointing me in ways toward wilderness, too?

In an undergraduate intermediate poetry workshop, Amanda writes,

I know the constant of fish
teeming in tea-spoons.

In the same workshop, Jeremy writes,

a window was recovered
from a two-sided stream.

Ambiguity: "to drive in two ways." Compassion's greatest ally. We can see its creative arcs across literature—most famously in Keats's definition of negative capability, in Coleridge's phrase for the imagination, the "esemplastic power" (Coleridge 161)—in Rilke's urging, "Take your practiced powers and stretch them out / until they span the chasm between two / contradictions . . ." (260–261).

I am thinking of being in two places at once. Of "Tea at the Palaz of Hoon"—of Stevens's reminder that we might always find ourselves, beyond the space of within ourselves, *more truly and more strange* (65).

Ben writes,

I imagine a butterfly
that breathes fire.
I name it Danaus Incendius
and invite it to nest
in my fireplace.

The eccentric finds us places we need not own to know.

From the eccentric we learn the art of dispossession. Of walking away from home, of becoming the hosted guest. As Akhmatova reminds us: *A land not our own / and yet eternally memorable* (85).

Emma writes,

> *beneath the words of the messenger*
> *whose command throws caution to the sea*
> *and feeds luxury to the wind.*

I am thinking of a question from Huston Smith: "We have first to ask how the boundary of the self is to be defined. Not, certainly, by the amount of physical space our bodies occupy, the amount of water we displace when we submerge in the bathtub. It would make more sense if we gauge a man's being by the size of his spirit, that is, the range of reality with which he identifies himself" (28).

Michael writes,

The slippery toothpaste
rubs across my teeth.
The parading beagle,
unseen shower cap on the mind.
Like a waffle ball bouncing
against les reglements.
See, Free, Content.

Be wilder, I say to the workshop.

Be wilder, their poetry says to me.

Against les reglements. By nothing less than free imaginings, let us outdo the laws of averages, of gravity, and of penalty.

Jon writes,

palm scents, palm leaves driven windward,
fiber husks plucking hides
to trill huracan *in the breasts*
of pocket finches—

In the strange economy
of teaching poetry—where giving to and receiving from
are this blessedly mixed up—as opposed to what's certain let us live
for uncertainty, as opposed to lost

let us be bewildered.

WORKS CITED

Akhmatova, Anna. "A land not mine, still." Trans. Richard McKane. *Anna Akhmatova: Selected Poems*. New York: Oxford University Press, 1969. 85.

Ammons, A. R. "A Poem Is a Walk." *Claims for Poetry*. Ed. Donald Hall. Ann Arbor: University of Michigan Press, 1983. 8.

Coleridge, Samuel Taylor. *Biographia Literaria*: or *Biographical Sketches of My Literary Life and Opinions*. Ed. George Watson. New York: Dutton, 1965. 161.

Faragher, John Mack. *Daniel Boone: The Life and Legend of an American Pioneer*. New York: Holt, 1992. 65.

Jamison, Kay Redfield. *Exuberance: The Passion for Life*. New York: Alfred A. Knopf, 2004. 59.

Melville, Herman. *Moby Dick*. New York: Signet Classic, 1961. 70.

Rilke, Rainer Maria. "As once the wingèd energy of delight." Trans. Stephen Mitchell. *The Selected Poetry of Rainer Maria Rilke*. Ed. Stephen Mitchell. New York: Vintage Books, 1982. 260–261.

Smith, Huston. *The Religions of Man*. New York: Harper & Row, 1965. 28.

Stevens, Wallace. "Tea at the Palaz of Hoon." *The Collected Poems of Wallace Stevens*. New York: Vintage Books, 1923. 65.

Thomas, Dylan. "Poetic Manifesto." *The Poet's Work: 29 Poets on the Origins and Practice of Their Art*. Chicago: University of Chicago Press, 1979. 190.

What's Difficult?

SRIKANTH REDDY

The fascination of what's difficult
Has dried the sap out of my veins, and rent
Spontaneous joy and natural content
Out of my heart. There's something ails our colt
That must, as if it had not holy blood
Nor on Olympus leaped from cloud to cloud,
Shiver under the lash, strain, sweat and jolt
As though it dragged road-metal. My curse on plays
That have to be set up in fifty ways,
On the day's war with every knave and dolt,
Theatre business, management of men.
I swear before the dawn comes round again
I'll find the stable and pull out the bolt.

Casting a cold eye on his years of toil laboring to promote the fledgling Abbey Theater in turn-of-the-century Dublin, Yeats confesses that he has squandered his youthful energies on the agonies of showbiz in the opening lines of "The Fascination of What's Difficult": "The fascination of what's difficult / Has dried the sap out of my veins, and rent / Spontaneous joy and natural content / Out of my heart." Tendering his letter of resignation to the theatrical world within the rigorous formal grid of the sonnet, however, Yeats never really renounces his ethos of difficulty entirely. Rather, he turns away from one kind of difficulty—the ordeal of "the day's war with every knave and dolt" at his beloved playhouse—toward the more private and fugitive "secret discipline" of writing lyric poems. There is, in the end, no doing away with difficulty altogether. By a curious economy of hardship, though, one's worldly troubles may be translated, displaced, or sublimated into the arduous contours of literary form.

As a teacher of poetry, I try to encourage my students to cultivate a fascination with what's difficult about this art, from prosody's endless demands to the toil of revision to the psychological challenges of self-disclosure. Though I myself may be an exception to this particular rule, I tell them, poetry isn't for wimps. Of course, the difficulty inherent to poetic expression is what makes this form of writing so marginal in our culture today. Few people have the time, the energy, or the "inner resources" to undertake the labor of slow reading that a poem like Berryman's "Dream Song 14" requires:

> . . . I conclude now I have no
> inner resources, because I am heavy bored.
> Peoples bore me,
> literature bores me, especially great literature . . .

The wages of ease, intimates Berryman's speaker, is *ennui*. At the same time, though, I've often worried about rending both "spontaneous joy" and "natural content" from the work of young writers through my own fascination with what's difficult. Burden these literary colts with too much pedagogical road metal and they lose the sense of improvisatory pleasure and natural self-expression which enliven all good art. A poetry workshop should, ideally, "pull out the bolt" from a student's literary consciousness, instead of constraining the writer with cumbersome technical problems unsuited to her temperament. While it is useful to assign restrictive formal exercises to one's students, it seems to me equally important to instruct them in the other forms of difficulty—emotional difficulty, conceptual difficulty, etcetera—available to us as entrants into the ancient *agon* of lyric writing.

In the end, it's difficult to know what kind of difficulty to embrace as a poet. Anybody can learn to write a passable sonnet, just as anybody can learn how to construct a conceptual poem—given world enough and time. It might, however, be worthwhile for an expert sonneteer to lay aside the difficulties of octave and volta in order to explore the challenges of new theoretical approaches to the lyric. And it might benefit a conceptual poet to momentarily abandon philosophical problems in favor of a more technical prosodic discipline. Oftentimes, the truest difficulty resides where we least expect it. To my mind, the hardest thing about writing poems, then, lies in locating the problem of difficulty itself, for oneself. Or to paraphrase Yeats, you have to find the stable before you can pull out the bolt.

A Note on Hanging and the Uselessness of Verse

ALBERT MOBILIO

In "A Poet's Notebook," French symbolist Paul Valéry claimed that a poem's true worth depended upon its content of "pure poetry," which he defined as the "perfect adaptation in the sphere of perfect uselessness." In the early twentieth century this notion of verse for verse's sake helped subvert dominant utilitarian beliefs about poetry's role and meaning. Poetry, to paraphrase Valéry, isn't a tool for storytelling, teaching social or moral lessons, or achieving self-understanding, but rather a bauble, an objet d'art whose seamless impracticality alone might command the attention of readers. Several decades later, with much contemporary art wired for visual immediacy and commercial viability, no aesthete need argue for poetry's splendid isolation; the genre has become—in mainstream culture—an almost universally accepted exemplar of self-consuming effetism. But Valéry's argument—that true poetry offers "apparent and convincing probability in the production of the improbable"—continues to hold meaning for poets, purposefully so in the classroom, where they attempt to impart some elements of their art and its practice.

One work surely to be counted as a pure poem is Chidiock Tichborne's "Elegy." Written in the Tower of London the night before his execution for plotting to kill Queen Elizabeth I, its three stanzas address the twenty-eight-year-old author's imminent demise with admirable equanimity: "And now I die, and now I was but made. / My glass is full, and now my glass is run, / And now I live, and now my life is done." Tichborne had no prospect of ever enjoying an audience's flattery, the perquisites of a literary career, or even awareness of a single reader. The poem was composed without expectations, written in and for the moment. Its stanzas did not save the poet's life or redeem his soul: the words, rhymes, and images merely embody Tichborne's adaptation in the "sphere of perfect uselessness."

Of course, the specter of being drawn and quartered doesn't animate the poetry workshop. Instead, writing students—all students—are encouraged to be future-minded. The pedagogical supposition undergirding the typical classroom experience is that the acquisition of knowledge or skill will prove necessary or useful. One learns geometry to perhaps, one day, design buildings. Anatomy might predicate a medical career. Studying literature improves verbal facility and might just as well equip bankers and advertising executives as literary scholars. In contrast, learning how to write, especially learning how to write poems, offers the student meager practical skill and knowledge. Of course, one might gain a sensitivity to, say, syntax and rhythm, and such things could be put to use by a future politician or motivational speaker. But those who study poetic craft are best advised to regard the art as its own end. Thoughts of publishing, as well as of a potential readership, should be put aside to focus on creating that "convincing probability," which must convince no one but themselves. If, in every other area of their lives, students are called upon to be responsible members of communities, this one class can permit utter solipsism — the freedom to disengage from expectation and perform that which is useless.

The sociopolitical dimension of this refusal to engage is clear: poetry can be an assertion of autonomy. The potentially compelling aspect of such an assertion (which, admittedly, is commonplace these days) is that it be *needlessly* articulate, *needlessly* artful. The quality of the assertion, its improbable elegance, constitutes the renunciation. Tichborne's defiance in the face of mortality is not to be found in the poem's thematic content. Indeed, the poem argues for the inevitability of fate—"I sought my death and found it in my womb." While there is a certain personal bravado on display—he wrote in truly fraught circumstances—resistance flexes most vigorously in Tichborne's graceful meter and witty, inventive tropes ("My feast of joy is but a dish of pain"). Perhaps in his last hours, the poet howled in fear, denounced his enemies, or called upon God—all serviceable acts; he also spent some of that time counting off syllables for the sake of metrical precision, his sole intent being to delight the ear.

Acquiring the rudiments of verse-making enables students to achieve nothing . . . except that. But if they read, listen, and write and *write*, they might do this useless thing beautifully. For themselves. For the moment. For pure poetry.

WORKS CITED

Harmon, William, ed. *The Top 500 Poems*. New York: Columbia University Press, 1992.

Valéry, Paul. *The Art of Poetry*. New York: Vintage, 1958.

Sidelong and Uncodifiable

ELENI SIKELIANOS

Of late, and perhaps of long, I've been trying more experiential approaches to the hours we spend together in the classroom. What is our goal there? In the thicket of writing programs, I sometimes wonder. What seems important to me, more and more, is establishing a collective, collaborative space in which we can explore some of the edges of our interior conditions (which include the emotional, the intellectual, and the spiritual) as well as engage in documentary (socio-, eco-) experiments, and to test those edges against what previous poets have done. As we all know, there are already too many workshop poems in the world eating up available reality (as Robert Creeley once said of Robert Frost). I want to see what other realities we can explore. At the University of Denver, I have the enviable challenge of working with PhD students who have either read nearly everything or are trying to read nearly everything, so I know they're in the process of figuring out the lineage. What I want to steer them away from is "product"; what I want to steer them toward is an exploration of consciousness (whatever that term may mean). With my undergraduate students, I also want to steer them toward at least a rough grasp of twentieth-century poetry (though I must confess in a particular vein, as outlined in anthologies like the *New American Poets* and the *Norton Anthology of Post-Modern American Poets*), with some indication of writers from other parts of the world, and I want them to know where to go to continue their readings. With either group, our work is to recognize and circumvent received ideas, and to play, at least some of the time, outside our comfort zone. I mean this for myself as a teacher, too.

Looking to my own studies in a writing program, it makes sense that my inclination steers away from packaging the poem. I attended the Jack Kerouac School of Disembodied Poetics at Naropa in the late eighties and early nineties, studying for a week or for a semester with poets like Allen Ginsberg, Anne Waldman, Alice Notley, Bernadette Mayer, Susan Howe, Jerome Rothenberg, and Anselm Hollo (who first introduced me to such life-shifting poets as César Vallejo, Paul Celan, and Aimé Césaire). Other inspiring figures were wandering around, and there was a certain thrill to watching William Burroughs cross the parking lot. There was very little focus on craft and a lot of focus on the poem as an exploratory form, a playground for intellectual, emotional, social, sensorial, and language experience. I learned from Allen Ginsberg a generosity of spirit—he didn't generally assume to be the master-poet, but posed questions and readings with an air of collective inquiry, and seemed to equally delight in revealing his own knowledge and his own ignorance. He could also be a brutal critic of student work; he wasn't always right, but he wasn't afraid to say what he thought.

Transmission was a common word, if an elusive concept. The poet modeled poetry by living it right there in front of you and with you. He or she didn't pretend to be anything else. The poets teaching at Naropa were generally interested in what happened around a poem, how one lived as a poet, in the building of community both among poets and through other forms of social intervention. There was encouragement to teach in prisons and public schools, to found magazines and presses, to open art centers. There was also an emphasis on the performance of the poem, how the voice and body carry the words. My schooling at Naropa didn't teach me to prepare poems for the *American Poetry Review* or to put myself on the market. Instead it directed me into the exploratory space of the poem.

I don't think I realized how marked I'd been by that schooling (which worked well for someone from a long line of social misfits) until I began teaching at DU, and as I've questioned how to teach (and how to write) in the professionalized atmosphere that the rise of the MFA has led to. (I was stunned to overhear a young poet recently calling an older poet I know "an outsider poet," because "she doesn't even teach in a writing program.") Many of us have probably been asked, "How can you teach someone to write poetry?" and obviously, the answer is you can't. Beyond any schooling, there is by necessity a measure of autodidactism on the path; it's the unorthodox mapping of personal electrical fields that makes a poet. In a recent article, French novelist Olivier Rolin calls up the work of Marcel Detienne and Jean-Pierre Vernant on the Greek notion of *mètis*, which in its original meaning indicated both magical cunning and deep thought. Mètis was Athena's mother. Odysseus, you may remember, was *polymetis*—many-wiled. It is an intelligence that is subtle, "sidelong, uncodifiable, unformalizable, not opposed to épistémè, to scientific knowledge, or to *dianoïa*—well-considered thought—but different from them." I am sometimes drunk in the face of trying to impart magical cunning, or ways to leap the gaps between life, imagination, and language in the class-room. I can't teach anyone to *be* a poet, but I can point out some poten-tially interesting trailheads, in terms of reading, in terms of accessing the mind and the world.

To the ends of making an exploratory space in the writing classroom, there are a number of texts and exercises I've found particularly useful.

— "Event" performances, as modeled on the two Events sections in Jerome Rothenberg's ever-rich *Technicians of the Sacred*. After reading those sections, I ask students to come to class prepared to perform an event. One of the most transporting: watching Christina Mengert *think* a series of questions and statements— exquisite to see thought and language move through the muscles of her face. (*Technicians of the Sacred* generally opens the possibility of the poem out beyond our limited time-space coordinates and into the tribal.)

— I recently tried hypnotizing students and asked them to write a correspondence with the dead in that state, taking Alice Notley's *Close to Me & Closer . . . The Language of Heaven* as a starting point. (I learned that young poets like to be hypnotized.)

— After reading Mei-mei Berssenbrugge's work, I've often laid out a series of objects on a table (a glass of milk, an apple, a light bulb, etc.) and then given instructions along these lines:

> *Write the planes and geometries between objects.*
> *Note what happens in time and perception as you move around*
>   *the table.*
> *Locate us in ordinary meaning.*
> *Add a memory and interrogate its phenomenon.*
> *Now write an abstract fable of memory and perception based on*
>   *these notes.*

(In response to this kind of exercise, my undergraduate students usually say, "*What?*" which I take as a good sign.)

— Other, longer-term assignments with which I've had excellent results: documentary projects after Charles Reznikoff and Brenda Coultas, "Land Art" projects after Williams and his one-time pediatric charge Robert Smithson, etc.

Teaching is often a painful experience for me. Like many, I feel my in-terior relationship to language and thought gets externalized in ways that are not always useful to me as a poet, and small forms of self-censorship arise. The occupation of facilitator is a bit like parenting, in which you must always strive to see your protégé and their needs as clearly as possible, but are yourself somewhat invisible to your charge. For those who can step in and out of roles fluidly, this may not pose a problem, but for those of us who can get stuck in identities, this asymmetrical equation may not always be conducive to leaping from facilitator back to poet. I also question my part in the industry. But teaching has also brought great revelations, some quotidian, some more profound. It took a second grader to teach me that the rhythms in Blake's "The Tyger" mimic the tiger's heartbeat and the pounding of the hammer making him. How could I have ever missed that? (I should have read my Northrop Frye!) More recently I learned, from PhD student Logan Burns, a new way to think about that first utterance in "The Red Wheelbarrow": as "the subject everything else gossips around." How beautifully apt.

Creative Unknowing
COLE SWENSEN

A good part of the teaching I've been doing for the past fifteen years has been in poetry workshops, and I've come to revolve those workshops around two principles: one, that a workshop should be a course in applied poetics, and two, that it's a poetics of unknowing that forms its core.

The traditional workshop model, to the degree that there is one, puts the students' texts in the center and develops critical skills and analytical principles off of critiques led either by the professor or by the students themselves. And this can work very well because it assumes that the poem is *right*. Done well, the method doesn't begin with a priori notions of what a poem should be, but begins with what it actually is and works from there to see what it (and, by extension, all poetry) can do.

But this approach can also downplay both the complex history of poetry and its relation to, not so much the other arts, but other ways of thinking. These two come together in poetics, in which language as an act of art can be scrutinized, not in order to prescribe the proper poem, but, on the contrary, to shift the parameters of poetry away from such notions of propriety to increasingly indeterminate characteristics based on its function in the world, and yet to do so in a rigorous way that keeps indeterminacy from becoming a simple dissolve.

In practical terms, my workshops increasingly have a series of theoretical approaches at their center. I begin each class meeting with a short lecture / presentation and then examine how the principles presented are operating or could operate in the poems in front of us. I start with the most general questions of poetics: What are the moving parts of the machine that is language? And what distinguishes the language of art from the language of information?—in Roman Jakobson's words, "What makes a verbal act a work of art?" I start with Jakobson's essays, his six functions of language and his distinction between the axis of selection and the axis of combination. This gives the students a vocabulary with which to break down their own work in an informed, nuanced way. In subsequent classes, we go over metaphor, metonymy, juxtaposition, stress patterns, inscape, and other principles.

Those are all topics that have a wide range of applicability and inform most genres of writing, but the core of the class is a series of principles uniquely central to poetry, all of which focus on the unknown, on the point where knowledge as a function breaks down, and with an emphasis on the ways that this point can further specifically poetic thinking. The principle I start with is ambiguity because it's the most general and flexible of them and underscores the distinction between the language of information, which can tolerate little or no ambiguity, and the language of art, which thrives on it, and from there introduces instability, incompletion, and inaccessibility as three faces of potential.

I follow the talk on ambiguity with what could be considered four specific modes of it, each conditioned by its culture and time: Keats's negative capability, Rimbaud's *dérègelement de tous les sens*, Shklovsky's *ostranenie*, and Lorca's *duende*. Each of these takes the point at which knowledge, including one's own bearings, begins to slip and uses that exact slippage as a vehicle to get to the interstices of language, to occupy, even if for just an instant, a place where language cannot go. But, coming from four different cultural traditions, each approach gets there in an entirely different way: Keats, with his air of calm suspension, as if a kind of radical acceptance could leave us hovering in a zone of distilled space and time; Rimbaud, casting off all the controls that regulate the senses and welcoming an ungovernable onrush of sensory data; Shklovsky, seeing in rigorous attention the possibility of returning to the objects of this world their bottomlessness, their unknowability, the true uncanniness of which our lax attention has robbed them; and Lorca, suggesting that we can tap into a power beyond the individual to participate in the soul of an entire people, or, more precisely, an entire art.

Each of these approaches has its own hidden assumptions: Keats's, that there are uncertainties, mysteries, and doubts to be wallowed in; Rimbaud's, that there's a tumultuous world of impression and sensation always trying to bombard us; Shklovsky, that every little thing has a unique and limitless nature; and Lorca, that there is a soul, both individual and collective. Despite their differences in detail, all these approaches rest on a radical faith in the world, not necessarily the faith that it's safe or good, but simply that it *is*, and that the experience of its *is-ness* is fundamentally different from the knowledge of it. Furthermore, the work of these poets and their writings intimate that language, with its constant production of knowledge, blocks us from experiencing that is-ness, and yet, paradoxi-cally, can be used to get beyond the very blocks it sets up.

On a more mundane level, focusing on knowledge and its limits shifts the class's perspective, taking the attention away from notions such as craft, which, while they have their place, can also be distracting, and in-sisting instead that language be entered as a mode of thinking itself, and of thinking beyond itself, which is the poetic thrust, for it is only when language has gone beyond itself, however slightly, however briefly, that it ceases to be information and has a chance of becoming art.

{ How to Teach
"Difficult" Poetry and
Why It Might Not Be
So Difficult after All

STEPHEN BURT

Any poem is difficult to talk about, to like, and hence to teach if you don't know how it operates, if you don't have the words to describe it, just as any poem is easy to talk about—though not, perhaps, easy to love—if you have the words and the experience to describe what the poem has been doing. What we find difficult, what we find enjoyable, what we find comprehensible (not that we can't enjoy what's not yet comprehensible), flow inevitably from what we already understand, what gives us a purchase on art, what gives us a way in.

The appreciation of any art, the ability to get inside it and see how the work is put together, what it is trying to do, comes in part from our experience of prior, related—maybe distantly related—art, related art with which we feel more comfortable, art we think we in part understand. That's true for artists (see E. H. Gombrich, *Art and Illusion*), it's true for students, and it's true for readers, listeners, and viewers of almost anything: If you know how to like Johnny Cash, you are more likely to know how to like both Bright Eyes and Hank Williams, Sr.; if you already know how to like Seamus Heaney, you are more likely to know how to like William Wordsworth (and the other way around, though readers outside classrooms are more likely to encounter Heaney first); if you already know how to like William Carlos Williams and Emily Dickinson, you are more likely to like Rae Armantrout.

We are also more likely to enjoy any kind of representational art if we are familiar with what it represents, or at least with prior depictions of what it represents (see Gombrich again). If you are teaching Armantrout to people who have never read, or never learned how to like, Williams or Creeley or Dickinson (or Niedecker, but almost no one loves Niedecker without already enjoying Williams or Dickinson), you should consider yourself lucky if those people are familiar with the plastic sameness of our warm-weather suburbs and new-model cities; with left-wing critiques of such sameness; with feminist critiques of the patriarchal family and the ideology of motherhood; with the student movements of late 1960s and the early 1970s, the reject-everything-old, build-something-brand-new ethos within and against which Armantrout's skeptical, terse sensibility formed (see Armantrout's memoir *True*). Once you have figured out what might be represented in a poem—and "what," for Armantrout, can be anything from "patriarchal ideology" to a bit of cactus, a dream about cartoon characters, or a lamppost—you are on your way to seeing how that "what" gets represented, how the verbal and formal choices within the poem (line length, choice among synonyms, order of details, notable omissions, etc.) add, to that "what," a "how" and a "why" and a "who." But you might need some help (from a teacher, for example) in figuring out what to look for, what might be represented, first.

As you might gather, I do teach even "difficult" modernist and contemporary "experimental" poetry as representational works: it seems to me that even the poets most distant from prose paraphrase—Rae Armantrout and Ron Silliman, but also Mebdh McGuckian, and Dylan Thomas—still use words, and that words have meanings, separately and in combination, and that our students should figure out what those meanings are. Sometimes the meanings in combinations of words have little to do with the meanings, and the apparent referents, the words would have singly, or in most prose, and much more to do with perlocutionary acts (Silliman's book-length poem beginning "Not this"), or with jokes about the social or literary contexts the words acquire in groups: "representations" of the perlocutionary acts corresponding to "Go away!" or "Ha, ha!" or "Yuck!" or "I'm taking my marbles and going home," for example, are ways into Flarf (I have not taught a Flarf book yet, though I might teach Katie Degentesh that way someday soon).

What you find difficult depends on what you already find easy; what you find comprehensible or enjoyable depends on what you already know. Randall Jarrell used to say that when he taught in Austria, his students found "The Waste Land" easy and Frost hard because they were used to Eliot's moves, having encountered them in other languages, other art forms (e.g., modern painting), or in daily life: Europe as rubble, the world as disillusioned collage, the poet as Tiresias, helpless latecomer to history. Frost's people, Frost's world, and even Frost's kinds of poetry (American eclogues, dramatic monologues, and neo-pastoral lyrics) were not what the Austrians thought modern poems could be. The most difficult poets for moderately well-prepared undergraduates to appreciate are not contemporary poets of any sort: they are the poets from before 1800 who fit neither modernist, nor Romantic, nor "confessional," nor avant-garde, frame-breaking, shock-the-audience modes. Among all the poets who have exerted a great deal of influence over the course of the English language, the hardest to teach now is almost surely John Dryden.

All poetry is difficult if you don't have a way in, a sense of what's represented how (which allows you to ask why); all poetry can be enjoyable, if not easy, if a teacher can make clear that way. I have seen West Coast poets with impeccable "experimental" pedigrees declare with some pride that it's easier to teach beginners how to read Stein, or Williams, or Armantrout, than to teach the more advanced students schooled, or deformed, by reading (say) Heaney or Frost: the poets who say such things think that they are making a point against older forms of poetry, older modes of education, but really they are just demonstrating that teachers give students (among other things) expectations, and that students, in our culture, pick up few expectations about poetry outside of class.

That means that the analogies most useful in teaching many contemporary poets are not analogies linking one poet to others, one kind of page-based poetry to another kind, but analogies between a kind of poetry, a book of poems, and some other kind of art form—kinds of pop songs, kinds of non-song-based pop music, kinds of prose (love letters, op-eds, satire a la *The Onion*, blogs), kinds of film, or kinds of scenes in films. You shouldn't stop with those analogies, since all good poems use tools specific to poetry, but they can make the best places to start.

{
**Teaching An
Improvisation**
JULIE CARR

From 1988 until 2000 I spent most of my time performing, studying, and teaching dance in New York City. I was dancing under the shadow of the Judson Church era of experimental dance and performance, training in something called "release technique," in a scene where democratically organized collaboration was the dominant ethos, and abstraction, juxtaposition, and improvisation were preferred over narrative, lyricism, and regulation. The dances I watched and participated in, whether improvised or choreographed, were one of my primary ways of experiencing art and others. I understand that much more now than I did then. Now, when I meet a new person or am struggling to understand someone, I often dream of him or her dancing or dream that we are dancing together. And, when I think about my teaching, it is often in terms of dance.

When we created a dance it was generally first a shape, a texture, and a series of timings. Rarely, if ever, did we begin with an "about," or a narrative. Instead: heavy here, heavier there, four people for five minutes, two for two minutes, slow over here, then still (the most still thing is the thing that has just finished moving or is just about to). Whatever it was we had to say in these dances we said by way of the abstractions of time, space, and numbers. Narrative and emotion were the direct results of these things. (If you do not know what I mean, watch any dance by Trisha Brown or Merce Cunningham, or rent the video "Fall After Newton," which features seminal improvisers Nancy Stark Smith and Steve Paxton.)

Once, Jeff Bliss, who had been offstage, shot upstage at full speed and without warning dove headfirst into a rather still line of people. After that, the space was utterly changed; everything that happened before his appearance and everything that happened after would now be in reference to him. That one spontaneous and indecipherable choice organized forty minutes of movement. Such a thing can happen on a page with the surprising introduction of a series of words, a single word, or even a sound.

Teaching poetry writing is, for me, first about teaching this kind of listening: a listening for language's abstractions. I want my students to become more attuned to language's nonsayings. In writing or reading a poem, I want us to focus first on the visual or textural aspects of the words and page, or to focus on sound. (Often these are indistinguishable; sound and shape cannot, in poems, easily be divided.)

One rule of improvisation that I attempt to carry into my teaching: assume the other's perfection. Everything your fellow improvisers do is, by definition, perfect. If you do find yourself critical of your fellow performers' choices, if you perceive them as in error, it is you, and not they, who will end up looking foolish. Instead, you must find a way to meet and support the excellent choices that the others are making.

Similarly, when I am teaching, I assume the poem in front of us is already masterful. It is my job to support its mastery. Sometimes that mastery is hidden. There is some noise in the way or some excess. Sometimes the poem's brilliance lies only in one phrase, the rest being a kind of protection, a kind of padding. As a class we work to reveal that bit of clarity. We listen for it and articulate it, so that it can, in turn, speak itself.

I assign ten to fifteen books a semester. Each one I hope to be challenging, difficult, and astounding—at least to someone. And each book should make evident some aspect of the history that has created our contemporary writing situation. I am not only assigning books as *examples* of what can be done, I am also assigning them as portals into the history of poetry. Just as the dancer who knows the vocabularies of ballet, soft shoe, mime, Cunningham, Paxton, or Brown can reveal that knowledge with a single sweep of the arm, the poet whose memory includes Dickinson, Browning, Hopkins, Akhmatova, Celan, Olson, Beckett, Stevens, Guest (this list is purely improvisatory and cannot be completed) can express these memories in a direct line of description.

People often say that teaching is an honor. I agree with this, and I add that it is also a way of honoring other people. Teaching provides opportunities for a kind of abstract affection, circumscribed by precise rituals, thriving within very particular walls. When I am teaching I do not imagine that I am turning nonwriters into writers. Rather, I am attempting to look through whatever obstructions present themselves in order to discover the expertise of any person in the room. This requires a constant humility: For if I cannot see what the person is doing, or what the poem is doing, then it is not the fault of the writer, but of myself. If I am rushing, or too absorbed by my own preoccupations, I will miss it. And that will be my loss. I will be the one who has, in failing to recognize another's perfection, failed to create something meaningful out of the time available.

Improvisatory dance, like jazz, gives the audience a chance to observe the mind of the performer observing itself in action. It might seem that writing cannot mimic the movement of improvisation. Its stillness on the page freezes that process, presenting only thought after the fact. But writing that is still in question, that is open for transformation, retains this sense of adventure and curiosity. One of the goals of my teaching, then, is to encourage even finished works to somehow hold on to this quality of exploration, this not-yet-arriving. The writing I like best, like the dances I like best, reveal the curious process of the mind watching itself move.

A teacher from high school once told me that if you can't write well, you can't think complexly. I find this to be deeply true and would take it further: If I am not writing, I am not thinking much. I write in order to think. And I teach writing in order to regularly observe the often-spectacular travel of other minds.

The Craft Can Be Taught but Not the Art

TIMOTHY LIU

I grow more and more convinced that while poetic craft can be taught, the writing of poetry cannot. What I can provide as a teacher is something akin to being an eye, a friend, an editor, a cheerleader, a collaborator. What cannot be taught is how to beef up the imagination, let alone have a real vision (in the religious sense). When I was called to be a Mormon missionary, I reported to the MTC (Missionary Training Center) in Provo, Utah, in order to receive an eight-week crash course in not only learning how to speak Cantonese but also in adopting various local social customs pertaining to various dos (bring fruit as a gift when invited to dinner) and don'ts (but never bring four pieces of any fruit because the number four signifies death). And yes, while I was diligent in my studies and curious about the new adventures that it seems I had already been embarking on, such training did not turn me into the missionary I'd become; it only laid the ground. All of us there received whatever training there was to be had, but not all of us succeeded in subsequently bringing souls to Christ. So this is pretty much how I feel about other types of training like the MFA, such as having worked for WITS (Writers in the Schools) in Houston when I was a graduate student myself at the University of Houston (having worked with the likes of Richard Howard, Cynthia Macdonald, Ed Hirsch, and Adam Zagajewski). Or having pursued an additional stable of Pulitzer stallions throughout my formative years (Donald Justice, Mark Strand, Charles Simic, James Tate). Or having the eyes of Gordon Lish on everything that I wrote while he was editing *The Quarterly*. As a nascent poet, I was a collector of books, of texts, of lives lived, of tales told. It was as important then to have veteran eyes on rookie work (and my eyes on their work) as it is now. I can't imagine living the life of poetry without having hung out with other living artists. Or cozying up with the great dead through their own accounts in verse and prose and through biographies and sundry missives. I love how Allen Tate's wife called Allen over to their kitchen window one morning and said, "Allen, look! There's a tent pitched on our front lawn!" only for the couple to later discover that it was the young Robert

Lowell who had shown up in the middle of the night, eager to make contact. I remember meeting Linda Gregg in Aspen, Colorado, back in 1990, following her around town and crowning her mane with daisies. We only get to be green once. If there were, say, a school for prostitution, we could all possibly learn the tricks of the trade, but only a few of us would be able to emerge as memorable world-class whores. In related literary endeavors, Roland Barthes's *The Pleasure of the Text* stands in my mind as the seminal training manual. Or Rilke's *Letters to a Young Poet*. Or Stevens's *The Necessary Angel*. I'm sure that the other pieces collected herein this anthology (which I will not have had the chance to peruse until it is published) will be both valuable and just as likely not. It all depends. On whatever else the reader and / or writer is or is not willing to bring to the page.

Texts dialoguing w/ other texts

{ **Alien Eggs, or, the
Poet as Mad Scientist**
DAWN LUNDY MARTIN

1. My first very real poems were written on an IBM computer (this was before the laptop computer or any handheld communication device more sophisticated than a telephone or a walkie-talkie). This seemingly, now, ancient word-processing device forced me to have a prewriting ritual that included a putting in and removing of big floppy disks on which my boot-up mechanism—the DOS program—was housed. The computer itself was deskless, as was I, and so I was required to sit cross-legged on the rug, hunched over the keyboard as would a new ex-smoker digging into a stocked ashtray for a not-so-smoked butt. In any event, my environment was stable, like any laboratory. The ritual of my laboratory practice—a kind of meditation—and the constraints imposed on me by the machine (and its positioning) are instructive to me, now, as a teacher. Since I can't, of course, force my students into a—perhaps pathological—ritualistic performance of the prewriting moment, I create my own laboratory, or more precisely, a laboratory-like environment for students to work in the classroom.

2. This might initially present itself as an oversimplification (and perhaps it is), but when I teach I ask students to write. Writing is the way I ask them to experiment, to investigate the world around them, to figure out what they think, and to read the writings of others. Toward those ends, I might ask students to "read" a text via exegesis—to write their own associated lines between the lines of another writer's poem. What I hope they'll discover is not only what they already know, but what they don't know they know about the text at hand; how poetic texts are often in dialogue with each other; and that dialogic production is original in its own sense. Additionally, this is a trick that one might perform to surprise one's self out of potentially well-worn habits of writing the poem. These laboratory-like environments are *entrées* into the unknown, where one might mix things up and see what happens, what's yielded is this process, which is, in some

ways, in striking opposition to the idea that one should "write what they know." Kathleen Fraser says this:

> The laboratory is a workspace in which to look closely at the evidence you've assembled. I cannot conceive of a "nothing space," but perhaps it is like a large internal screen continuously being filled with the writer's bits of thought, overheard speech, observation—all somewhat loosely and raggedly noted but not, as yet, brought into any kind of focus or coherence. The evidence is there, waiting, until some word or physical response brings one's focus to the screen—thought hunts and selects and assembles language and a shape begins to build, whose edges might describe a parameter.[1]

This for me is the most interesting thing a writer, or any artist, can do—to figure out ways to explore what you don't already know, to assemble evidences. Students often want poems to "come to them" and are excited when they fill an inspired page of verse in their notebooks or on laptop screens, as if they've been "touched by the poetry gods" with the gift (oh, muse!). When that inspired feeling is not fueling the brain's tank, I encourage them to dig their hands into the scrap pile of their imaginations and pull out *whatever*'s there—the bits and pieces, the unintelligible—and when that doesn't work, to seek sources (literary, medical, historical, silly, pop cultural, whatever) and explore them. Hold them in hand, manipulate them, break them into pieces, or use them in a nontraditional way. (*I am sitting on my orange today.*) The workshop, then, becomes a laboratory in the sense that we do a lot of writing in the classroom, that the classroom becomes a place for exploration, writing together, sharing what we've written and thinking metacognitively about what happened in that writing moment. This writing is primarily driven by exercises that I have either created or stolen from someone else, or borrowed from ex-colleagues at the Institute for Writing and Thinking at Bard College. Often the writing exercise is in relation to the reading that we have done for that day. In my undergraduate workshop, for example, I introduce writing as a form of expansive engagement with poems. It serves as an alternative to the traditional modes of analyzing or describing poetry and opens students up to ways of knowing that are unfamiliar and surprising.

3. As any good scientist knows, challenges are crucial to anything that might be called success. In fact, it is likely in the failing and failing and

failing that scientists figure something out, whether it's what they sought to figure out at the beginning or not. Try to write ten poems in one day when you have nothing else on your schedule. Run up twenty flights of stairs with your notebook and pen and then sit down to write. Have a friend sit on your chest while you write. Write at an altitude unfamiliar to you. Write in a language that you don't know. Make up a language. Write when you've had nothing to eat. Write when you're stuffed with chicken and pizza. Carve your poem into your arm with a splinter (write another poem using the bloody splinter itself). (Actually, I wouldn't advise my students to do that last one, but you get the point.) Some of my students have, indeed, invented challenges like these, and the results, are, I am thrilled to say, like breaking open the egg of an unfamiliar animal.

NOTE

1. Kathleen Fraser and Lauren Shufran. "Into Form: A Conversation." *Verdure: A Sporadically-Published "Magazine" of Poetry and Poetics* 7 (April 2005): 15.

Uncreative Writing

KENNETH GOLDSMITH

I teach a class at the University of Pennsylvania called Uncreative Writing, which is a pedagogical extension of my own poetics. In it, students are penalized for showing any shred of originality and creativity. Instead, they are rewarded for plagiarism, identity theft, repurposing papers, patchwriting, sampling, plundering, and stealing. Not surprisingly, they thrive. Suddenly, what they've surreptitiously become expert at is brought out into the open and explored in a safe environment, reframed in terms of responsibility instead of recklessness.

Well, you might ask, what's wrong with creativity? "I mean, we can always use more creativity."[1] "The world needs to become a more creative place."[2] "If only individuals could express themselves creatively, they'd be freer, happier."[3] "I'm a strong believer in the therapeutic value of creative pursuits."[4] "To be creative, relax and let your mind go to work, otherwise the result is either a copy of something you did before or reads like an army manual."[5] "I don't follow any system. All the laws you can lay down are only so many props to be cast aside when the hour of creation arrives."[6] "An original writer is not one who imitates nobody, but one whom nobody can imitate."[7]

When our notions of what is considered creative became this hackneyed, this scripted, this sentimental, this debased, this romanticized . . . this *uncreative*, it's time to run in the opposite direction. Do we really need another *creative* poem about the way the sunlight is hitting your writing table? No. Or another *creative* work of fiction that tracks the magnificent rise and the even more spectacular fall? Absolutely not.

One exercise I do with my students is to give them the simple instructions to retype five pages of their choice. Their responses are varied and full of revelations: Some find it enlightening to become a machine (without ever having known Warhol's famous dictum "I want to be a machine"). Others say that it was the most intense *reading* experience they ever had, with many actually embodying the characters they were retyping. Several students become aware that the act of typing or writing is actually an act of performance, involving their whole body in a physically durational act (even down to noticing the cramps in their hands). Some of the students become intensely aware of the text's formal properties and for the first time in their lives began to think of texts not only as transparent, but as opaque objects to be moved around a white space. Others find the task zenlike and amnesia-inducing (without ever having known Satie's "Memoirs of an Amnesiac" or Duchamp's desire to live without memory), alternately having the text lose and then regain meaning.

In the act of retyping, what differentiates each student is their choice of *what* to retype. One student retyped a story about a man's inability to complete the sexual act, finding the perfect metaphor for this assignment. Another student retyped her favorite high school short story, only to discover during the act of retyping it, just how poorly written it was. Yet another was a waitress who took it upon herself to retype her restaurant's menu in order to learn it better for work. She ended up hating the task and even hating her job more. The spell was broken when purposefulness and goal-orientation entered into the process.

The trick in uncreative writing is airtight accountability. If you can defend your choices from every angle, then the writing is a success. On the other hand, if your methodology and justification is sloppy, the work is doomed to fail. You can no longer have a workshop where people worry about adjusting a comma here or a word there. You must insist that the procedure was well articulated and accurately executed.

We proceed through a rigorous examination of the circumstances that are normally considered outside of the scope of writing but, in fact, have everything to do with writing. Questions arise, among them:

> What kind of paper did you use? Why is it on generic white computer paper when the original edition was on thick, yellowed, pulpy stock? What does it say about you: your aesthetic, economic, social, and political circumstances?

> Do you reproduce exactly the original text's layout page by page or do you simply flow the words from one page to another, the way your word-processing program does? Will the texts be received differently if it is in Times Roman or Verdana?

For a task so seemingly simple, the questions never end.

A few years ago I was lecturing to a class at Princeton. After the class, a small group of students came up to me to tell me about a workshop that they were taking with one of the most well-known fiction writers in America. They were complaining about her lack of imagination. For example, she had them pick their favorite writer and come in the next week with an original work in the style of that author. I asked one of the students which author they chose. She answered Jack Kerouac. She then added that the assignment felt meaningless to her because the night before she had tried to "get into Kerouac's head" and scribbled a piece in "his style" to fulfill the assignment. It occurred to me that for this student to actually write in the style of Kerouac, she would have been better off taking a road trip across the country in a '48 Buick with the convertible roof down, gulping Benzedrine by the fistful, washing 'em down with bourbon, all the while typing furiously away on a manual typewriter, going eighty-five miles per hour down a ribbon of desert highway. And even then, it would've been a completely different experience, not to mention a very different piece of writing, than Kerouac's.

Instead, my mind drifted to those aspiring painters who fill up the Metropolitan Museum of Art every day, spending hours learning by copying the Old Masters. If it's good enough for them, why isn't it good enough for us? I would think that, should this student have retyped a chunk—or if she was ambitious, the entirety—of *On the Road*, wouldn't she have really understood Kerouac's style in a profound way that was bound to stick with her? I think she really would have learned something had she retyped Kerouac. But no. She had to bring in an *original* piece of writing.

At the start of each semester, I ask my students to simply suspend their disbelief for the duration of the class and to fully buy into uncreative writing. I tell them that one good thing that can come out of the class is that they completely reject this way of working. At least their own conservative positions become fortified and accountable; they are able to claim that they have spent time with these attitudes for a prolonged period of time and quite frankly, they've found them to be a load of crap. Another fine result is that the uncreative writing exercises become yet another tool in their writing toolbox, upon which they will draw from for the rest of their careers. Of course, the very best result—and the unlikeliest one—is that they dedicate their life to uncreative writing.

NOTES
1. Marc Chagall.
2. Philip Yeo.

3. Richard Florida.

4. Dr. Wayne Dwyer.

5. Kimon Nicoliades.

6. Raoul Dufy.

7. Gail Sheehy.

**Radical Strategies
Toward a Poetics
of Play**
KAREN VOLKMAN

Some of my earliest teaching of poetry took place in elementary school classrooms. I spent five years working with schoolchildren in New York City through the organization Teachers & Writers Collaborative, founded in the lost years of humanistic idealism in the 1960s by Rosellen Brown, Kenneth Koch, Herbert Kohl, Philip Lopate, and Grace Paley among others. One of T&W's key terms is "educating the imagination," and their ambition is to bring the imaginative freedoms of poetry and the ethical expansiveness it allows into the early experience of language, and so to the early acts of articulating experience and perceptions. I taught in public schools in neighborhoods ranging from the South Bronx and East Harlem to Belmore, an upper middle-class suburb of Long Island. And I discovered what happens between the first acquisition of writing (the very painful crafting of letters in kindergarten and first grade—literally physically painful—I have so many vivid memories of kids putting down their pencils and shaking out their sore fingers) to the point of writing with relative fluency by sixth grade.

Working with hundreds of kids taught me that the weird and fascinating panoply of knowledge the mind receives in American grade schools— marine life, volcanoes, planets, numbers, colors—as well as neighboring streets, music, food, and the grandparents' donkey in Mexico are completely equal and exciting and allowable phenomena within a child's poem. The borders aren't there. They start to develop around the end of sixth grade when we are taught to define experience in terms of categories.

Like many poets, my deepest wish in teaching is to reawaken such a state of immediate engagement with language, as though we were first discovering the word *krill* or *lava*, and taking pleasure in the new realm of sensation it ignites in the mind. Velimir Khlebnikov, the great Futurist visionary and one of the most singular imaginations of the twentieth century, was fascinated by children's writing and its expressive and imaginative freedoms, its borderlessness. Dada sound poems, as well, sprung from a desire to return to an even earlier state of language experience, prior even to structuring sound into words. In these avant-garde movements, radical experimentation truly seeks a return to some fundamental root, rediscovered as a fertile, generative force—before the plant grew into a usable structure to be harvested and pruned.

To bring students back to this point, I use a range of methods, often drawn from experimental practices of different artists or schools. One course, "Radical Strategies," focuses on avant-garde movements of the twentieth century, starting with Futurism. In a recent version of this class, Futurism, Dada, Surrealism, students explored these three seminal movements (which can be collectively viewed as the childhood of the avant-garde) and wrote from experiments drawn from their works, including poems, prose, paintings, short films, music, manifestos, and speculative writings.

From the manifesto "The Futurist Reconstruction of the Universe," students imagined how language could respond to one of the various proposed reconstructions, including "The Futurist Toy," "The Artificial Landscape," and "The Metallic Animal." An exercise based on Khlebnikov's "Alphabet of the Mind" set into play an associative relationship with sound and letter and word, breaking out of traditional logics into a more extensive mode of relation. Another exercise made use of the "Surrealist Art Questionnaire," based on the example in Mary Ann Caws's anthology *Surrealist Poets and Painters*; questions posed for De Chirico's "Enigma of a Day" include "Where is the sea?" and "Where would you make love?" as well as more scatological queries. For this project, students worked in groups of three, each proposing questions about a work of Surrealist art, which they each then responded to and compiled (I also invited them to have friends, roommates, and partners contribute, widening the circle of response). This approach helped break through any reverence for or intimidation by the painting or sculpture, resulting in a greater intimacy and freer interaction with the relational energies of the work.

For another exercise, based on the section in Andre Breton's *Mad Love* in which Breton and Alberto Giacometti wander through a flea market chancing upon resonant objects, I asked students to go to one of Missoula's junk/antique stores with a partner, in search of some instigating Thing. As Breton describes, the presence of another person results in the receptive faculty being "primed"—a different field is opened and charged by the emanation of the other with his or her own references, associations, extensivities, hauntings.

As a form of "educating the imagination," a poetics of play provides a new set of engagements, de-emphasizing the I-centered perspective while still allowing a dance of sensibility, a tracing of a ranging intelligence touching and touched by phenomena—including language and sound relation as event and phenomenon—but not compelled to subvert these sensations to a reductive or boundaried conception of self. It prompts a shift of mind to the importance of encounter with the material of phenomena, of inhabiting not a self but a diversity of selves created by engagements with the sensuous. It is poetics as a process of initiation and invitation, alive with insights, hints, glimpses into new relational realms.

In Thought a Fine Human Brow Is Like the East When Troubled with the Morning

PETER GIZZI

Whenever I begin a workshop I ask everyone to recite a line, phrase, or sentence that they have retained from their reading. This is almost always met with diffidence, but once the initial awkwardness is overcome we go around and around reciting our favorite pieces of language. The title above, one of my favorites, is a sentence from "The Prairie," a chapter from Melville's *Moby-Dick*. In it, Ishmael attempts to read the face of the whale.

Teaching is always an act of reading, memory, body, room tone, gestures, volume, and faces—mostly faces. I learn more about what I have to say, think, when looking into a face. I find meaning there. It is a formal experience. I have spent years now at this practice and a new face is a new mind to transpose William Carlos Williams talking about poesis. There is so much to discover in an open, or closed, countenance, a history actually—the forms of time, generation, the present. Always to know that they see the world in a way that no one else will. What I read there is the last of what they see—that's as good a definition of generation as I know. That I am the last of what I see, we all are. There is no going back. "Onward," Bob Creeley used to say when he'd sign off. I wonder if that's what he meant, there's no going back—you're *it* and what will you make of yourself.

I never accepted the argument that poets shouldn't teach. I mean where else does poetry live if not between people, faces, in a room, a stanza struggling in a condition of awakening, of annunciation really. It is a difficult task but a privilege and a gift, therefore a responsibility to never be alone there in the face of loneliness, a body coming to this understanding as itself among others who have come here before. In "Ode: Salute to the French Negro Poets," O'Hara writes, "The only poem is face to face whose words become your mouth and dying in black and white we fight for what we love, not are." That what I find in the face of the poem is deeper in me than I am.

{ **A Note on Derrida
and Teaching Poetry**

LISA FISHMAN

Recently I was reading and rereading a small portion of Jacques Derrida's essays, books, and interviews and thinking about his work in relation to contemporary poetry. I was preparing for a conference in Sweden
on "writing after Derrida," where I wanted to challenge the "after" in the
program by seeing what would happen if poetry—so important to Derrida's way of reading—were brought to the center of the discussion. In that
context, it was natural to bring some of Derrida's work into the graduate
poetry workshop I was teaching and to invite the second-year MFA students to think with me about points of contact between deconstruction
and poetry. Some points of contact may further open onto teaching as a
critical and improvisational practice.

Derrida says of deconstruction, "What matters is the trajectory, the
pathway, the crossing—in a word, the experience. The experience is then
the method, not a system of rules or technical norms for supervising an
experiment, but the pathway in the process of happening, breaking a way
through."[1] His description seems relevant not only to poetry that emerges
of its own internal necessities but also to teaching that emerges from the
experience of being present in a room with other people while something
is happening. What is happening, in a poetry workshop, is that language is
being listened to (or even better, made in class), whether by way of "outside
reading" or student work under discussion. The hope is that such work has
come into being as an act of listening—immense activity—and that when
the rest of us hear and read the work in class, the internal experience *of*
the work (the *work* of the work; I mean its listening)—remains as active
as language as when it was being formed.

Derrida's notion of the pathway or process of something happening as
itself that which matters (so that deconstruction is just that experience,
not a program or set of results) was helpful in getting students to think
about what makes poems more or less alive. Thinking alongside Derrida,
students were able to imagine that if a poem was written without being
willed into some external notion of what sounds good or funny or smart

or vivid, then the poem's true activity—what I've called its listening—may come through in the reading of it as uncannily as in the making of it. The intersections between deconstruction and poetry gave us another angle for approaching the notion that a poem must constantly, recurringly transmit the activeness, the unknowingness, the discovery-of-itself, even as a "finished" poem being read—or it was never innately written. In other words, made more articulable with Derrida, if the poem was not an experience while it was being written (instead of a "project" or goal or directed body of words), then it has no experience (of coming into being) to be read. To be read should be to happen again—as if being made again—for a poem. We saw that this is Derrida's hope, too, for his readings of any text: to enable the renewability of the experience of close reading is to read deconstructively, for him.

In Derrida's practice, poetry's movements and crossings and silences and traces—its way of working as trace or ash, as he describes—are deeply informing of deconstruction. That is, largely by means of what he heard and felt in his early reading of Paul Celan, Edmond Jabès, and Stéphane Mallarmé, Derrida learned to read deconstructively; he learned to read the gaps and silences between words. He learned to listen to their accretions and multiplicities and to the work that their gaps, silences, and undoings perform. And so for class we read Celan, Jabès, and Mallarmé alongside Derrida, with a small selection of Freud and a lot of Blanchot. It was good to read that material with MFA students, who found Derrida more hospitable in that company, I think, than when he is either isolated as a monolith or taught only in the context of literary theory. We knew we were leaving out endless layers of his work's embeddedness in philosophy, history, psychoanalysis, and linguistics. But we could see, as I proposed in Sweden, that Derrida's thinking comes in crucial ways from poetry: it's a poetic practice he describes when he says, "Deconstruction always consists in making more than one movement at a time, and writing with two hands, writing more than one sentence or in more than one language."

It's also a pedagogical practice, insofar as teaching poetry consists in making more than one movement at a time (into the present and into the past), writing with two hands (one that feels capable and one that doesn't), and writing more than one sentence or in more than one language. In poetry workshops, I like to have the class dwell in some form on the latter by means of exercises designed to permit a fresh encounter with English, as if it has become a foreign language. In the graduate workshop I taught while preparing for the Sweden conference, Derrida and the French poets, and Gertrude Stein and others, invited us to such exercises and processes in various ways, at times involving the breaking of *our* language down to its most rudimentary elements. Anything to estrange the students from their material so that their experience in it can *be* an experience, an action, with nothing to go on but their attention to their newly "unknown" material (language) itself. Anything to help the deepened listening that can occur when the ear provides the primary pathway or mechanism of orientation.

NOTE

1. Jacques Derrida. "Others Are Secret Because They Are Other." Interview with Anthony Spire in Derrida. *Paper Machine*. Trans. Rachel Bowlby. Stanford: Stanford University Press, 2005. 137.

Unlearning to Write

RON SILLIMAN

There are, I think, two very different dynamics involved in the making of a poet. One is learning that you already know everything you need about writing *before you even begin.* The other is an extended reading of the literature, to understand what has been done, why, and what its implications might be.

The first sounds easy, but is in fact the harder of the two tasks. Many starting writers never solve this problem at all, which means that they're destined to fail. The difficulty is what happens in that instant between the moment *before you even begin* and the moment once you've begun, into which is inserted every vague notion you may have about what writing is, how it is done, who does it, and every conceivable fantasy you might harbor about being a poet or a novelist. Before you begin, the blank page or screen is in front of you, absolutely free of any irrevocable marks, literally virgin territory. Once you begin, however, you instantaneously discover yourself burdened with thousands of ghosts and beliefs about *what writing is.* It's like trying to swim with a team of elephants on your back. The opportunities for drowning are immense.

Much of the actual process of learning to write is involved in examining these beliefs, one at a time, almost as though you were peeling them away. You would be surprised just how many of the things you do, unconsciously, as a poet, are in fact decisions you've made predicated on these beliefs.

So one of the things I always do in a classroom is to work through a series of exercises intended to make people conscious of the decisions they make. This is something I picked up from three of my teachers, Wright Morris, Jack Gilbert, & especially William Everson (Brother Antoninus at the time I was his student). Following Everson, I let students know at the start that what they write for my class is not going to feel like their work. It's going to seem uncomfortable and alien. If it doesn't, they're not doing it right. Their discomfort is really an index of how well they're doing their homework.

I start with the actual physics of writing. How do they do it? On a computer? In a notebook? On a legal tablet? Whatever it might be. I ask them to change this: if they usually work on a computer, try doing it by hand; If they usually work in a notebook, try writing on a PC. Robert Creeley has an interview somewhere in which he recommends this as a mechanism for getting out of writer's block, and I can see how this exercise might be useful in that circumstance. I recall that once, back when I was a student at San Francisco State, I inadvertently dropped my typewriter and suddenly had a couple of hundred typewriter pieces all over my apartment. Since I had almost no money, it took me to the end of the semester to be able to afford a new machine. So I was forced into switching my basic method of creating first drafts, which I'd been doing on the typewriter since I was in tenth grade. I switched over to legal tablets, a process that also gave me more flexibility as to when and where I might write. Since I was living in Berkeley at the time, getting to school meant a long ride on the F bus (this was before BART), followed by a long ride on the Muni to get out to the Sunset District. For the first time, I began writing on public transportation, inspired in part by the fact that three of my favorite poets, Robert Duncan, Phil Whalen and Paul Blackburn, had all written about doing so themselves. It was a fascinating process and took my work forward very quickly, although I noticed that once I typed up my manuscripts, virtually all of them fit perfectly on a single typed page, often filling it completely both vertically and horizontally.

Later, when I was at Berkeley and thinking about writing in prose, I made a point of buying one of those smaller black-bound sketchbooks, the size of a trade paperback, and sat on the roof of our apartment building on Highland Place in Berkeley, usually watching the sun set over downtown San Francisco, constantly writing and rewriting what I hoped someday would become the *perfect* paragraph. Though I worked on this project years before I would begin *Ketjak*, there is one (incomplete) sentence in that work taken directly from this project.

Depending on the length of the class, we examine a variety of such variables. Do you write in the morning or at night? Do you have to have silence? Do you like to have music? What kinds? Do you need total solitude? If you use paper, what size, color, etc.? Do you write under the influence, whether it be coffee and tea or something stronger? One can switch one or more or even all of these variables and it's worth looking at the impact of each one.

Making students conscious of the terms and conditions of their writing is one step toward making them responsible for every single element on the page or screen or in the air. Do you capitalize at the left margin? If so, do you know *why* you do so? If you don't know, why are you doing it? A writer needs to own everything he or she does.

The second task, the extended reading, takes far longer. There are people—Bruce Andrews was one, Rae Armantrout another—who are writing in their mature style very early on, but in both cases you will find that they were voracious readers also. This is where I think that Malcolm Gladwell's gimmicky ten thousand hours of work to become good at any one thing, whether or not it's writing, comes into play. You need to understand the range of poetry that you are seeking to become part of—a process that becomes harder each year as the number of contemporary publishing poets grows—and you need to be able to trace the history of this landscape backward at least two hundred years. I would go further than that myself—I'd argue that you need to know enough Middle English to reach Chaucer in the original and really grasp (a deliberately vague term) your own place within this constellation. If you can't, you haven't read enough, written enough, thought hard enough.

To do this, your *reading needs shape*, which is to say that if you can't articulate *where* a poet fits into the universe, their work either is not distinct enough or you haven't read enough to place them. Conversely, you need to be able to challenge claims that want to lead you astray. Anyone— anyone!—who argues that either Dickinson or Whitman leads you to the School of Quietude (though they won't call it that) is a fraud. Though it is worth noting that Dickinson and Whitman will lead you to very different parts of the post-avant spectrum. So read the New American Poets as a project. And the Objectivists. And the Imagists. And the Romantics. Even the New Formalists. If a writer falls outside any cluster, as many over the last two decades have, figure out what makes them so misanthropic. Is it really, as I suspect, a *natural* (but defensive) reaction to the conservative ascendancy that began with Reagan? Are flarf, conceptual poetry and *hybrid* writing the first steps toward a post-Bush era literature?

Ultimately the poems you or anyone will write will be the poems *you* (or anyone) needs. I always think of this as the blind spot in the totality of verse, a place toward which each of us is driven & where we never quite fully arrive.

A Po Pedagogy

SANDRA DOLLER

"The poem is a meteor," and "the poem is a pheasant," wrote Wallace Stevens. If we take both of these statements to be true, what then are we to make of the poem? In the classroom, I seek to surprise students into loving poetry—as one loves a meteor, as one loves a pheasant. Beginning with a question that directs students to recall their first word ever uttered (or their first favorite word, or their favorite word yesterday), I take it as my mission to encourage delight in the very syllables of our shared and personal languages—from the mundane to the literary. Poetry need not be comprised of abstractions or noble sentiments or hidden messages, as many students have long feared or even been taught to idealize. Using poems from Wallace Stevens's *Harmonium* such as "Life is Motion" and "Depression Before Spring" to enlist a giddy pleasure in the sensuality of language, often beyond its logical sense, I hope to free students of their preconceived notions of language as a rational system of communication, whose rules we must obediently follow. This is not to say that I urge students to only write nonsense verse or to merely flout conventions in their poems (though both are useful resistances to deploy in writing and reading alike); I do, however, urge madness at the level of the writing prompt in an effort to exercise the muscles of rebellion, so that even experienced students find access to freshness at the level of the word, the syllable, the morpheme when they need to most—in the making of their own work. Such writing prompts include: homophonic translations (translating based on sound, with no attention to semantic sense), left-handed lipograms (using only the left-hand side of the keyboard), centos (collaging bits of language from source texts), performance pieces (composing notes for performance, with the notes and the action inter-acting as the poem), list poems, manifestos, and "This is just to say" apology poems.

There is no such thing as a writer reading too much or reading being a hindrance to writing. I have heard some poets say that reading Emily

Dickinson is the equivalent of writer's block—and while I agree that The Godmother of American Poetry has a stunning stag-in-headlamps effect on me, this is not altogether an ungenerative effect. It is my task to urge students to read as much as they can, as much as they want to—and of course always more than that—especially when making work of their own, if merely to distract them from the (mis)perceived gravity of their own projects. No one is going to lose an eyeball from reading a book (whose grandmother said that?). The notion that writers write in a vacuum, far from the world and its concerns, far from books and the history of literature in an "anxiety of influence" does no good, I feel, for the student writer. Student writers should be engaged in the world where writing is real and made, whether this is in their own politicized cross-outs of classical texts, their lists of potential car names (à la Marianne Moore), their imitations of forms both traditional and contemporary, or an engagement with ethnopoetics and translation. For the verbal artist, there are no texts that are sacred in and of themselves and cannot be reconceived in one's own creative art. There is a necessary element of rebellion in the writer that leads her to question received ideas yet possess a secret reverence for the smallest things and to dare to write at all.

We are responsible for knowing the history of our art forms, with particular attention to those (yet to be) dignified and (yet to be) canonized moments—such as the early twentieth-century experimentalists, the early twenty-first-century bloggers, and the collagists of all forms. I encourage students to follow their obsessions, to become interested in a particular time period or style of writing, to apprentice themselves to one writer as mentor by digesting her entire oeuvre, to expand their ideas of *worthwhile* literature. For even academically accepted poetry is ever-altering in its reception, and *value* is a notion writers must trouble—see how Emily Dickinson has been traditionally categorized as light verse and yet her letters and fascicles are still being exposed today in the depth of their variations, contexts, and intentions.

"I is an other." So quoth Rimbaud. I hope to instill in my students a humility toward their art form (and, by extraction, themselves), the work that preceded them, and the work that they and their peers will make. Not only does an abstract conception of the self free the writer to experiment

with her subjectivity, but it allows for a politicized reconfiguration of the
self as a natural entity. If students of writing—are we all students of writing?—can begin to decay the strong bond of the "I" that inheres (in some
ways necessarily) in our waking world, they can approach the oneiric ecstasy that is the creation of a persona, a language, a form, a poem.

In workshop, I hope to create a nonteleological, process-driven environment of mutual respect for one another's risks, to arm students of all
backgrounds and levels of proficiency with the analytical eyes necessary
to improving their writing through peer discourse, and to inspire students
to question themselves, me, each other, and our notions of what a poem is,
what literature is for, and what makes it interesting at all. The workshop
model can become too static, and it is worth mixing it up by asking students to submit work anonymously, to make detailed comments in writing, to give the occasional cold read and the opposite extended hot read,
to present on one of their peers in depth, and to masquerade with each
other's work as their own. To misquote U2 quoting John Lennon: I don't
believe in [talent].

I don't dig anthologies, with anything by Jerome Rothenberg being the
exception. Hazel Smith's essential text *The Writing Experiment* is a book I
agree with to an unusual extent, and I find this agreement useful in teaching it. Some writers I consistently teach and reteach include Harryette
Mullen, Ronald Johnson, Theresa Hak Kyung Cha, and Russian Futurist
and Zaum poets, because:

In Harryette Mullen's work, voice is a driving factor, as she seems to
wrestle with every syllable in her formal poetic architectures, working
through vigorously codified and stanzaic constructions in order to achieve
crystallized moments of tone and diction rather than conventional image.

Ronald Johnson's work has compelling roots in the concrete poetry
movement of the 1950s, bringing up essential theoretical issues of word-
image via a compelling practice. Johnson's pastoral long poems proceed
along architectural lines that cohere mathematically, bringing a man-
made constructedness to the lyrical sensibility—much as his troubling of
letterforms intertwine with his poetry. Johnson's rewritings of Milton and
Thoreau in cross-out are valuable records of a canon received, and reconceived.

Theresa Hak Kyung Cha's foreshortened career left us with a body of documentary writing, art, and film that achieve a poesis on their own terms, navigating personal, cultural, and national histories in a single bound. The starkness of Cha's attention to language as accultured and acquired is a sharp inquiry into the very (im)possibility of human connection and bereavement.

Stemming from the histories that precede and accompany these concerns, I also include Alexei Kruchenykh and Olga Rozanova's Russian Futurist bookmaking, collaboration, collage, and Zaum or transrational poetry in course texts, in an effort to remind students what semiotic freedom looks and sounds like—good old-fashioned Russian freedom.

NOTE

The title to this essay is in reverent sonic reference to Edwin Torres's spectacular and inimitable book *The PoPedology of an Ambient Language* (Atelos, 2007).

Question and Answer

AARON KUNIN

Part of what one does in a job is pretending to do the job. Pretending to be a teacher or a cop or an assistant in an office or a store. Pretending to be busy. Pretending to listen. I suppose it is an element of play in work. It explains why workers need evidence "that they are still in the trade they were trained for," as Erving Goffman observes. Stacking chairs, moving pianos—is this part of my job? Goofing off—is this how I spend my time? Everything that I do without caring demoralizes me, and I look for evidence that I care about something.

Sometimes the answer is yes. This pretending can be good for me. Pretending to know something or to be interested in something. I depend on this process for my intellectual development. If I stopped pretending, I might never learn anything new. So much of what I do as a teacher boils down to inventing reasons for my students to care about something that they may never previously have imagined as a valuable thing. The Shakespeare survey that I teach comes as a relief because it is a rare occasion when I do not have to add value to the book we are reading. My students bring their own reasons for thinking that Shakespeare is important. In fact, the value of teaching Shakespeare does not have to be explained to anyone outside of the profession.

Part of my job is there only to convince me that I am actually doing my job. This is the worst kind of pretending. In school, where I work, this pretending takes the special form of question and answer. My students ask a question and I invent an answer. I ask my students a question and they invent an answer. I listen to an interesting lecture, ask a question about something vaguely relevant, and get a brilliant improvised answer. I listen to a boring lecture, invent a question out of pure spite, and ignore the speaker's response.

Some of these questions are sincere and productive of knowledge. Others, without intending to produce knowledge, may do so inadvertently. They are all seemingly designed to produce false issues. School is very good at creating situations where talk is required, and these situations are ripe for intellectual dishonesty. Because saying something is automatically superior to saying nothing, because no one takes my protestations of uncertainty or ignorance seriously, because it is never acceptable to refuse to answer, because the continuation of the form of question and answer is the only thing about which anyone reliably cares, I invent false issues. Then, because what I say is coercive—it seduces me more than my audience—because anything that exists tries to convince me to adjust to what is already there, because what I imagine saying but keep to myself has its own dimmer coercions, I pretend to care about the false issues. I add to them. They become my life's work.

It is possible to dedicate your entire working life to things that make no difference. Things that (you would think) no one could possibly care about.

The same problem may be observed in writing. I once knew a writer whose entire style, on the level of the phrase, was about multiplying things that make no difference, moving them into view, and pretending to care about them. Always at the center of what he wrote, he narrated the production of his own narration until he somehow managed to dress the needless in the clothes of the fundamental and crucial—describing this attention to the needless, finally, as an ethics.

Something that is not well understood about writing is that when you write something, you have to inhabit it. This rule may sound like magical thinking, but it isn't. If you write a book about Paulette Goddard, someone might ask you to give a lecture about her. Someone organizes a symposium on movie stars from the thirties and invites you to give a paper. Pretty soon, before you know it, you've written enough material for a second book about Paulette Goddard. Then you read about a conference on women in classical Hollywood cinema and start grumbling because they *didn't* invite you to participate. Meanwhile members of Goddard's family have been sending you old letters, clothes, all the stuff they don't want and can't fit in their garages, and it piles up in your house until, really, the subject of your book has taken over your entire life, and you may truthfully say, "I am Paulette Goddard." This sort of mimetic regression is expected in reading. If you read a book about bees, you start to notice them. It's as though the bees are following you around. If you write about bees, the effect is even more profound.

When you write something, you have to inhabit it. An ethics for writers should start here. Cares for what readers might do with what you write are misplaced. Thus, I am opposed to the idea that the relationship between writer and reader models a better kind of social relationship. That from reading books I learn to read people better. That in reading I encounte something other than myself, and learn to recognize it, respect it, empathize with it. And the related idea that writers should prepare for the activity of readers. That I should empathize with readers, anticipate what they will care about, and reward them for their attention.

These ideas are not only wrong but harmful. Wrong because how you feel about other people is not a reliable foundation for an ethics. It isn't possible to have a personal relationship with everything. It isn't even true that my actions would be any better if I learned to empathize with my victims. No. Better to treat people well regardless of how I felt about them. Regardless of whether I cared. Even if I couldn't stand them.

Harmful because everything I write without caring demoralizes me. There is nothing worse than writing, trying to write, something if I do not care about it. At these times my imagination of how readers are likely to respond, sheer paranoia and projection irrelevant to my own pleasure and conscience, torments me.

One of the first things you learn about lyric is that it is an address to something that does not appear. Writing that professes to accommodate readers, to reward them for their attention, has already given up on this possibility. Accommodating readers is not ethics at all; it is rhetoric. About which I am skeptical, and, like everyone, suspicious.

Things That Have Their Origin in the Imagination

LILY BROWN

The curriculum of the first poetry course I taught balanced reading and analyzing poems with writing and workshopping poems. I had had other teaching experiences, including teaching poetry to elementary school students, and teaching composition courses. But as I embarked on teaching a poetry course for the first time, I found myself reflecting on my past teachers rather than on my own past teaching.

In college, I took seven poetry workshops with four teachers, all of whom taught a different kind of workshop. In graduate school, I took four poetry workshops with four teachers, all of whom, again, taught a different kind of workshop. In designing my own course, and in developing my own teacher-identity, then, I've found myself borrowing and combining the most valuable things I learned from my eight workshop teachers—not to mention my literature teachers from elementary through graduate school.

Here is some of what I've learned from my teachers.

For beginning students, sometimes praise for what is working in a poem is just as important as criticism of what is not. Furthermore, when in workshop or discussion the class begins to reach irritably after fact or reason, a teacher's defense of a poem can be incredibly valuable, not only for the student writer, but for her classmates, as well. Someone often feels discomfort when the language of felt experience overtakes literal language and experience. When I was in college, I took three workshops with D. A. Powell, who gave eloquent defenses of the more difficult poems we encountered in class. Redirecting the discussion away from "This doesn't many any sense" and toward "How is the language here working?" can go a long way toward modeling the validity of poetic logic.

I should say, too, that in all of my classes—whether poetry or composition—I make a point of discussing the workshop process itself and require that compliments be offered before criticism. Once I talk about the workshop process, students often express their anxiety about sharing their work with a group. In a class that largely concerns taking risks with language,

I feel that it's important to discuss how we might talk about a poem and offer criticism without being unkind. I learned this from all of my teachers, but particularly from Brenda Hillman, who embodies a generosity and kindness with her students that I hope to emulate in some way. Brenda would pass poems back covered in penciled-in notes of ideas for revisions and new directions to try out. I also vividly remember her generosity in sharing her own tricks for revision (rewriting a poem by hand to try to get back inside of it), and for ordering a manuscript (laying the poems out on the floor and having "an intuitive conversation" with oneself). In the temporary community of the classroom, I believe in both modeling how to be considerate and offering some guidance in terms of how we treat members of our group.

In revision, a different poem often lurks within the poem on the page. Rearranging a poem's lines demonstrates how moving language around can and will reveal another poem (or poems). What feels key here is upsetting the idea that just because a poem is written in a certain order, it needs to stay in that order. I learned how to relinquish control over my poems in a workshop with Jorie Graham, who always found more vital poems within whatever I handed in for workshop. Why can't the last line become the first line? Why can't the first line become the title? Further, why can't a poem be more economical in its language? When I was a senior in college, Peter Richards taught me to do a "negative capability" revision by taking a page-long poem with long lines and paring it down to an eight-line poem with short lines. I went home and cried. Yet, the lesson was an invaluable one, and I got over the surgical trauma quickly: we don't need to keep everything we write just because we write it.

In graduate school, I learned from Graham Foust that teaching is an act of creation in itself. Poems are hard to write. Good classes are hard to design. I revise my own poems extensively and obsessively, and I do the same kind of revisionary thinking about teaching. While teaching a set of literary terms is important in an introductory poetry class, modeling thinking seems just as important. If a teacher indicates his or her own puzzlement over a given line or phrase, and puzzles through that line or phrase with the class, others seem more willing to think through a poem verbally, as well. I think this willingness to dwell in the uncertainty of the poem translates into students' own poems and prose writing about poems, too. Moreover, discussion that engages in curiosity about poems and their language is beneficial because it shifts the focus away from normative logic.

My own expectations for the workshop were changed in a class with

Michael Palmer, who taught me that a workshop doesn't need to follow the traditional model. Discussing how a poem is working, indeed noticing what a poem does, rather than concentrating on how we might change it, can actually lead to a greater willingness to experiment. A class with Norma Cole further changed my expectations of the workshop. Norma had a thoughtful, nonjudgmental way of guiding class discussion that ultimately allowed the students to take more responsibility for our interactions with each other, and to focus less on the praise, criticism, or opinions of the teacher in the room. Rather, I learned to be a better listener when my classmates commented on my work, and ultimately to trust my own instincts about and reflections on my writing.

In the class I'm currently teaching, we began the term with a piece by Wallace Stevens, "A Comment on Meaning in Poetry." The piece begins as follows:

> Things that have their origin in the imagination or in the emotions (poems) very often have meanings that differ in nature from the meanings of things that have their origin in reason. They have imaginative or emotional meanings, not rational meanings, and they communicate these meanings to people who are susceptible to imaginative or emotional meanings.[1]

I think that everyone must, on some level, be "susceptible to imaginative or emotional meanings" and my hope, in my teaching, is to encourage this susceptibility, which all of my teachers encouraged in me. The cultural pressure to conform to "rational meanings" (and to the language used as a vehicle to convey these meanings) is huge. The poetry classroom is a place where—at the very least—language can be allowed to mean in other ways.

NOTE

1. Wallace Stevens. "A Comment on Meaning in Poetry." *Stevens: Collected Poetry and Prose*. New York: Library of America, 1997. 825.

Ekphrastic

The Image, Setting Forth Selfhood

RICHARD GREENFIELD

There is little currency in the term *image* now. Certainly some hear *image* and think this term means simply engaging in a process of representing things or replicating sensory perception in language. In poetry workshops, especially for beginning poets, implementing images in a poem is often emphasized as a skill of craft. Yet, the notion of the image as a purely rhetorical tool is clearly limited. Moreover, Romantic and Modernist concepts of the image were historically charged with a suspect quotient of authenticity. Although Ezra Pound's precept of the image (early in his career) is no less conspicuous in this regard when he finds it "presents an intellectual and emotional complex in an instant of time,"[1] it is a good beginning for thinking of the image as impetus for engaging the self in poetry, for where else might intellect and emotion dwell in time if not within a presence of the self? His term "complex" is a broader abstraction in this formula than the rest. It suggests a kind of structure; it also suggests space in which a union of the mind and the heart takes place—an ancient metaphysical dialogue finally crystallizing (perhaps problematically) in a disembodied image. I am interested in the premise that the image is ultimately the extension, or redoubling, of the self (also a multivalent complex of the mind and the heart). I want the image to be much more than representation. I believe the image can "set forth" selfness—activating self and engaging self by encouraging empathy with the object under scrutiny.

One way I pursue this interest in my own work and in the poetry workshop is through teaching *ekphrasis*. Aphthonius's *Progymnasmata* suggests this kind of writing will "set forth" the object from its representation. As such, ekphrastic writing is an opportunity to do more with the object.[2] In my hope to merge my subjectivity with the imagined subjectivity of a work of art, I once read all of Van Gogh's letters, and then began to imagine how the worlds in his paintings might be representations of my own experience. Van Gogh's *Cornfield with Crows* has been viewed as his "suicide note." His letters written while working on this painting often referred to varying kinds of "disappearance." I looked for disappearance in the painting, and I could see it everywhere. A green road going nowhere, a formless cloud dissipating into the blue. And I could see the death of my cousin Brenda—the only "sister" in my life—as the unsolved disappearance in my childhood. She was lost in that field. The poem I wrote borrows language from the letters as it describes a field where a "little girl" has been lost—where searchers (myself among them in the poem) had set up a "grid." Van Gogh had written: "Plus elle apparait, plus elle disparait."[3] I too tried to conjure in a poem she who could not be returned to this world. I had to put the disappearance into the work, with as much intent as a brushstroke, and Van Gogh's "line" became a part of my poem. I suppose that writing a poem this way is putting theory into praxis—a form of inquiry into the *work* (the object that is the work as well as the effort that is work) and a form of inquiry into the self. The ekphrastic response to the work of Sigmar Polke in Mary Jo Bang's *The Eye Like a Strange Balloon* is a good example of this. The speaker's attempt to comprehend (and apprehend) the speechless mystery of Polke's *Katastrophentheorie* series leads to important inquiry into the making of art: "How catastrophic can that be?"; "Do you wish to stay connected?"[4] On *whose* behalf are the questions asked?

Often times, this inquiry into process leads to "metapoetic" language; other times, the inquiry leads to an intense conversation with the self rather than with the work of art. But why should such an inquiry lead one *away* from representation—a seeming contradiction to the entire purpose behind ekphrasis? In its silence to the viewer, art conceals its maker and its subject's historicism beyond the frame. The poem as a response does the work of voicing the silent history there. Adrienne Rich's poem "Mourning Picture" brings to the surface what is at stake for *all* of us in the death of Edwin Romanzo Elmer's daughter, Effie, who appears in a painting of the same title. Effie's detachment from her family in the background is given new dimension by the epigraph of the poem, which reports her recent death. But Rich also inhabits the ghost voice of Effie, who recalls the moment within this frame (the world of the living) from another frame (the afterworld). The frame only reminds us of the constructed-ness of a painting, the page the constructed-ness of a poem. There are several selves at play here, each speaking with a unique perspective on *making* when they say, in unison: "Should I make you, world, again, / could I give back the leaf its skeleton, the air / its early-summer cloud, the house / its noonday presence, shadowless, / and leave *this* out?"[5] *This* is the inquiry the poem engages. The ekphrastic poem, with its emphasis on writing visually, can be a foil of the object from which the self is reflected in its own experience, reaching that *other* who is the maker, the viewer, the speaker, the listener, all at once—this other that is the essence of *selfhood*.

NOTES

1. "A Retrospect." *Literary Essays of Ezra Pound*. Ed. T. S. Eliot. New York: New Directions, 1938. 4.

2. Ruth Webb. "Imagination and the Arousal of the Imagination in Greco-Roman Rhetoric." *The Passions in Roman Thought and Literature*. Eds. Susanna Morton Braund and Christopher Gill. Cambridge: Cambridge University Press, 1997. 120.

3. The Letters of Vincent Van Gogh. Ed. Ronald De Leeuw. London: Penguin, 1997. 102.

4. Mary Jo Bang. "Catastrophe Theory IV." *The Eye Like A Strange Balloon*. New York: Grove Press, 2004. 42.

5. Adrienne Rich. "Mourning Picture." *Necessities of Life: Poems 1962–1965*. New York: W. W. Norton, 1966. 32.

{

The Page as Poetry's Artifact

JENNY BOULLY

If you're spending too much time on the page and not enough time outside the page, then you'll need to find more time to find poetry. The page isn't poetry: rather, the page is poetry's artifact, poetry's afterthought. The page is what happens after the fact.

Poetry happens outside the page. Poetry is an instant. It strikes us oh so quickly; it makes us mourn. It happens when life too painfully or too blissfully filters through us. By the time we've acknowledged it, poetry's passed.

That's why we turn then to the page. We want to filter that poetry through the page so as to give that poetry a place to live because it has since stopped living.

The page is artifact to poetry, that is, to what has been.

Can you give to someone else *what has been*? That's the task of the poet. Over six thousand light years away, almost one thousand years ago, a supernova explosion occurred in the constellation Taurus. When it happened, that was poetry. The Crab Nebula is artifact. We can wonder at its explosion because of that artifact.

Poetry should allow others to wonder at explosions.

Did something explode inside of you? Did something recently die? Is there, today, enough poetry to confront the page?

The line will break; the line will break, and you will need to answer why. Can you answer why? I came upon an answer once, and it was too true; so I stopped with all the line breaking because it frightened me too much. You should know why the line breaks; you should be able to say why. If you don't know why, then you should face each day, not the page, but the break.

Because things will break, and their breaking will make you a poet.

 Are you generous enough? Have you enough to give? Or have you lost trust and, as a result, cannot give enough? Sometimes, a poet loses trust. A poet often does not give enough. Giving takes a long time to learn. Giving may not be something that's taught.

When life filters through you, and it has given you a gift (and you've already been gifted, you see, as a poet, that is, with language's swift abilities), will you be poet enough to return this gift, say, on the page? Life will filter through you and deposit gifts your way. You must be astute enough to see what each thing has to say.

Poetry is an instant. It is an instant in which transcendence is achieved, where a miracle occurs, and knowledge, experience, and memory are obliterated and transformed into awe. The instant passes quickly, so quickly, and then you are just your regular self again. This instant is what has been; the page is artifact to that.

Is it love that you're after? Immortality? Friendship? Acceptance? Fame? I want to know what your motives are. You should have no motives. Your communion should be wholly sincere.

Sincerity takes time. Sincerity doesn't come easily. The addressee still evades, eludes, escapes you. Is your addressee somewhere enjoying life without you? Or does your addressee flitter somewhere between two clouds? Your prettily packaged artifact: I want to know who it is intended for.

These things can be learned: rhythm, rhyme, imagery, metaphor, form, synecdoche, line. The tools of the poetry trade are there; they are easily given over to you. But do you know what use there is for metaphor or what form is for? What equivalents exist of these tools in the stars?

So nice of the ancient Greeks to have left us Draco and Scorpius, Cassiopeia and the Pleiades, arrows aimed finitely toward infinity.

They knew that artifice is what we use when dressing the artifact.

The page is where we turn to resuscitate that.

It's Not That
I Want to Say
FRED MOTEN

It's not that I want to say that poetry should or can be disconnected from having something to say; it's just that everything I want to say eludes me. But if I caught it I wouldn't want it and I imagine you wouldn't want it either. Maybe poetry is what happens on the bus between wanting and having. I used to think it was what happened on the bus between Oakland and Berkeley. And it was, too, like violet and Texas in peoples' voices, a whole bunch of subtle transmissions broken off by stops and bells, the percussion of riding, mobile contact, slow symposium. But now, even in the absence of my private office, I still want to move and so I have to move but never get there in this whole extended region of not being there, of stopping and saying not there, not there, and of that being, in the end, pretty much all I have to say. What I want to say is that having something to say is subordinate in the work of being true to the social life in somebody else's sound and grammar, its placement in my head, my placement in the collective head as it moves on down the line. The itinerant ensemble arrangement of the forty, and sometimes of the fifteen, is where I began to learn to move and live and think in poetry. Now I want to transfer what I'm learning as a practice of revision on the edge where ethics, politics, and aesthetics are in parallel play. Some kind of homeless shift between reading and writing that emerges in a class or set as our cut-up schedule, a diverse list of things, point-to-point restlessness, interlocking schemes of material breaks, the constantly renewed syllabus of a new composers guild in the middle of enjoying itself. What we will have come together to try to do would start to look like what we were doing when we came together to enjoy ourselves, handing over saying what we want for one another, to one another, in and out of words.

Nothing That Is Not There and the Nothing That Is Some Notes on Teaching Poetry

LAURA MULLEN

My title cites a famous poem by Wallace Stevens: perhaps a "mind of winter" starts to describe what's needed in the encounter with poetry. Though if you need a mind of winter for some poems then you also need to know that you'll want a mind of summer for others. Which is to say something like *the* poem *is everything that is the case.* That begins to get at the way poetry compels clear presence, accurate response, and (often enough) intense (and sometimes public) vulnerability, but if I'm really going to talk about reading, I'll want to start earlier. Maybe with Robert Pinsky expressing his frustration (circa 1983) with teaching Berkeley undergraduates? "They look everywhere," I remember him saying, jerking (in imitation) his own jaw side to side like a nervous thoroughbred, "*except* at the poem. If you could just," he continued, "get some kind of contraption to hold their heads down over the page." There's something to that: the reluctance to *look.*

Maybe what keeps people from wanting to read poetry is the same blindness that keeps them from seeing other kinds of waste (I want to invoke the connection between potlatch and trash here: *excess*). Most of the language we come to in our lives is treated as if it were a disposable container (say, to borrow Brenda Hillman's brilliant take on Keats's "Ode on a Grecian Urn," a Styrofoam cup): drink the hot message and chuck the cold words out. But the point of a poem (find one, find another: to say "'the poem is too full of meaning,'" a friend said he told his students, "is like saying 'the sex was too intense'") is the frottage across possible interpretations, to be repeated and experienced differently, no neat resolution of the relationship between beauty and truth.

Carol Krumhansl's essay "Memory for Musical Surface" touches on language studies proving that "subjects remember the meaning or gist of a sentence and not its surface structure—that is, the exact way the meaning is expressed," *except* where subjects attend to "wording" as per instructions or where the way the meaning was expressed becomes important. Poetry, as Stéphane Mallarmé famously said, is made of words and not ideas: in

└ relate back to
quote "we remember
how we felt"

other words (there are no other words) poetry is "the exact way," and not "the gist." It's this exact way that's hard to slow down enough to experience: too much rushing at premature 'meaning' (information or theme), too little time spent, as Gertrude Stein says, addressing and caressing.... (If I had to sum up Stein's genius in a phrase it would be this: you cannot paraphrase her without *immediately* discovered loss).

Slowing down means getting out of goal mode: Carol Snow and Cole Swensen, through attention to the visual arts, have developed productive guidelines for ways to start students reading for something other than content, and Charles Bernstein's witty "Poem Profiler" (from *Poetry and Pedagogy*) offers a seriously useful list of what to look for, but Craig Dworkin's *Reading the Illegible* suggests vision is developed by meeting blindness with blankness. Asking students to read—and write down everything they know about—Man Ray's "Lautgedicht" is transformative. Once we've established that this arrangement of what seems to be censored phrases is the poem, understandings of stanza and measure reveal themselves, and no one looks away from the site. "So while the physical opacity of a text prevents communication from ever being perfect, meaning is always being communicated by that very materiality," as Dworkin puts it.

Feminism has a lot to do with making the space to attend to the materiality of a text or reminding us that awareness of that aspect is unavoidable. To say we have to be in our bodies is absurd (where else are we?)—*and* bears repeating. "For the most part, we are not where we are, but in a false position. Through an infirmity of our natures, we suppose a case and put ourselves into it, and hence are in two cases at the same time, and it is doubly difficult to get out." What Henry David Thoreau calls the "two cases" are presented by poetry as language's essential duality ("Syllable" and "Sound" as Emily Dickinson says), not to get out of but *into*: to face.

"Have we talked about the French nose?" It's a question I ask my students: in Paris I noticed that, rather than diminishing (by surgery or some arrangement of hair and makeup) what might be regarded as an imperfection, the exquisitely gorgeous French women *play it up*. "Do I have a large nose? Very well!!" Every controllable aspect (hair, makeup, dress, accessories) seems arranged to call attention to and celebrate that special *flaw* which makes a person unique. Too often what happens in a poetry workshop can be the worst sort of plastic surgery, leaving the poem (O, Sharon Stone!) unrecognizable: bland, brittle, and false. (We start too soon to make suggestions, Rikki Ducornet suggests, and perhaps she is right in saying that we shouldn't talk about first drafts.) We need to read carefully to find the flaws to dazzle with: to make the most of whatever it is that makes us, as writers, unexpectedly exciting and unlike anyone else.

In order to recognize truth and beauty (in whatever form), you want a seasoned mind: the kind of openness only exposure to a wide variety of possibilities provides. Knowledge and courage allow good teachers to attend to their actual students and to suggest that real and resonant strangeness go even farther. Only by keeping the door open to "the sound of the wind"—without projecting "misery" on what might seem at first to be senseless—can we hope to hear "the sound of the land." Thud of "The the" here—heard—counter whisper of *s*: *sounds*, *lands*. Incommensurable: exquisite in their difference.

WORKS CITED

Dworkin, Craig. *Reading the Illegible*. Evanston: Northwestern University Press, 2003. 75.

Krumhansl, Carol L. "Memory for musical surface." *Memory & Cognition*. 1991. 401–411.

Thoreau, Henry David. *Walden*. New York: Heritage, 1939.

Roadie

MARK WALLACE

In most creative writing classes I teach, the majority of students have read no more than a few poems before and are likely never to have heard a poem out loud. That presents some challenges. I'm trying to help students gain an interest in poetry not only when they're not writers but also when they're not, to any significant extent, readers, and not just of poetry but of anything else.

Some people might scoff. They might bemoan the general lack of literature in American life or think it's hopeless to teach poetry writing to students who barely know what a poem is and may be only marginally functional writers. And often it is hopeless. But even if most of the students I teach never become writers, a significant number of them gain at least a little respect for poetry. Americans who don't know what literature is can't be expected to like and respect it if we make no attempt to show them what it is. In that sense, helping people see that there's value in literature even if they don't end up writing it may be worthwhile. Oddly enough perhaps, every year a few of my students decide that they actually do like poetry. They become involved with it both as readers and writers, and it becomes part of their lives. Frankly, it's not possible to know who will or won't become a writer unless you deny people the opportunity to find out what writing might be like.

The difficulty: people who don't know what poetry is usually think they know. Misinformation about poetry is very much alive even in places where there's little or no poetry. People who have never read poetry believe frequently that they know they don't like it and know why. The issue I'm always faced with is how to replace this powerful antipoetry misinformation with at least some awareness of what poems are and why people might love them.

As it turns out, the best breakthroughs I make usually occur when a student learns that poems create sounds. Many people are never taught anything about the sound of words. Instead they're taught to read silently and that the goal of using words is to make meaning. Talking about rhythms, syllables, and line breaks—or anything else about the structure of poetry—becomes meaningless with people who have never learned that sound has anything to do with words or that the structures of poetry are usually structures of sound.

All my students have heard music though, even if not much, and that's where I start. I make a loose comparison between notes and syllables, measures and lines. And it's crucial to have students listen to poems out loud, both poems they have written and poems being performed by experienced poets.

While comparing poetry and music often grabs the interest of at least some students, the comparison obviously has limits. Some students will head straight for the idea that poems are like pop love songs, and the most annoying ones too, full of abstract generalizations and emotional overstatements while lacking details, since the detail-free song is supposedly most universal. So we have to talk about the difference between poems and pop lyrics. Music has elements besides the lyrics to carry its feel and meaning. But many poems rely only on words to create their effects. The words have more work to do.

I'm aware that there's nothing original or innovative about what I'm saying. Sometimes ground-level work has to be done, and in my job there's a lot of it. Teaching poetry isn't like high-wire acrobatics. Instead, on bad days it reminds me of the joke about the circus worker who was asked why he stays in a job that requires him to shovel mounds of elephant shit daily. "Ah," he says, "show business."

Where I think innovation does enter into it is in the range of sound that students can be exposed to. Not just a recording of a reading by Hughes, Stein, or Eliot, but readings and performances of many types, done by writers from many different cultural and class backgrounds. Dub poems, slam poems, experimental performance poems, labor protest poems, digital poems with sound elements, sound poems (that is, poetry not relying solely on words), L=A=N=G=U=A=G=E poems, collaborative poems, flarf. In many cases it's possible through the sound of poems to open students to work which has meaning(s) they don't need to entirely understand just yet. Sonic pleasure allows people to loosen up about meaning because people already understand that, in music, meaning isn't the sole source of pleasure. Exposure to many types of sound also encourages comparison, and comparison encourages understanding.

And I find that, strikingly, sometimes this exposure works. Students who came into the class thinking that the only goal of poetry was to find a trick meaning that in fact isn't there start listening to poems. A few close their eyes to hear better. And some start writing good poems, or at least better ones. Their sense of rhythm takes them in directions that before they wouldn't have known how to let themselves go in. They pick up rhythms from their own bodies and minds that they didn't think had anything to do with poetry. It turns out that they already know, and feel, a lot of things that have to do with poetry. All they really needed was someone willing to make the effort to show them the connection. Someone to help them set up the equipment.

So remember the moon is
beautiful and who knows what
would happen without it.
—from a poem by Navjot

Teaching Poetry at the California School for the Blind

CLAIRE BECKER

In order to make the task of opening my students up to poetry less daunt-ing, I've tried to isolate what I'd like them to gain from exposure to it. My students are blind or visually impaired with congenital as well as recent vision loss. They attend a state-run special school for intensive instruc-tion in expanded curricular areas—braille, assistive technology, orienta-tion and mobility, independent living skills, and more. In my class of stu-dents, ages thirteen through seventeen, we also follow state standards for English-language arts, math, social studies, and science. Sometimes it's hard to know how poetry fits in.

Most of the students with whom I work have little exposure to poetry in a classroom setting. Many find reading and writing to be a challenge, especially if they are losing vision or new to braille. It takes a rigorous ap-proach to master grammar, spelling, diction, and one's tools for writing, but in order to gain from poetry initially, mastery isn't required. Poetry can help students access new ways of thinking. Many people who interact with blind children focus on giving them a logical understanding of the world; they don't always share the mystery and strangeness of it. That is a great deficit. I hope that poetry exercises will help my students enter the mystery and strangeness of the world as well as find value in their own ideas and thoughts.

Exploring poetry on their own can be difficult for blind students. Once they're exposed to it and interested, students might be able to find famil-iar poets on the Internet and access their work through screen magnifiers or screen readers. They can read braille copies of poems and books in our classroom or school library, but they can't browse a bookstore shelf or friend's collection like their sighted peers. They can't have every experi-ence that's possible with print when they are writing. Most students write electronically on a braille note taker and navigate their documents one line at a time. Many students who prefer to write prose poems because they already experience text in short chunks (or they experience a poem's sen-tences, not its lines—a screen reader doesn't identify ends of lines). They can't write collaborations on the chalkboard or scribble comments on a friend's poem.

I worked on erasures with one student recently. To give examples of the exercise, I read her the original pages of text and the poems that were made by erasing many words in them. For a print version of an erasure exercise, one can photocopy a page out of any book and give it to a student. Braille can't be easily reproduced, so I took a page from a book about manners published in 1959. To erase braille, one uses a tool with a blunt end to push down the dots that have been raised to form the character. My student was tickled by the idea of ripping a page out of a book and erasing words on it but challenged by the labor of erasing. It took her twenty-five minutes to erase ten words. She enjoyed the project, but she stopped there, less than a quarter through the page. The experience isn't the same as with print.

My students tend to favor poets who use common diction and uncomplicated phrases, and the students turn out short poems with fairly simple diction themselves. Using short words is common in any assignment, especially among low-vision students. Some students write on dark-lined paper with a felt-tip pen. They write large enough so they can see their writing, or they use a magnification device to enlarge it. A student may not choose a word that takes up a whole line of the page. Following this paragraph are three poems by Leonardo, a student with low vision. The assignment was to write loose a haiku about a reflective moment. The haiku exercise was successful because it didn't ask for many words to be written. It also taught condensation and revision, even in an already short poem.

I was by the car
I went back home
It was windy

Outside the door
Trash cans nearby
I look up at the sky

I walked to the park
The food tasted bad
I was bored

Many students included actions of looking in their poems, such as, "I look up at the sky," "Looking at the snowflakes / Falling from the sky," and "Soon I finish and stare at the sun." Whether a student has vision or not, he or she is exposed to descriptions of people interacting with the visual world and often understands the feelings and emotions associated with these actions. Visual descriptions can be prevalent in poetry, and my students include them in their poems too. For students who are born totally blind, writing about the visual aspects of the world can be an exercise of the imagination.

I'm interested in where the students will go with their writing in the future. The qualities of the braille code could be influential. Shortcuts and contractions change the length of English words. For example, the word *knowledge* is written as *k* with a space after it; the word *know* is longer, a dot in position five of the braille cell, followed by a *k*. Many common words (designated as common nearly a century ago) take up little space, just one, two, or three characters. Among these are the words: and, also, altogether, but, braille, can, father, for, little, mother, of, people, quite, rather, receive, receiving, some, the, together, very, with, word, work, world (and many more). Some spaces between words are omitted. However, uncommon roots with uncommon affixes can contain as many characters as they do in print.

I want my students to get comfortable writing without having to argue for their choice of words and phrases in a logical way. This is important for teenagers, whose words can be scrutinized by their peers for anything out of the ordinary. They may struggle translating thoughts and ideas into academic language. They need an opportunity to enjoy writing, to record their thoughts, and to be confident in their own voice. Whether they are wondering about the visual world, expressing emotion, or playing with the sounds of language, students can use poetry as a way to explore their own thoughts. Exposure to poetry may help students with visual impairments understand themselves a little better, and it may complicate the way they understand the world.

Integrating Other Arts

{ **The Poem as Canvas**
Interdisciplinary
Pedagogies
HADARA BAR-NADAV

I am a poet and painter who happily studied poetry and painting side by
side in graduate school. During my doctoral work, a typical day might con-
sist of painting for four hours in an art class, teaching a poetry workshop,
and then participating as a student in a graduate poetry workshop. Or I
might sit through a class on the history of photography, then a class on
postcolonial poetics, and then teach a poetry class. As a graduate student,
I looked for ways to bridge my areas of interest. I rushed from an art history class to the poetry class I was teaching to tell my students "God is the
details" (qtd. in Blake) during a discussion on imagery. And when these
poetry students told me they were feeling uninspired and had "seen it all,"
I countered with Brassai: "If reality fails to fill us with wonder, it is because
we have fallen into the habit of seeing it as ordinary" (qtd. in Guatrand).
I also handed my students viewfinders (slides without the film in them)
and asked them to write what they *actually* saw—to capture the luminous
details—versus generalizing their vision (a painting professor had given
our painting class viewfinders the week before). Time and time again, I
learned that pedagogical approaches from my art classes could be usefully
adapted to poetry workshops. Now a professor of poetry, I have continued
to develop my interdisciplinary practices into an interdisciplinary pedagogy. For this short essay, I will share two ways that I have implemented
interdisciplinary methodologies in my workshops.

1. THE ART OF DOING

Painting students assume they will be required to paint in painting classes;
however, poetry workshops generally have become a site for talking *about*
writing rather than engaging in the *act* of writing. Writing has been per-
petuated as a private and solitary act. For some student writers, this might
not seem like an issue, except that a different set of expectations is required when students are asked to shift gears and participate in a communal workshop.

    Similar to a painting class, I claim the poetry workshop as a creative art-making space. Moreover, I propose the writing *and* revision process as potentially communal acts (not only among workshop members but also beyond the workshop: poetry as a form of communication that inherently seeks and creates community). When students write and revise in class, it emphasizes the importance of process, inspires them to be playful and take advantage of the creative energy of their peers, and encourages collaboration by providing access to a community of peer-editors.

Recently my graduate poetry class read an essay on tonal variety in Tony Hoagland's *Real Sofistikashun*. After we discussed the essay, I asked the students to consider revising their poems with tonal variety in mind and gave them ten minutes to do so. I wasn't expecting a masterpiece, and I didn't collect or grade these drafts. I only asked the class to spend a few minutes thinking about how Hoagland's idea might benefit their poems.

For some of my students, this activity was groundbreaking; it hadn't occurred to them that they could immediately and directly apply something they just learned to their own poetry. Apparently, students would apply new ideas about craft to each other's poetry or to the poetry we were reading, but not necessarily to their own work. Taking time in class to have students revise snapped them out of familiar modes of making and gave them the opportunity to practice incorporating tonal variation. Furthermore, it enabled them to recognize that they could in fact practice new ways of writing and revising in class as well as on their own.

2. THE POEM AS OBJECT

Poetry on the page has a shape. It is a physical object as well as a verbal / ideological construct. A poem made of thin tercets has a much different weight and presence than a long prose poem (for example, consider poems by Sylvia Plath and Gertrude Stein). I would argue that we register the shape of a poem before we even read a single word and that the shape of a poem prepares us for the poem ahead, filling us with expectations, sensations, etc. And while it isn't difficult to convince my students that poems have objectness and are multidimensional, most tend to write poems that hug the left margin (a Microsoft Word default) and rarely venture out across the page. Certainly there is nothing wrong with writing poems that are left-justified. But must all poems be left-justified? What kinds of poems should be left-justified? And what would happen to language, syntax, and form if students pulled away from the left default and explored the entire canvas of the page?

To give shape to the discussion of a poem's objectness, I collect art books from home or the library and show paintings to my students (I tend to select nonrepresentational art to isolate the focus on shape / object). Without stating the name of the artist or work of art, I ask students what the shapes in a painting by, for example, Mark Rothko signal to them—two or three wide luminescent shapes reaching from margin to margin. I might show them a couple of Franz Kline's—his lightening bolts jagging across the canvas—or a Helen Frankenthaler—her waterfalls of color that emanate and echo. I then show a few poems on the document camera, throw off the focus so students cannot make out the words, and ask them what the shape of the poems suggests. Afterward, we read the poems and discuss how closely our visual expectations match the actual content (commonly the two overlap). We might also discuss how form relates to content (i.e., Bob Hicok's long column-like chatty poems) or creates tension between our expectations and the content (Mary Jo Bang's seemingly neat elegies). Though this discussion may spark a surge of concrete / Vispo / calligramatic poetry, it ultimately invites students to consider leaving the left side of the page, playing with form, and seeing what else poems can do, what words might be waiting, what discoveries they have yet to make.

WORKS CITED

Blake, Peter. *The Master Builders: Le Corbusier, Mies van der Rohe, Frank Lloyd Wright*. New York: Norton, 1996. 200.

Guatrand, Jean-Claude. *Brassai: Paris*. Hong Kong: Taschen, 2008. 20.

Hoagland, Tony. *Real Sofistikashun: Essays on Poetry and Craft*. St. Paul: Graywolf, 2006.

The Human Teacher

TYRONE WILLIAMS

The current teaching models, which still employ human beings as teachers, might well be equivalent to capitalism itself, assuming (and it is by no means certain) that the current models are an improvement over older pedagogical / economic models. Under the current system, teachers are analogous to, perhaps equivalent to, the bourgeoisie, emerging from feudalism as obstacle and vehicle of socialist revolution. But the question of whether or not current models of teaching at the secondary public schools—and to a larger extent, at public primary schools—and public colleges are better than those prior to the professionalization of teaching remains open. I am not concerned with ethical or moral issues here. I am concerned with the alleged objects of teaching.

To some degree, especially at the college and secondary public school level, the object of teaching resembles that of the early nineteenth century in the United States when teaching was an explicit means of acquiring or solidifying social and cultural power. Today, if teaching is more about information than knowledge, one wonders then if human beings as teachers do not present an obstacle to the reception of information, understood here as the aggregate of facts concerning a spectrum of fields and disciplines authorized by the physical and human sciences.

The insistence that the human face of the teacher is a *sine qua non* of learning calls into question exactly what it is that one, a student, for example, is supposed to be learning. In relation to information the teacher may well constitute an obstacle; this may be one reason, perhaps, that educators and others often oppose information to knowledge, the alleged object of education. Knowledge would thus be something conveyed from one human to another, that something being composed in part—but not wholly—of information. Information would thus be gleaned from reading or viewing a Web site, book, or museum exhibit, but knowledge would depend on seeing and hearing a *person* relay information. Or put another way: knowledge would be information that has passed through the transformative powers of the teacher.

It is not assumed that the student is illiterate, cannot read or view on her own. Rather, it is assumed that the current teaching models do not provide enough time to glean both information and knowledge from mere reading. But this is the more generous interpretation. It may well be the case that the suspicion toward reading and readers—which has a long history, one inextricable from the development of the current secular and religious systems that dominate world history—still survives in the presumption that students cannot learn (gain knowledge) from reading alone. These assumptions are significant.

For example, it may be that American students starting school at the arbitrary age of five years old could accelerate their learning through reading and listening in the absence of human teaching—or at least in the absence of institutions of learning. This is one of the tenets of home schooling, though it only exaggerates the *human* factor by both humanizing and personalizing learning. As public educators remind us, students are supposed to learn more than mere *book knowledge*, a term whose pejorative connotation cannot be missed by even the most hapless of students. Education—which should not be confused with the acquisition of knowledge—is indeed a mode of socialization. In this context, book knowledge may often be antithetical to education.

In brief, the current teaching models not only contradict one another from elementary school on to graduate school, they are also self-contradictory to the extent that they link knowledge (which is primarily thinking) to education. These self-contradictions are openly acknowledged; in fact, higher education (post-secondary) is, in certain disciplines, explicitly posed as the almost total repudiation of secondary and primary education. That "almost" is indicative of a countervailing assumption: that higher education, even in these disciplines, remains fundamentally dependent upon secondary and primary education.

One might respond that the above descriptions are needlessly exaggerated, that only a maverick immaturity or willful iconoclasm would see contradiction where there is only the enabling tension of increasingly challenging, increasingly complex and difficult, modes of knowledge. Education would thus be analogous to the competitive spirit that animates, for example, evolution as natural selection; to wit, in "the marketplace of ideas" the best and most useful ideas, the ones most adaptive to a given historical epoch, will invariably triumph.

Yet it is precisely analogy within and migration throughout the arena of human knowledge that fuels argument, contention, and disagreement.

These battles are not easily assimilated to mere competition with its implication of a graspable, if temporary, victory. It is not that evolution serves here as the ground against which the figure of education would appear as its double or shadow. If anything, we would have to reverse polarities, for education, as an object of human knowledge, is *older* than evolution. Evolution, like analogy, would not exist without education. At the same time the migration of terms and concepts between education and evolution—most significantly, the concept of development—reminds us that the autonomy of disciplines and fields is, at best, relative. We are reminded that analogy per se undercuts the absolute autonomy of any sphere of human knowledge.

Thus the Aristotelian—not Hegelian—contradictions I am referring to are relatively new in the history of formal education. And to a large extent they are confined to the human sciences, though one should not underestimate the internecine conflicts within the physical sciences the closer they attempt to discover or explain the conundrums of the origin of matter, of life, to say nothing of existence. As it happens, these concerns dovetail with those in the human sciences and they take many forms. Ever since the division of the academy into ever specialized fields and disciplines (in this country, the late nineteenth century and early twentieth century are particularly crucial) these forms have multiplied, and the skirmishes and all-out wars between and within them have subsequently multiplied exponentially. But what they have in common, and what they have in common with the physical sciences to the extent the latter broach those metaphysical concerns above, is this: the human abstract vis-à-vis knowledge. It is precisely how we know and its relation to what we know that is in question throughout the spectrum of the human and physical sciences. And the word "relation" presupposes the concept of analogy, whether that relation is affirmed, disputed, or deemed irrelevant.

The tripartite structure of analogy implies a medium—and in formal education the teacher serves as the figure of mediation. As we know, however, education accomplishes one of its ends with the disappearance of the teacher. He or she too must, finally, be repudiated—almost—for such repudiation takes the form of an abstract, a remnant, interiorized by the epigone. If we insist that there is no *must* about this at all, that the teacher can always be completely erased in the name of removing the last obstacle between a student and an object of knowledge—let's still call this object a book, even if the ubiquitous Web site and Amazonian Kindle loom on the horizon—we will have already, however unwittingly, inserted the metaphysics of the *pure* rupture in history, an idea replete with religious overtones. As a matter of tradition and custom, belief in the possibility of an absolute break constitutes one understanding of history, one whose effects are everywhere visible in the various wars—physical and metaphysical—being fought on so many terrains across the earth, to say nothing of those being waged on the lands currently called the United States of America. This interpretation of history as absolute rupture, as history *sans* that "almost" so crucial to the enabling, productive, contradictions of higher education, is, by definition, anti-intellectual, anti-higher education, even if these are not the same thing. It is on this basis of this interpretation of history, which dominates that other interpretation of history (history as neither rupture nor continuum), that we are told so often, as a frustrated but persistent teacher tells his or her recalcitrant students, history repeats itself. Does not that "itself" say it all?

Becoming the Poem

SPRING ULMER

I did this maybe twelve times in a university composition classroom: Photocopied Emily Dickinson's "Master" letters without her name on them and then handed out the photocopies. I said, "Read this as if you were a teacher, make marks on it, give it a grade."

My students generally failed her.

(Poetry teaches teachers—with our red pens—humility, hopefully.)

I volunteered for a year teaching creative writing to kids on probation. One kid, M., wrote and breathed poetry. I invited him to my university composition class to give him an idea of what college was like. His probation officer gave him permission. I picked him up in my truck and brought him to class. He participated eagerly, even volunteering to read his in-class writing out loud. Afterward I asked if he wanted to see anything else on campus. Eyeing a map, he picked the Little Chapel. We walked there together. Once inside, he said, "Spring, you don't know the Psalms? I've got to read some to you. They are poetry."

And so I heard the Psalms for the first time.

(Years later, I was eating dinner at a Mexican restaurant when a young man approached me. It was M. "I just wanted to tell you," he whispered, "I'm at community college now.")

Khoor used to come to see me during my university office hours. He wasn't my student. He knew me because I had once taught English to Sudanese refugees. He, too, was a refugee, but his English was excellent. He'd fought in the Sudan People's Liberation Army and was now getting his master's degree in mathematics. He also wrote poems. He would come with a stack of new poems once each month or so, and we would sit together tightening them, tweaking their grammar. He wrote about longing for a wife, about losing family. Once, he told me a war story. It took place in a town in Sudan. A small child, wanting to help the liberation army, blew himself up in an armored tank the Russians had given the Arabs. It was the Arab's only tank. After telling me this, Khoor said that he would go back to war, if he had to. Better to die fighting, he said, for the liberation of your country, than to die of disease. If you die of disease no one will remember you. Yet one of Khoor's poems (and don't we write poems to remember and be remembered?) is about how love and hate can't solve anything, only respect and understanding can.

I miss sitting under flourescent flickering lights, bent over Khoor's poems with him. Now I am in another state and he is setting up a business in Sudan.

■

The day I played Nina Simone's "Four Women" and then Talib Kweli's "For Women" on the boom box, there was an uproar. Some students noticed other students weren't listening. "It's not like it's important to them, anyway," one student said. Another student, who had been talking while the music played, lashed back: "My grandfather was persecuted in the Holocaust!"

This: The undeniable starting point for a class attempting to read the lyric politically.

■

Kizzy, an old student of mine, emails me her poems. She also writes to say, "I hope you like our dinners and that they make your life fun." They do. They are almost the only times these days when I laugh. She, Erin (another former student), and I dye our hair, make strange chili, act silly. How could this have come about? It's magic—this extension of the classroom, this extension of the poem.

■

The setting is a classroom. White walls, whiteboard, a crowd of trapezoid-shaped tables, uncomfortable chairs, buzzing lights. Some unattractive posters hang on one wall. A television is screwed and bolted into the ceiling stage right. Emily's drawn the colonel's broken glass wall on the room's window with erasable marker. "Something for your poetry, no?"[1] Ryan narrates.

Kalisha is playing the part of the colonel. Martin's the cop show on TV *and* the Spanish commercial. In the place of ears, Kalisha throws coins onto the ground. The pennies hit the floor and clatter. "Silencio!" she yells.

Afterward, we sit circled, the students and I, shades drawn. "What in this poem 'The Colonel,'" I ask, "do you identify with personally?"

"I'll talk about how I relate," Kalisha says. "My grandmother told me about this place that I don't know if I'm strong enough to go to. It's a place where they burned slaves who were worn out, of no more use. She said they cut off their ears, their fingers, body parts, and handed them out as souvenirs . . . I just can't stand that it still happens, that the cycle continues."

There is silence. Then we find the words to thank Kalisha for her comment.

The next day of class, I pass out a photocopy of a *New York Times Magazine* photo of the Sassaman family at home in Colorado Springs. We all look at the photo and write down whatever comes to mind. *They're perfect, middle class, the father's in a uniform . . . It's the ideal American family, boy and girl, suburbs . . . The mother has definitely worked on her appearance, she's tanned, maybe has had plastic surgery, trying to look young* . . . Only after we've come up with these interpretations, do I tell everyone the information the image doesn't relay: "The father in this image is a colonel," I say. "He is being tried for the murder of an Iraqi."

I ask whether anyone sees a connection between this colonel and the one in Carolyn Forché's poem. *They both have families, they seem middle class, both have a son and a daughter and a wife*, students answer.

"Is this man in the photo what you thought of when you imagined the Colonel?" I ask them.

P. and I meet on Sunday. She wants me to look over her paper comparing her own personal suffering to her people's suffering as it's represented in a poem about the Long Walk. I begin to read her paper out loud and then I stop as it becomes more personal. "Could you keep reading it out loud?" she asks.

"Of course." I come to a place where she's written: *Obviously he didn't love me.* "He loved you," I say.

"I know," she says.

We talk. She is sitting in the shade and I am in the full sun, squinting at her from across a white table. She tells me of riding horses with her boyfriend and going to expensive dinners at restaurants. Then she gets out her iPod. She wants me to hear traditional singing. She's downloaded some onto this green little piece of plastic. We sit there, one button in my ear, one in hers, listening to her iPod. She plays me song after song. She sings along, and then tells me which songs she's learning, which she'd like to learn. I ask if she drums. Women haven't been allowed to drum, she says, but now there are a few girls. Sparrows and two bees around us. And one black ant on a white sneaker. In my ear, old men singing traditional Navajo songs whose messages P. translates.

(Teaching poetry teaches me to listen, to let poetry do the talking.)

NOTE

1. Caroline Forché. "The Colonel." *The Country Between Us*. New York: Harper Collins, 1981.

As Many Questions as Answers

BIN RAMKE

I was recently moved to say, in a moment of annoyance, that I no longer believe in poetry, and ten minutes later to say the same about teaching. And yet for the past thirty years I have taught, most consistently I have taught the writing of poetry. I am not being merely, or mainly, provocative. But by way of provoking I will say that what has always annoyed me about teaching, as with religion, is authoritarianism—the way, for instance, the language of monarchy is the default language of preaching and teaching (a word such as *Lord* is offensive, anti-democratic, and suggests a need for obedience; the medieval titles and trappings of the university can be similarly suggestive). Poetry is always about liberty, sometimes anarchy, and while both teaching and poetry are intensely concerned with structure and pattern and historical context, these elements are only acceptable alongside the resistance to specific structure, repeatable patterning, and ahistorical impulsiveness.

At its best, teaching *enables*, and is a collection of practices of the rights of and the obligations toward the self of the student. At its worst, poetry is a display of skills which separate poet from reader by enforcing an arrogant authoritarian ownership of language.

Anyone attempting to teach others how to write a poem must face the probability that young students hope to use writing to face a rising sense of metaphysical loneliness which may be indistinguishable from standard adolescent angst. The teacher of poetry writing must help the new writer learn to make various distinctions about the self and the world beyond the self through language. The new writer must learn that thinking for the poet occurs on the page, in the language, in the voice and the body which contains and enables the voice. Which means the teacher of poetry writing is in effect fighting the teacher (or at least the teachings) of standard rhetorical composition. Freshman composition is perhaps not THE enemy, but will do for now. Poetry is not argument, and the voice of the poet is not an instrument to silence the voice of the reader, and yet the rhetoric of much teaching-of-writing is a rhetoric of domination. Similarly, the voice of the teacher should not be allowed to become an instrument to silence the voice of the student.

The teaching of how to write a poem involves a continuing series of subversions and sub-versions. At least, this is true if one is trying to teach the kind of verse which hopes to do something in the world, not merely to ornament it.

Read

For several years now I have used Laura (Riding) Jackson's "As Many Questions as Answers" as a way to begin undergraduate poetry workshops. I have the students read the poem, discuss a bit about the question-answer format as a poetic form, have each student write a brief poem in that form, have them read the poems to each other, and then I require them to tear the poems in half and read questions paired with unintended answers. I claim no originality in this procedure, but I do intend it as more than a mere exercise to get a writing process started. It matters, for instance, that Laura (Riding) Jackson eventually (and complicatedly, serially) repudiated poetry, and I speak to my classes about this fact. It matters that I force the students to give up (in a sense, and for a time) their individual ownership of poems. But it *is* only an exercise, and eventually other poems arise out of individual concerns and responses, questions and prejudices. The process of teaching writing is a process of introducing the student to him or herself, to her own concerns and intentions, and then of challenging the student to confront what these concerns and intentions might mean in a larger (social, cultural, aesthetic) context, and how those concerns and intentions fit into some sort of artistic continuum—a tradition, if you wish. Leading students into asking themselves more complex and finally more significant questions is a kind of teaching.

But I have also been requiring students to bring into the classroom what I am calling contexts (but which involve much more than texts), which will allow the rest of us to more quickly and completely engage their work. These contexts might be the music the new poet listened to while writing, or short films, or images in books, or essays. Since all writing arises from complex and even contradictory situations, it is useful and enlightening for the writer to become more conscious of the situations that surrounded the writing. A delightful result of such a process is that the presentation of poems becomes livelier, a part of a multisensory enactment. It is fun.

I wish I believed more in authority in the classroom because I suspect I could then predict much more accurately when things will go well and when they might not. But my anxiety as a teacher has always been high, and it seems no amount of experience makes me less fearful, less anguished about whether I am actually doing good, whether I am responding to the individual, specific needs of the students—whether as a teacher of so-called "creative writing" I have a legitimate place in the world of work. Sometimes I believe in it, especially when I see former students' writing out there in the world.

WORK CITED
Jackson, Laura (Riding). *Poems*. New York: Persea Books, 2001.

Myth and Permission

JULIE DOXSEE

For the past year and a half I have been teaching at a private university in Istanbul, where, owing to my status as a foreigner, I must approach poetry with as Turkish an eye as possible. Colleagues warned me of the obstacles that would crop up in a Turkish creative writing class. I was told, first, that the public education system in Turkey requires a penchant for memorization and robotic exam-taking, not for self-expression. Owing to methodologies which reward rote learning, Turkish students are afraid to write (especially in English), and they don't understand abstraction. Kids do not choose their majors, rather their parents and exam scores assign futures as engineers, computer scientists, business administrators, etc. Given these cultural underpinnings, I was not expecting to encounter positive experiences in the introductory poetry classroom.

My only previous experience with a beginner poetry class occurred in the States, where the inevitable presence of skeptical, half-willing participants tended to drag down the motivation of the entire class. I expected a roomful of such skeptics in my Turkish classroom. To my sigh of relief, though, I now believe that the educational differences in Turkey, rather than damning up the muse, leave a thirst for creativity that is uniquely quenchable in the creative writing classroom. Further, the aforementioned obstacles are no match for Turkish warmth, humanity, community, and cultural inheritance of the notion that "nothing is uncool." What I mean is that when given instructions for an exercise, my students do not automatically resist à la the skeptical student—they are willing to try anything.

A poetry professor once told me that for one to become a successful artist one must live as a risk-taker—to do so one must shed the fear of embarrassment. Embarrassment, as a construct of Western culture, is a term associated with ridicule and klutziness (to me these associations are poetic contaminations par excellence—which speaks volumes, perhaps, about my own fear). When I pass pro-embarrassment advice on to my Turkish students, they respond as though they are already far beyond this fear—either they are beyond it or they understand, in a very literal sense, that embarrassment vis-à-vis risk-taking is good because the advice came from an authority figure. When given permission to do something, they perk up: they go to dark places, speak from the gut, gesticulate, philosophize, and crack open new emotional worlds from which to inspire one another. For example, in a class I taught last summer based on neo-mythology and cosmology, students, inspired by Italo Calvino, wrote their own "invisible cities." Groups of students transformed their cities into elaborate poetic civilizations and even invisible planets with their own economic, ethical, emotional, and cosmological systems. The response was not a passive, paper-only experience, it was an accumulative, collaborative, epic activity extending into dark humor, visuals, and performance. In the same class I asked students to write, after Pliny, poetic encyclopedia entries for different attitudes and / or emotions. They wrote contemporary rituals based on Jerome Rothenberg's *Technicians of the Sacred*, they read Mathias Svalina's *Creation Myths* and wrote their own versions. In yet another exercise, they were prompted to write a poetic (Platonic) dialogue between a famous person, an animal, and a child.

Because Turkish university students who come from the public education system are allegedly "afraid to write" I have refrained, in the beginner classroom, from conversations of excision in order to draw out as much writing as possible. When given a set of constraints and time limits, my students focus (like good exam takers) and set out to produce accordingly. Turkey lies within the vast seat of Greek and Roman mythology and philosophy, and I believe my students, as undergraduates undergoing identity-formation, feel particularly moved to contribute as contemporary myth-makers. The work I've seen so far is mined from untapped reserves and bears an originality perpetually surprising to me. Following my hunch to allow students to unearth as much poetic substance as they possibly can, I applaud the raw and ungainly nature of unedited attempts. From the raw writing they build performances, plays, choreographies, films, and other "translations" that broaden what poetry is and what it can be. Permission to consider poetry a cross-medium genre is met with explosive energy, intent, plans for collaboration.

When we were not screening short films and / or student films in our classroom last summer, we held readings and performances in a gazebo overlooking the Black Sea. Occasionally students became so enraptured they would dance around our gazebo reading poems, shouting, and cheering each other on. This energy led to a long, elaborate end-of-semester poetry day involving hours of feasting, singing, shouting, tearing up, and fishbowl-style reading on the shores of the Bosphorus. The majority of my students are not shy, and they do not employ filters that tell them such behavior is embarrassing or outlandish. My students do not sabotage one another to get ahead, rather they stand together and seem to gain an extraordinary amount of pleasure from the experience of airing out their pieces communally. To be honest, beyond bearing in mind cultural idiosyncrasies, I am not certain what my role is in provoking this celebration of poetry. I serve as the voice of permission and possibility, and they do the rest.

At the end of my first semester teaching poetry here I praised my poetry students for their bravery, and for their willingness, really, to say anything. I told them the experience of teaching poetry here was so unlike my experiences in an American classroom. A student replied, "We are a warm people—this is the way we need to live."

NOTE
With thanks to Teoman Türeli

A Pedagogy Torments Itself with a Question That Questions Itself

DAN BEACHY-QUICK

Poetry is an art overseen by a pantheon: Apollo, Hermes, the Muses, Dionysus. To teach poetry is to find oneself devoted, and convincing others to devote themselves, to an art whose faith demands contradiction. Poetry counters wisdom with foolishness. Poetry counters truth with falsity, counters clarity with drunkenness, memory with forgetting. A teacher of poetry is all of these qualities at once: wise-one and fool, stoic and liar, seer and lush, mnemono-maniac and aphasiac. Other contradictions abound. Heraclitus notes: the bow-string and the lyre-string are one. The teacher of poetry knows what sings must also wound. The poet is one who is wounded by song and in singing is one who wounds. The page the poem is printed on is a threat. The teacher draws the lines of the poem back—as the archer draws back the bow, as the poet draws back the string—and in doing so the line is alive.

Other contradictions abound, and the teacher is devoted to them. The contradictions do not cancel each other; they embrace each other. The Muses, descending from Mount Helicon to speak to Hesiod, say "we know how to tell many lies that pass for truth, / and we know, when we wish, to tell the truth itself."[1]

The teacher of poetry may not be a Muse, but in the classroom conducts a Muse-like, maze-like, activity. The mother of the Muses is Memory. Memory confounds vision with expectation. A student most often sees what she already knows she sees. A teacher undoes that knowledge and releases vision from the limits of recognition. Then vision thinks and the poem is the record of that thinking through the eye. It is not a painless process. The eye is also a wound.

Aristotle claims that philosophy began in wonder. We see the fact of the world in front of us and marvel at it—and in marveling, we ask a question. Aristotle says that wisdom is the ability to generalize about the universe, to find truth without needing to resort to experience. We like to say a teacher is wise.

William Blake says that universals are for blockheads. The poet dwells among the particulars. We seldom mean it as a compliment when we say a teacher is a fool, but a teacher is a fool.

These oppositions coincide in the poet. In the classroom, the teacher is one who finds no difference between the wise-one and the fool. The teacher is both. Poetry, too, relates to wonder. Wonder is where poetry returns us to. It disables something in us that knows what to say about the world. At the end of the poem—one we write or one we read (as if there were a difference)—our wisdom feels foolish. I love that silence best when I hear it in the classroom, that silence of gaining some unspeakable thing. I like to find that silence in myself; I like to find myself in that silence. It is wonderful. It is also tormented. For within that silence a question gains urgency, a question about how this exact leaf the storm pasted against the window relates to that other image-leaf blown against the window in the mind. The teacher stands between the particulars of the world and the generalities of the universe. The teacher of poetry is the one in whom those realms collide and maintain their livid connection. The bow-string and the lyre-string are one. The teacher of the poem and the poem do a work that cannot be told apart—the same is true of the student of the poem (as if there were a difference). For a moment truthfulness and truth collide—it is not wise and it is not foolish. It is both. And the wise fool feels the prick of the world. The wise fool asks that question whose end is to question itself. Our wonder suffers doubt. Then the teacher says: now is when our poem begins.

NOTE

1. Hesiod. *Theogony, Work and Days, Shield.* Trans. Apostolos N. Athanassakis. Baltimore: Johns Hopkins UP, 1983.

The Box

FORREST GANDER

To show students how to get inside the work, that's the challenge. And it has exacted an enormous price, has levied an incomparable torque on my body: my heart straining its blue moorings, the reverse peristalsis, my internal organs pressurized almost into a lube.

But I should begin with a general comment about writing poetry. At the absolute center of the work, in the vortex from which any form is spun, there is a shaping hand which is neither godlike nor joyous. The poet's primary engagement is with violent, mute fear.

It is my pedagogical practice to enter the classroom in a simple white robe beneath which I wear only a mawashi. I carry with me the potential work, a transparent plexiglass box. It is a two-and-one-half-foot pellucid cube. I stand six-two. The class usually expects a trick.

In the beginning of my career, I used to have nightmares. I dreamed of squeezing into a work that wasn't my own, into an altered box whose hinged panel, when I'm ready to exit the work, I cannot find. Scientists say that claustrophobia is a disease that involves an actual physical swelling to accompany the mind's equation of body and surrounding space. I remember dreaming of being so crammed into a box that all my muscular convulsions are throttled and the students imagine me at peace, untwitching even as I howl breathlessly against my naval.

I rarely dream anymore. Discipline is freedom, as Marianne Moore teaches us. I have trained myself to withdraw my testicles through the naturally occurring inguinal hernia. This is part of the physics of entering the work.

And like every poet, I'm a repository for the writers of the past, the dead who are carried inside me and who account for some real particular of my volume. The secret to poetry being breath, temporarily, only temporarily, it is possible to exhale the dead from the body. In the tidal interval between their departure and their return, the body becomes more limber, less encumbered by influence, and smaller. A poet my size can slip into a very tight work.

Volume, after all, is a sort of illusion of surface areas created by molecular vibration in near emptiness. It is like a subway train moving with such velocity that it appears to be on all tracks at once. But by slowing down the breath, by blowing out the clatter of the dead, I concentrate myself onto one track, one line, into a single position, the small circle on the subway map indicating YOU ARE HERE.

This is the brief moment of *poésie pure*. Brief because, like water displaced by the finger of a poet writing his name in water, the dead come rushing back. In that momental wake of their egress, my memory usually goes.

Closing the door to the classroom and discarding my robe, I step onto the chair and then up onto the middle of the table, the plexiglass box under my arm. I sit lotus-fashion with the students around me. I take them through some breathing exercises. When I begin to feel, inside myself, the diaspora, then the absence of influence, I open the side of the box and slowly fold myself inward. To the class, there seems to be not enough room even for my long legs. But the dead are being pressed out, my memory is fining away, my torso swaying tarantellasmically at the mouth of the box. Slowly, my head, shoulders, and knees make the crossing. The body, as Hart Crane reminds us, makes its meek adjustments. The final thing I do is reach lightly with my right hand, my writing hand, to close the door. The last motions are wholly mechanical. There is an audible click of the latch and the class is always hushed now. I do not remember who I am, I am inside the work.

To keep the dead at bay, to keep them from blowing back into me, expanding me with their authority while I'm still cramped in the work; to keep them from crushing me, I have been forced to develop increasingly elaborate exercises. All my practice is like a circle of pig's blood the ghosts cannot penetrate. And within the circle, inside the box, I contract into a tight fetal position, my hands over my ears and my eyes clamped like fists, while all of hell screams for entrance.

Around the silent space of my work, the hideous chorus stalks. No observer could perceive my bottlenecked spasm. While my students watch, the work takes place. The box finally opaques with the tiny steam of my breath.

Exercises / Praxis

The Ax

RAE ARMANTROUT

At UCSD we have a large undergraduate writing major. We're planning to start an MFA, but haven't yet admitted our first class. Consequently, most of the students I deal with are beginners. They come in (many of them) thinking that poetry is a highly subjective form of "self-expression." I try to get them to see that, if they turn outward and write *about* the world, they'll find themselves in it. You can't get away from yourself, after all.

I begin by having students read a few poems from Francis Ponge's *Taking the Side of Things*. I point out the way Ponge describes objects with an almost scientific precision, but also takes great liberties with them. He is both objective and outrageous. After we discuss the Ponge poems, I pull out a child's school eraser and a loofah sponge and ask students to write about one of these in the spirit, if not the style, of Ponge. I find that, in attempting to respond to the eraser or the loofah, they begin to confront their fear of mistakes, imperfections, things that *need* to be erased. Such fears can be the greatest impediment to writing original poems.

Later I encourage students to see bits of language as modular and recombinatory.

What happens when markedly different kinds of subjects / tones / discourses come into contact? Sparks may fly. Maybe *B* doesn't come after *A*. Maybe *X* does. Then you have an ax.

The Low-down
on the Warm-up
EVIE SHOCKLEY

My creative writing class meetings almost always begin the same way: we write. *Okay, people, take out some paper and a pencil or pen.* I call this writing our "warm-up," but regularly—and increasingly as the semester progresses—we find that some of us may be red-hot from the get-go. *An abecedarian is a poem whose formal structure is based upon alphabetization, typically a twenty-six-line poem in which each line begins with a different letter, proceeding in alphabetical order.* I can use this brief segment of class to quickly introduce forms and concepts that I will return to more thoroughly later on, or to remind students of tools we covered early in the semester that they may have forgotten. *But your assignment is to write a twenty-six-word abecedarian—the first word should begin with an "a," the second word with a "b," and so on through "z."* The idea is to give them a task that is short and sweet, but involving an element of the impossible (or the wildly difficult). *You have three minutes. Go!* When time is up, I have everyone read her poem aloud, either going around the circle or taking volunteers. *Sounds like you accidentally skipped "j"! Poor, neglected "j"!*

I always perform my own warm-up assignments along with the class and read my poems aloud as well, going first or last as my intuition guides me. *I think you snuck in an article in that last phrase, but I like it!* I comment frequently, but very briefly; the idea is to create and reinforce an environment in which good humor, enthusiasm for language, and risk-taking are encouraged. *Do you think you would have used the word "viscosity" if you hadn't had to find something that started with "v"?* It's obvious to everyone that I haven't allotted enough time for anyone to create a masterpiece, so it gives everyone permission to loosen up their brains and do whatever wacky thing will fulfill the basic terms of the assignment. *There certainly ought to be a "rudely shaped trumpet" in the world, if there isn't one. . . .*

Ten minutes, more or less, at the beginning of each class: we bond; we laugh; we get past the idea that everything we write must make sense; we experience liberation through form. *Your assignment is to write a five-line poem comprised solely of one-syllable words. Go!* We become conscious of language; we relinquish habitual phrasing because the constraints won't accommodate them. *Make a list of every sound you've heard today—at least ten of them.* We open ourselves to poem-drafts that take their direction, at least initially, from something outside our own will. *Now write a poem of no more than nine lines using five of those sounds and the color red. Go!*

We surprise ourselves with how individual our pieces are, though we're all using the same or similar materials. "*Red bells from the towers, red / splash of tires through slush, red ragged / ripping of scotch tape from the roll: the holiday / colors everything. . . . .*" We learn that impersonal constraints can accommodate our personal preoccupations. "*. . . the news from the Middle East pours into my ears like blood.*" We discover that creatively "cheating" the prescribed form may be not simply appropriate, but fabulously successful. *Listen to this short poem.* We see that sources of poems are all around us; that poems can begin with choices as arbitrary as drawing a card from a deck. *Write down the three words you found most memorable. Don't think—just jot them down!* We find we have the cure to writer's block: the world and everything in it. *Now write a quick kwansaba, which is a seven-line praise poem with seven words per line and no words of more than seven letters—and include the three words you gravitated towards in the poem I just read.*

Lines from these warm-ups become the germs of more fully realized poems that go through workshop and end up in students' portfolios. The quirky structural limitations I typically place on these assignments help nudge students into different thematic territory and break down the fear and aversion sometimes inspired by such traditional forms as the sonnet or the villanelle. Being required to write quickly and without a clear sense of where the prompt might take the poem drives home to students the point that first drafts need not be—and usually are not—perfect. (That's what revision is for!)

Ultimately, the warm-up period serves as a transition zone, in which we really get geared up for the work of the class session—whether analyzing pieces by published poets, exploring the ins and outs of a new form, or workshopping each other's drafts—by focusing with quiet, ritual intensity on the poet's resources from the moment class begins. After a few minutes of pen-scratching-paper hush, followed by a room-filling collective medley of voices and words, my students are prepped not simply to think creatively, but to share their thoughts in a lively discussion. The warm-up—part mental muscle-stretch, part poetic sugar-rush—releases the knots in our brains and raises our energy level for the work at hand. *Write a twenty-six-word <u>reverse</u> abecedarian. Go! Go!!*

On the Elasticity of the Sonnet and the Usefulness of Collective Experimentation

LAYNIE BROWNE

Where is the serious playfulness in form? As writers, or explorers of consciousness, what materials do we have? The material within which we are operating is time. So in a sense life is already a time-based experiment. All form is time. I think of the modern sonnet as an increment of time within a frame. Something that often physically fits into a little rectangle (but not in thought). Something you can utter in one long convulsive breath or hold in your palm. When my hand covers the page it disappears. It's a controlled measure of sound and space within which one can do anything. An invitation.

When you begin to write sonnets I invite you to think about writing series of sonnets. One reason I like to think in series and sequences is that it tends to pull us out of the problem of preciousness. In other words, if I have written ten poems or one hundred poems it becomes easier to cut one up or throw it away, or to see how a particularly bad poem I have written might have been necessary as a means to moving toward something more interesting. We also learn how poems talk to each other by writing and thinking in batches (think poems for immediate consumption). If you write slowly, perhaps you'll write a batch of fractional sonnets. The idea isn't density, but movement and momentum. Working in series also creates a big field in which to spread out, get comfortable, and mess up. We don't really learn anything by doing what we already know we can do. Therefore, I invite us all to wake each other up and begin something untried. If it feels uncomfortable, this is all to the good. The poem won't necessarily be good, but the process is essential. I say that because there is a potentially infinite number of poems you could write. Language is a medium we are continually awash within, always available.

The process of collectively taking on an experiment is very different than doing so on one's own. The sense of collectively writing and reading, in my experience, is much more important than applauding or critiquing each other's work. From this perspective I could argue that all of us have written each other's poems. Everyone's success or failure belongs to all of us. This isn't just true for writing, obviously. It is a way of looking at endeavor as an offering, less in an individual sense and more on a level of sound or cell. Of course it's also true that these are my words, and those are your words. But the problem is, we are already know this to be true. We don't need to practice it. And thinking collectively might change the way you speak about someone else's poem. I'm not suggesting that every poem should be rewritten to be the one you would have written. Just the opposite actually. Try to read the poem with the intent to help fulfill the vision of the poet, not your vision. In an ideal world the poem and language belong to no one. And no one knows exactly what they are setting out to do because poetry is a living transmission whose evolution is linked to other bodies in time. I approach all writing as the unknown. I am constantly returning to the question: can I do something I haven't done? Process is intimate, messy, and hopefully surprising. Sometimes I'll abandon something or hear it incorrectly but years later it arrives very strikingly as a possible way of reading, listening, or writing.

Here are two approaches to writing, two common modes that come to mind. One is deep immersion in a field of words, which might involve reading and editing something already somewhat formed, whether that be an aesthetic approach or an actual draft of a poem or manuscript. The second is what I'll call a rash impulsive generative mode. Try the second, or generative mode as a means of discovering some new territory. Both modes are necessary, and we can also get stuck in either. There is a false assumption that unless we dwell in deep serious immersion or intentional mode we aren't doing *real* serious writing. However, most adult people spend all too much time being serious and as a result approach things the way they have always approached things. Generative experimentation is all about discovering permission to expand from the borders of the known. As in Duncan's "Often I am Permitted to Return To a Meadow."

The generative mode encourages permission and fluency. Fluency encourages getting comfortable with process (rather than product) oriented endeavor. Why are we writing? If the answer is to arrive at a predetermined idea or location we are missing a considerable amount. The "meadow" isn't a place or an accomplishment; it is a way of experiencing and perceiving all that is available to us regardless of our circumstances.

What is our job as writers? Hannah Weiner writes, "If you are a poet would you have the three obligations, work on yourself to become more conscious, work in the world to change it free and equal include ecological survival, and work in poetic forms that themselves alter consciousness."

She continues, "techniques of disjunctive, non-sequential, non-referential, writing can directly alter consciousness, whether by destroying long habits of rationality, by surprise tactics to which the brain responds differently, or by forcing a change to alpha level by engaging both hemispheres of the brain, choose your science" "If Workshop" (*Open House*, 161).

Form is a container, a direction for words, a frame. Think of form as different ways to direct your lens of vision. Something to try on, walk into, a temporary dwelling, a borrowed manner or means of locomotion. One form may be a bicycle and another a current of air or movement of thought. What is the sonnet? (What is the sonnet for you this minute, today, and what is it tomorrow?) Try moving about in fourteen lines, take notes and let us all know.

SONNET EXPERIMENTS

(with gratitude to Bernadette Mayer)

1. Time experiments: Write a sonnet during a limited amount of time. Begin with one- or two-minute increments, lengthen to five or ten. Try writing a sonnet every day at the exact same time. Or write one word or line or one stanza a day for fourteen days. Try writing a sonnet in an unlikely circumstance. For instance, if you wait in line every day for five minutes write a sonnet then, on a bus, waiting to buy coffee, or before or after brushing your teeth while standing at the sink. The idea is to write not in the usual spaces or circumstances where you fall into a habitual pattern. Standing up trying to write on the wall or on a little pad can be part of the experiment. Try dictation into a recorder. Have someone write down what you are saying. Try writing upon waking or before sleep. Set a certain number of days to try a practice, such as a week or more.

2. Create a sonnet through erasure and / or palimpsest from / upon another text. As an example of erasure, look at Jen Bervin's from the book *Nets*.

3. Write a sonnet by lineating found text or prose or a prose poem. Write several versions of the same poem, experimenting with line length, breadth, prose. You can use found material, a poem you have already written, a piece of prose, etc.

4. Write a *dictionary divination* sonnet. Open the dictionary at random. Write a poem using only the text that appears on the facing pages in front of you.

5. Write an *I see* sonnet by writing using only words for things you can

literally see wherever you are. Try this in different settings (indoors, outdoors) and at different times of day and night.

6. Write a sonnet in response to a sonnet. Some ideas on how to do this:

   a. Use a line from a sonnet as springboard or as the first line of your own poem.

   b. Use the text of a sonnet to cut up and create your own sonnet.

   c. Use end or beginning phrases or words from another sonnet in your sonnet (see Aaron Shurin's *Involuntary Lyrics*). Use a chance operation to rewrite or create a new version of a sonnet by yourself or anyone else. Write a sonnet which repeats a mood, rhythm, or idea in a poem you admire. For example, see Jarnot's "O'Hara Sonnet" and O'Hara's "You Are Gorgeous and I Am Coming."

   d. In all of this writing from another poem, consider the following possibilities:

      i. Write a sonnet inspired by another sonnet.

      ii. Write a sonnet inspired by a piece of writing that is not a sonnet.

      iii. Write a poem inspired by a sonnet that is not a sonnet.

      iv. Invent a new form that somehow begins with reading or writing a sonnet, then morphs into something else.

7. Write a mock historical sonnet, a sonnet you are writing as if some other (living or dead) person has written it. Experiment with voice, tone, assuming authority, meekness, antiquated or futuristic speech. How do you imagine someone else would write your poem?

8. Write a homophonic translation in the form of a sonnet. Experiment with online translation dictionaries such as babblefish. Read from Jackson MacLow's *French Sonnets* and his explanation of process.

9. Translate a sonnet as a commentary on a sonnet. In other words, read a sonnet or any text, then write your own version of the thrust or intent of the poem. This can be done with poems you like or dislike. Don't think of this as paraphrasing but another way of reading. And also possibly a way to reversion, or re-vision—responding in writing to a poem. Read Sparrow's "Translations from The New Yorker" in *America a Prophecy*.

10. Write in someone else's voice, kids' voices, borrow from children's literature and media, or write in overheard language, particular professional language, code, or character. Be someone else for the

duration of fourteen lines. Be anyone (for the sheer liberation of it) and see what happens.

11. Write a collaged sonnet composed of one or various found texts. Experiment with cutting up text, picking words or phrases at random from a series of books, limiting yourself to a limited *found* vocabulary, and so on. Try this: Go to a library, pick fourteen books at random (preferably from different areas / subjects, include a reference or technical book). Place the books in a stack. Systematically open each book and randomly point to a sentence or phrase. Transcribe one sentence or phrase from each book. Then translate your found sonnet by writing a line responding to each found line or phrase. Include some of the text you have found in your poem. Or practice getting lost in the accidental relationship created by the juxtaposition between the lines. And write from that place of collision / adhesion. This experiment works well to supplement / enliven any text you are working on. It works in bookstores, waiting rooms, dumpsters, Goodwill, the street, etc. Enlist a friend to help you rewrite their sonnet and have them rewrite yours.

12. Write a collaborative sonnet. You can do this in person as an exquisite corpse, via email, voicemail messages, various ways.

13. Write a sonnet in a gallery or museum in response to something you see: art, people, noise, etc. Intersperse found text, art titles, catalogue copy, segments on the history of art, into your poem.

14. Write a sonnet during meaning, while doing something else, such as listening to a poetry reading, a concert, watching a dance performance, etc., and allowing the experience to filter into your writing. This can be done while doing dishes, waking up—don't discount any activity as material (though writing while driving can be hazardous). The idea is to allow the outside to be filtered into your work. Experiment by writing while listening to Ted Berrigan read his sonnets online at: http://writing.upenn.edu/pennsound/x/ Berrigan.html. Explore rich resources for listening to other poets read their work online. Let poetry fill the air while you do other things as a means to inspire. Try listening while not trying to listen. How is this different? How is it different on more than one listening or reading? Read from Lee Ann Brown's *Philtre*: *Writing in the Dark* (forthcoming from Atelos).

15. Create a visual sonnet.
16. Write a sonnet that defines your vision of a sonnet. Your definition can include: the purpose of the form, affirmations and prohibitions, a list of reasons to write sonnets, comments on favorite or despised sonneteers, new thoughts on rhyme, meter, lineation, and themes.
17. Write a fractional sonnet, for instance, one-half sonnet, 6/14th sonnet, one-and one-half sonnet, etc. Experiment with the number of lines written, implied, missing, added. How does this change the form and the intent of form?
18. Write a sonnet in which each line functions independently, serves as a title for another poem, or refers to another poem or cycle of poems.
19. Write a sonnet that hinges on associations and definitions of one word. Explore word play, various spellings, families of words, etymologies, sound.
20. Write a sonnet, then write several versions of the same poem from memory. Or rewrite the sonnet as a homophonic translation: from English to English (based on sound) or to any language you like. Do this collaboratively or independently.
21. Experiment with repetition (read Gertrude Stein's *Tender Buttons* or Lyn Hejinian's *My Life)*. Pick a word, a phrase, or a line to repeat through a series of sonnets.
22. Write a sonnet composed entirely of questions, or composed entirely of answers.
23. Write a sonnet or a series of sonnets addressed to a person, or for a particular occasion.
24. Write a sonnet that is a series of guesses to an implied, mysterious, or stated riddle / question.
25. Write a sonnet that is a list poem: list of days, list of reasons, calendar, list of favorite or most despised something, etc.
26. Write a sonnet or a series of sonnets using the daily news (print, internet, radio) as source material. Write a commentary on a commentary. A response to a news flash or editorial. Consider how poetry is legislation or propaganda. Rewrite an article in the form of a sonnet or series of sonnets.
27. Write a sonnet over and over again in various styles such as in Queneau's *Exercises in Style*.
28. Write a sonnet in love with numbers. Explore the number fourteen, equations, counting, numbers of letters, or the qualities you

associate with numbers, significant historical years, sums, numerical questions.

29. Create a poem by mishearing or misreading. One misreading experiment: You need three people: a speaker, a scribe, and a text holder. If you wear glasses or contact lenses this experiment is easier. Begin by taking off your glasses. Have the text holder hold any text just far enough out of your visual range that you can barely make out the letters but not exactly read. Begin to recite what you see, not reading, but guessing and speaking. The scribe will transcribe your creation.

SUGGESTED READING AND WORK CITED

Hilson, Jeff, ed. *The Reality Street Book of Sonnets*. East Sussex, UK: Reality Street, 2008.

Weiner, Hannah. *Hannah Weiner's Open House*. Ed. Patrick Durgin. Chicago: Kenning Editions, 2007.

Teaching John Ashbery
GRAHAM FOUST

When I teach contemporary poetry in my introductory courses—whether they be literature courses (in which I more often than not make a point of making students try their hands at writing some poetry) or creative writing courses (in which I more often than not make a point of making students grapple with some literary theory)—I more often than not find myself teaching one of John Ashbery's books. I do this for several reasons, including the fact that he is arguably America's most well-known living poet. Given that I'm very likely teaching some non-American writers, some not-so-well-known writers, and some dead writers, Ashbery seems a decent starting point, and given that I'm likely to be teaching a range of books that runs the gamut from mainstream to experimental and back, Ashbery seems a good fit (and/or fair game) in that he has dedicated readers at both poles. (And yes, it's true that this is a problematic claim that makes use of vague and potentially pointless labels—but it's probably also true that you know very well what I mean.)

In my admittedly brief and limited experience, I've found that Ashbery tends to polarize the classroom, which is to say that he usually has eight or ten rabid fans and eight or ten enemies once we've made it through the first half of the book. That said, these two camps usually have something in common, in that both tend to have trouble articulating their reactions to the work. Those who are taken with it can't seem to get beyond the notion that it "just sounds good," while those who don't much care for it can't seem to get beyond the notion that it "just doesn't make any sense."

In order to help my students figure out what makes Ashbery's poems tick—and I think this metaphor works for both friends and enemies, given that a clock's tick can be comforting or irritating depending on one's timing and one's temperament—I developed the following exercise:

Write a John Ashbery poem. Try to sound as much like Ashbery as possible. Avoid references that members of this class can instantly associate with you so that it might be possible for them to "mistake" your poem for a poem in one of Ashbery's books. When you're done, email me a copy of your poem. Please observe the following requirements:

1. Your poem must have a title. It must also be composed of two (2) stanzas of any length and twelve (12) lines of any length.
2. Your poem must contain or allude to one proverb, adage, cliché, platitude, or familiar phrase / saying.
3. Your poem must contain two of the following nouns:

pills	*bark*	*thing*	*plan*
house	*sick*	*whistle*	*street*
salt	*shadow*	*stick*	*afternoon*

4. Your poem must contain the proper name of a person or place.
5. Your poem must contain at least two tenses.
6. Your poem must contain an ellipsis . . .
7. Your poem must contain two of the following verbs in any tense:

to whir	*to bark*	*to cough*	*to pick*
to know	*to roll*	*to strike*	*to wonder*
to climb	*to expect*	*to chew*	*to allow*

8. Your poem must contain a question.
9. Your poem must do something so overtly *poetic* as to be silly. The use of the phrase "O my love" (as in "Let's handsel it, love, O my love, I said" from "The Earth-Tone Madonna") or over-the-top alliteration (as in "More morbid mongrels munching" from "Any Other Time") would be two examples of this.
10. Even as it's being silly, your poem must be deadly serious.

Once I receive the poems, I remove all the writers' names, convert all the poems to the same font and font size, and assemble them into a packet, which I then copy and distribute to the students. In addition to the student poems, the packet also includes John Ashbery's "Little Black Dress" (from his *Hotel Lautréamont*), which they've not read and which, to my mind, meets all ten criteria above. I then inform them that somewhere in their packet lurks an actual Ashbery poem, and, for the next class, I ask them to read and think about the poems carefully and to choose two poems that they suspect might be Ashbery's. Here's the math: Over the course of ten years and roughly three hundred students, "Little Black Dress" has appeared in 90 percent of these "top two" lists. And 75 percent of that 90 percent had "Little Black Dress" as their number one guess.

As to whether or not this means anything—and if so, what—I'll let you and your students decide, but I will say that the classes in which the students revealed and discussed their guesses have, to my mind, proved useful and instructive 100 percent of the time. (It's also the one class of the semester in which I really don't have to say much of anything.) Somehow, this exercise seems to help students to begin to come to terms with— which is to say to begin to come to terms *for*—some of what makes Ashbery Ashbery. Mind you, this exercise is not intended to be—nor does it seem to function as—a way of getting people to like Ashbery. (That is, I've found that most students don't change their allegiances with regard to whether or not they "like" Ashbery's poems.) What it does seem to do is to get students to begin to identify and articulate some of the things a particular writer is doing and how he goes about doing them. In almost as little time as it takes them to form an initial *opinion* about a poet's work— which may or may not change over time—the students manage to initiate a *lexicon* that will, one hopes, expand and last as long as they do.

WORK CITED

Ashbery, John. *Hotel Lautréamont.* New York: Knopf, 1992.

Six S's

CATHERINE WAGNER

"Six S's" is a mnemonic for six overlapping line break categories: speed, sound, syntax, surprise, sense, space. The S's are easy to introduce to students: take a poem, remove its line breaks, and ask students to break its lines in a way that foregrounds one *S*, then another. Students can compare their decisions with the authors' and decide which breaks best suit their understanding of the poem. If you've got a computer and a projector, students can take turns deciding on a particular poem's breaks while all of you discuss the resulting effects. Trying out line breaks as a group means everyone can weigh in on how the poem morphs as its line breaks move. It becomes immediately obvious to students that changes in the texture and structure of language mold and redirect thinking. I don't know that many of my students will continue to write poetry, but I hope they leave my courses believing that we think in form(s) and that the structures we live with and in are revisable. Here are some of the questions I ask about each line break tactic as I introduce it.

Speed: (Compare two or more poems.) Are shorter lines speedier, or longer lines? Are enjambed lines or end-stopped lines slower? How does speed affect tone and mood?

Sound: How might you end lines to emphasize soundplay (rhyme, consonance)? How might you make soundplay less overt through line breaks? Remove line breaks from a poem that has a strong rhythm and consider how you might break it to emphasize or de-emphasize the rhythm.

Syntax: Is the poem broken to align with its syntactic units (whether standard or unconventional) or against them? Do the prepositions in a poem usually occur at the beginning of a line? If so, is this common strategy used to make a difficult passage easier for the reader to absorb, or in order to make the poem imitative of pauses in speech? Or does it mean that the writer is in a lazy default mode, breaking wherever "natural" pauses occur? If the poem breaks against syntactic units, what's the effect?

Surprise: When a particular line breaks at an unexpected point, what's achieved? Does the line break manage to do more than simply create surprise?

Sense: How do the line breaks help the poem present its argument (not necessarily a logical argument: it could be a sonic argument, or an argument that hinges on wordplay)?

Space: What visual impression is created by the line breaks? What can you gather about the poem based on its appearance? Does the space between and around lines create any expectations that are fulfilled or countered by the text? Space tends to create a sense of drama; is the drama appropriately managed? Does space represent time in the poem, and if so, is the poem aptly scored? Does space mean?

The Baggage Switch
NOAH ELI GORDON

Early on, I want my students to be aware of the intuitive motivation behind the choices they're making. Later, as they progress, I'll hold them accountable for figuring out how to articulate this motivation. In the beginning of the semester, it's enough to acknowledge that the agency one has within a poem carries some heavy baggage. The best thing one can teach is attention. I do this by purposefully sending my students to the wrong carousel, pointing at someone else's luggage, and asking that they live with whatever ill-fitting clothing is found inside.

Every noun calls to mind a default lexicon, a swirling mass of expected words that bury it in mundane, dull, deadening language. The sun shines, glints, rises, sets. A river flows, swells, churns. Snow falls. Cars speed. Gears turn. Birds chirp. So what? A noun's attendant network of verbs is the enemy of poetry. Thus our general shouts: "Show, don't tell!" But what does this mean? An eagle that soars is little more than information, an intellectual concept, something immediate yet flat; this is banking, not poetry: you deposit two hundred dollars; you know what your statement will read. Some poems need information. Some information needs poetry.

To make this clear I use a practical exercise called the *baggage switch*. It can be an addendum to any poetry assignment, but it is best to use in conjunction with one of the semester's first writing exercises. Here's how it works: Students should come to class prepared to read aloud one of their own poems. Perhaps they've all written villanelles, followed a list of line-by-line instructions, or have been set completely adrift—whatever the case, the room should be electrified by the nervous energy and anxiety of their initial moment in the spotlight.

Before reading their poems, ask them to circle each verb. If this presents a problem, as it has in my introductory creative writing courses, at least you know what you're in for, and can adjust the curriculum accordingly. Next, have them copy each of their verbs onto a separate sheet of paper. Multiple appearances and various conjugations are irrelevant, but if anyone asks, one "is" is enough. After they've done this, collect the pages and redistribute the lists, making sure no one receives the verbs from his or her own poem. Then, have them replace each of the verbs in their poem with one from the new list. This will inevitably raise a few eyebrows and elicit chuckles, which is a good thing, as the classroom should be a place of both discovery and dismantling.

The following stipulations should help: One doesn't need to use every verb on the list; feel free to conjugate verbs differently; it's okay to use any verbs from the list multiple times. What I stress here is the deliberate avoidance of those verbs which would simply replicate the poem's original statement. If your line reads, "I climbed up the mountain," then replacing *climbed* with *walked* isn't doing enough work. Try *shuddered* or *sank* or *roped*. Remember, the clothing isn't yours. It's not supposed to be a perfect fit and one stray accessory—a tie clip here, sock garter or scrunchie there—might make all the difference.

Now, they can enjoy the spotlight as it illuminates their goofy Technicolor outfits, which is to say they're to read their poems aloud with these new verbs. Yes, there's something here akin to the silly camaraderie of a round of Mad Libs. However, there's also a pedagogical imperative, that of attention's necessity, attention to the choices one makes, and attention especially to diction, to its ability to trump expectation and enliven language. Although these substitutions will be momentarily humorous, most end up pretty forgettable, with one or two stunning exceptions. It's important to point these moments out, to explain to students why they're so much more compelling.

For example, *the clock on the kitchen wall struck twelve* is an innocuous enough line. Clocks always *strike*, don't they? Maybe not so much in the digital age, but there's something so anachronistically familiar and mundane about the line that one can only consider it a product of writing, a construction, and an attempt at passing off information as poetry. What if the author of this line had been given the verbs *stretch, fill, think, dance,* or *scream*? A clock *stretching* an hour is wonderfully loaded and, as one stares at it in anticipation or trepidation, somehow more accurate. If it does a little damage to the original intention of the poem, so be it; such damage is a gift.

As with any exercise, the goal here is not to create the perfect poem. We must practice our scales, composing symphonies comes later. At its core, the creative writing classroom should continually stretch the apogee of the possible farther into the unknown, equipping students with numerous ways to think on the page. That a seemingly disparate verb might launch one's noun into metaphoric territory is so obvious we often forget to mention it. *The baggage switch* is simply a reminder, as much for our students as for ourselves.

The Holograph

BRENDA HILLMAN

I encourage students to recopy their poems using script over and over until they are satisfied with the versions before them. It doesn't matter whether they want to call this activity writing or rewriting.

Handwriting a poem, like drawing or making music with an instrument, allows the language to shape its own nature.

Some writers think a poem emerges pure and complete the first time out, and that no revisiting of words will produce something more interesting. Writers from across the aesthetic spectrum are drawn to this "sanctity of the first draft." I am drawn to the idea that recopying is also writing and certainly no less pure than the first drafting process—and that the freshness of a piece will be enhanced by multiple visits.

Isn't it true that if you visit a person or a place multiple times, the first visit loses nothing? I encourage all writers to recopy their poems in script, allowing changes to enter in their own handwriting—either on new sheets of paper or on recycled paper—until the point when they will copy the poem in the form of print.

Some writers fear the initial impulse will be tainted if they rearrange or exchange words.

It is always surprising to hear experienced writers—including innovative writers—holding a belief, almost akin to religious fundamentalism, that there is only one version.

Computer use is certainly enjoyable, especially the practice of final formatting and reformatting poems, but I encourage students to use handwriting through many stages of the process, for reasons all having to do with why drafting poetry is such an amazing and gratifying activity:

I.

Handwriting puts you into haptic contact with the texture of the page, with the air and space of letters, allowing a technique of script—sometimes sloppy and shallow, sometimes sharp and branching—to operate anarchically. Emerging signs are very close to the nerves of the hand.

Seeing a letter formed in stages, seeing words accrete meaning, seeing the ink—the demotic ink of the cheapest ballpoint, the lightest or heaviest pencil—pulled into the thread or wick, to the thing of the word itself—gives a sense of participatory process, that the poem is still unfolding, that all of its unconscious dream nature has not yet been foreclosed upon by your intention to keep it in its first form.

The mysterious origins of writing are contacted; the elements are inscribed in the signs again each time. Phenomena of air enter the upper regions, water and earth enter the stems of q and y and p below the line.

Many of the physical features of our atavistic connections to the written expression are rehabilitated through the handwriting technique. The contraction of the fingers and the tiny movements around the pen or pencil refresh expectation.

II.

The discriminating intellect can engage alternatives in a gentle, nonjudgmental way. The poet enters the free zone, dropping syllables, phrases, rearranging sections, allowing words to fall to the floor as the poem is copied, as if a principle of creation were providing an even better alternative. Then the judgment is engaged: should you go with the new version or the old version? Recopy it and your intuition and your intellect will give a clue.

Script in a notebook permits its other. Boring words fall away. *I've seen that before*, whispers the handwriting. A computer might have fooled you into approval, especially with its cut-and-paste functions.

Writing by hand, you draw up alternatives from the ground and air, from the infinite place of refreshing choices. Handwriting gives the opportunity for otherness and firstness to coexist, almost like a form of knitting and/or other handicraft.

I learned to do this by setting the previous draft of the poem to the left of the blank page, recopying the poem in a hypnotic way, allowing more interesting materials to drop in, allowing tedious materials to fall away, doing this over and over as many times as it might take for the fresh discovery to arrive so that the poem could be true to the mental experience that sparked it, however dire or unusual. Fear and doubt might be folded in: fear that something will be lost, doubt about whether the project is worthy.

If you question even the concepts of authenticity and originality, sometimes what is really true and fresh greets you.

I read thousands of poems a year—as an impassioned grazer, as a teacher, as an editor, as an addict. I sometimes wonder whether the writers stopped too soon, finalized too fast, were too easily satisfied, didn't try one more visit. Nothing is to be feared by slowing down the process and allowing temporary dissatisfaction and wildness to instruct you. The curvature of new letters can enter when the practice of handwriting lets the writing see back into itself.

III.

The phenomenology of sustained hopefulness has an enchantment. It is writing itself, being in the act of it, that graces you. You think of letters and words as various rooms and things come from the margins.

Going into a slightly hypnotic state as you copy a poem directly from the page is a useful action.

Using your marginalia, you admit the inadmissible.

IV.

Some might say: My handwriting is unreadable; it is discouraging to decipher. But far from being a reason not to use handwriting, this is all the more reason to employ it. The elements of surprise and invention are part of the practice.

If you cannot read your own writing, you have more opportunities to arrive at a satisfying word or to invent a new one. Like small harmless gopher snakes the words emerge from the underbrush. My own handwriting has become messier over the years. The mystery of writing returns with the production of each draft, from the pen held by hand.

V.

Writers of prose or long poems may consider the holograph technique to be an impractical method. Of course the production of prose will be slowed by it. Since when did you become a machine, producing material so fast as to forget thought? Since when were you supposed to turn your writing out on an assembly line? Why did you come to writing in the first place?

If you are involved in a long poem or piece of prose, you may not want to copy the whole thing, but sections of your writing could be recopied by hand, to make them more accurate to your mental experience. My own long poems have benefited from multiple recopying. I recopied the poem "Cascadia" for eight months until the pieces of its multiple experiences settled into form. At a certain point it was placed in the computer, into the communal font, with elements only the computer can offer.

VI.
If you do not like alternative versions, you could return to the first draft or keep recopying just for the sheer pleasure of the experience. I also like to recopy poems other than my own onto new pages, because there is an intimacy about that as well.

Two Dozen English-to-English Translation Techniques

JEN HOFER

One of the most important elements in my teaching practice is devising ways to encourage students to write outside their habits or beyond their perceived formal, substantive, or aesthetic limitations. Not coincidentally, the idea of extending beyond comfortable boundaries is similarly a central aspect of my own practice as a writer and translator. I consider a capacity for curious adventuring beyond the familiar limits of what we already know to be of crucial political significance. In the realm of writing specifically, I am encouraged by the idea that we might encounter another writer's text as something absolutely foreign and other to our own practices, and at the same time, alongside that foreignness, we might find ways to make that text our own and incorporate some of its modes of inquiry and expression intimately into our own work. It is, in part, this simultaneous encounter with immutable foreignness and mutable subjectivity that makes translation such a politically compelling literary practice for me.

English-to-English translations are texts written in English through or toward other texts written in English, using translation techniques as a compositional method. Some of these techniques are very close to modes I use regularly in my translation practice between Spanish and English, while others are more fanciful or even completely unrelated to actual translation practices. I'm sure there are more techniques than the ones I have devised here. As these occur to you, please let me know (jenhofer@gmail.com) so I can expand this list.

ENGLISH-TO-ENGLISH TRANSLATION TECHNIQUES
Grammatical: substituting parts of speech—like Mad Libs—nouns for other nouns, adjectives for other adjectives, etc.
Structural: reproducing the structure of the lines or sentences exactly—the placement of punctuation, line breaks, etc.—but substituting your own words.

Meaningful: translate the meaning, as you understand it, of each line or sentence (or whatever unit you choose), saying it in a different way. Alternate idea: find the subtext or hidden meaning you feel a text does not present clearly and write the uncovered meaning of the text.

Denotative: as you read, ask yourself "what does this fragment / phrase / line concretely say?" Write a text that says this.

Connotative: consider the connotations (or harmonics) of each word in a text, or of particular words (all nouns, all verbs, etc.). Write the connotative version of that text.

Fanciful: use each word or phrase or line as a jumping-off point and let yourself jump as far as your imagination can take you.

Processual: choose a process to enact on the text. For example, translate each line into a single word. Or translate each word into a line. Or etc.

Concrete: use only the lines or words in the original poem to make your translation. You could make a cut-up using lines or phrases cut and pasted from the original, or you could do a complete word jumble and remake a new poem using all the same words.

Homophonic: take the sound of each word as if you did not know its meaning and create a text that sounds the same.

Musical: make a text that "rhymes" with the vowels and consonants of the original. Or take the rhythm and meter of a poem and follow those, using words of your own.

Dialect / Voice: translate the text into another dialect of English or a radically different voice.

Thesaurus: insert a letter into every word so that it's spelled incorrectly, then take ideas of words to use in your poem from your computer's spell check.

Synonymous: change each word into a synonym for that word. (You could write an antonymous poem by changing each word into its antonym.)

Responsive: talk back to the poem, word by word, line by line, or stanza by stanza.

Imitative Jump: use an entire line from the poem as the opening or closing (or both) of your poem.

Sideways Glance: slide each word or line into a word or line that seems similar sonically or denotatively. Define *similar* as closely or distantly as you please.

Etymological: begin with a text (written by you or written by someone else). Using an etymological dictionary, expand every significant word (all nouns and verbs, for example, or whichever words strike your fancy) to its fullest etymological definition. If desired, edit your text to streamline.

Crossword Puzzle: think of each line in a poem as the clue to a crossword puzzle; solve the clues.

Interrogative: think of each fragment or phrase or line as the answer to a question. Write a text that asks the questions. Write your answers to these questions.

Audio Filter: create a sonic space that relates to the text you are translating (that space might entail putting on a particular piece of music, going to a particular place, riding public transit, etc.). Begin your process with a headphone in one ear playing an audio version of the text you're translating and with the other ear open to the sonic space you've chosen to occupy. Allow fragments of what you hear in both ears to filter in and become part of your translation.

Concentric: think of each fragment or phrase or line in a poem as the innermost point of a series of concentric circles. Write the surrounding circles that radiate out from that point. Or, conversely, think of each as the outermost ring, and work inward to the center point.

Snowball: for each phrase or line of the text you are translating, add a word or two that illuminates or explicates the text further. As you continue translating, add more and more words until your illumination or explication snowballs vastly beyond the original text.

Congruent Correlative: consider how the text you are translating functions in relation to normative language use. Make a list of tools, techniques, or impulses that make it possible for the text to function in this way. Employ these tools, techniques, or impulses in your translation to create a text that functions congruently.

Translation and Retranslation: ask a friend to translate your poem into another language, then retranslate the text back into English without consulting the original English.

Three Questions

PETER STRECKFUS

What will it look like?
How will it speak to others?
Why are you making it?

From 2000 to 2004—after graduate school and before I returned to teaching—I worked as the writer and publicist at the San Francisco Art Institute. My favorite part of the job—because it was a real education for me—involved writing features and profiles of students, faculty, and visiting artists who were passing through. One of the interviews that sticks with me most from that period was with the artist Will Rogan (co-founder and editor of the literary object journal *The Thing Quarterly*), who had then just recently finished his undergraduate degree at SFAI but was already showing work around the country. Will doesn't remember this part of the conversation at all (it didn't make it into the published profile), but I've never forgotten it, or never forgotten what I took away from it at least: He was speaking about his experience studying with the conceptual artist Paul Kos and three questions (listed above and discussed below) that Paul led Will to consider whenever he was making new work. I've talked to Paul about these three questions and he doesn't recognize them either, so it's hard to know whose formulation they are, but in any case, this is how they've come down, channeled from Paul Kos, through Will Rogan, and finally through me to my students, although not always presented in this form and not always all at one time.

These three questions force the writer to take responsibility for her very subjective hand in forming the three relational legs of the literary triangle: the written object, the audience, and the author. In other words, they ask us to consider the relationships between form, content, and identity.

Here perhaps I'm intellectualizing the matter a bit too much; just keep in mind that the questions themselves are pretty straightforward. Even presented as they are, however, these questions may well have a deadening effect on some writers as they sit before the blank page. For them, the three questions may be useful as tools once the seed of the work has already germinated and it comes time for revision / shaping / expanding.

What follows are some thoughts on each leg and how together they affect one another. I leave it to the reader to consider what happens when we teach our students to focus on one or two of these while ignoring the third.

1. WHAT WILL IT LOOK LIKE?

This question is in many ways, when taken by itself at least, the most elementary. I often see work by students who appear to have only one or two models available to them for what their poems can look like. Part of this, I know, has to do with development. It takes time and commitment to build up oneself as a writer, years, decades. We identify our writing self with one kind of work, the kind we are most familiar with or the kind our teacher was most familiar with, and finally enmesh ourselves with that writing self. Students form poems the way they know poems to be formed, meaning they are limited by what they have read before. It's the mentor's task to offer students as many formal and procedural choices as possible, to lead them to think about how those choices affect and are related to their content (see Q.2), and how their sense of identity (see Q.3) as writers is invested in or perhaps limited by those choices. This question involves engagement with the conventions of one's language, which are as vast as the history of the language.

2. HOW WILL IT SPEAK TO OTHERS?

One might think of each of these legs, in fact, as forms of engagement. Question two asks us to consider how engaging form (see Q.1) and engaging ourselves (see Q.3) results in an experience that anyone (or perhaps certain others) would actually care about. How does the work engage with the world outside ourselves? When I teach, I refer to this engagement with the world by using the term "argument." For example, what is the poem's argument in terms of pleasure? But other terms work just as well or better, depending on the purpose: What does it propose as pleasurable? What are its concepts, its subjects, its stakes? Some poems create a logic so internal to themselves that they remain, at first glance, clearly formed (see Q.1), clearly self-engaged (see Q.3), but opaque (at least at first) to the reader. Here again we see two questions (Q.1 + 3) pressing on the third. So okay, the work is at first opaque—how then does this quality propose itself as part of the poem's argument? Perhaps it offers only a few, specific handles for opening the poem to further engagement.

3. WHY ARE YOU MAKING IT?

The final of the three questions is in many ways, I think, the most interesting, the one most difficult to answer, and the one that mature artists grapple with most meaningfully. It is the existential question. For the young writer, it often has to do with motivations: Have I chosen this subject (see Q.2) or procedure (see Q.1) to merely impress others or to honestly engage it because it's meaningful to me? The meaning may involve simple, honest curiosity, a desire to experiment, to explore, to see what's on the other side. In any case, it has to do with investment. If the writer isn't abundantly invested in the work for reasons that are meaningful to her, does she expect her reader to be? On some occasions the writer isn't sure why the content or form is meaningful to her but feels drawn to it nonetheless and won't find out why she is drawn to it until she begins to write. She may not find out until the twentieth draft, a year later, if she persists, or until she's twenty-four, or fifty-three, or what have you. At other times, when the writer happens to begin with this question—she knows for instance that a certain subject is important to her and why—she may develop a set of forms or procedures that used together are properly the work's own. On the other hand, left by itself, this type of engagement may lead to solipsistic, self-indulgent work (back to Q.2).

{
Poetry as Translation
and Radical Revision
RACHEL ZUCKER

Students often view the making of poems as a two-step process: writing and revising. Writing, they say, is the generative stage. Writing is free-spirited, creative, personal, and enjoyable unless the muse is withholding in which case writing can be supremely frustrating. Writing is somewhat mystical in that it depends upon imagination and inspiration, two difficult-to-define and difficult-to-control forces. Many students believe that writing (both the process and the product) can't or shouldn't be judged by others; writing is an expression of the self and is highly subjective.

Everything other than writing, according to this dichotomous model, falls under the rubric of revision, the process by which one perfects the poem. Revision is hard work, often boring, but necessary in order to garner a positive evaluation from others. Revision is an intellectual rather than creative endeavor, a necessary undertaking that is, by nature, antithetical to the spirit of poetry.

I find it useful to question and complicate this dichotomy and these terms. First, I suggest we limit *writing* to its more literal sense: the action of forming letters, symbols, or words on a page. I suggest that we call what students are doing when inspired to employ their imaginations *translating*. Students are translating experience into language. Translation is an attempt to render something in another medium or to convey or transfer something from one person, place, time, or condition to another; or as Willis Barnstone more elegantly put it, "Translation is the art of revelation. It makes the unknown known."[1] It is helpful to think of making poems as more similar to painting or dancing than to writing an essay. How does a painter make the unknown known? How does the poet make experience known?

Then, there is re-vision. I add the hyphen to distinguish this process from the more traditional sense of *revision* which, for most students, is a synonym for editing. Re-vision is also an act of translation. Re-visions are homolinguistic (English to English) translations of poems, which are translations of experience. The process of re-vision is as exciting and exacting as one's initial translation. The result of re-vision is not a polished poem or a fixed poem but a new translation, a new poem.

These are semantic distinctions, but I find that using new terms for the process of making poems can really open things up in the classroom. Describing writing as translation allows us to do away with the notion that some writing is immune to criticism. A poet is free to keep her poems private, of course, but even when writing for one's self, a translator is responsible for how accurately her language and images describe or enact the experience she is translating. A poet is responsible to his / her experience the way a translator is responsible to his / her original text. Also, by making writing and revising equally important and by describing both as acts of translation, we reanimate the process of re-vision and invite endless possibilities for play and experimentation.

I often ask students to write multiple, radical re-visions of a single poem. The result will be several poems that may not seem to have anything in common but are each translations of the original experience, which is anything the student has personally encountered, undergone, or lived through (including fantasies, dreams, thoughts, feelings, and direct observations). Translations may be undertaken with specific aims; perhaps the student wants to translate the poem for greater accuracy, more images, toward a highbrow or lowbrow diction. Perhaps the student wants to translate the content of the poem into a different form or different genre. Perhaps the student wants to play with a mechanical technique like a cut-up or fold-in or substitutions.[2] One re-vision might aim for the feeling of a word-by-word or direct translation that strives for greater and greater representational accuracy in the language. Or, on the other end of the spectrum, students might experiment with homophonic translations (substituting words for other words that sound like the original words in the poem). A student might try a "lost text" translation where they pretend to have lost the original text and write the translation without it or translate the poem by trying to be extremely accurate to the form of the poem while paying no attention at all to the content.

These kinds of re-vision are not about fixing a poem. I ask students to try re-visions that privilege the uneven spots, the places one's sock would snag if walking over the surface of the poem. I suggest re-visions in which one excavates the poem, searching the poem-site for signs of life, unearthing broken shards, and examining them from all sides. I urge students to be as creative and radical as possible in their re-vision practice. Translate your own poem as if you know absolutely nothing about the time, culture, or context of its origin. Translate a poem written by another student in the class. Translate the poems of your favorite poets. Once you get going, it's hard to stop.

When translating a poem from one language to another the translator needs to pay close attention and have empathy. Paying attention and developing and practicing empathy are essential to writing and living well. By thinking of all poems as translations of experience or as translations of other poems, I help students develop these vital skills and habits.

NOTES

1. Willis Barnstone. *The Poetics of Translation: History, Theory, Practice.* New Haven, Connecticut: Yale University Press, 1993. 265–271. http://www.poets.org/viewmedia.php/prmMID/15984.

2. See Charles Bernstein's list of experiments for more re-vision ideas: http://writing.upenn.edu/bernstein/experiments.html.

Doing Things in Silence

TONY TRIGILIO

My first artistic training was in music, and I was a professional musician before I ever taught a creative writing class, so it's natural for me to think in terms of music instruction when I'm teaching poetry. This is no great revelation, of course, with poetry's grounding in song. Whether harmonious or discordant, poetry is to language as music is to noise. Yet if silence is as crucial as noise in music, then why is silence often considered a symptom of a failure of speech, of a blockage, in writing? When I incorporated in the creative writing classroom the lessons of my meditation practice, I came up with some provisional exercises that helped work with these ambiguities and contradictions without unnecessarily trying to resolve them. In-class guided meditation can heighten students' ways of seeing; and their heightened perception can confront and redirect the silencing power of our everyday distractions.

In the silence of doing nothing, of just sitting still, the mind can be at its most active. I don't mean *active* in the sense of what Zen warns is our debilitating and restless "dog mind": the mind that chases hurdy-gurdy every stick thrown its way. Instead, I mean *active* as a description of a pointed and focused state of mind, the momentary lucidity of Zen mindfulness, and at the same time a state of mind vulnerable enough to admit oppositions, contrarieties, irrationalities, and all of what Keats so famously describes in his negative capability letter as our ability to abide "in uncertainties, mysteries, doubts without any irritable reaching after fact and reason."[1] These active uncertainties, mysteries, and doubts—the active still-point possible during meditation—are integral parts of the active silence that both meditation and poetry (the reading and writing of it) produce in me, and that I hope to encourage in my students.

In-class and journal exercises inspired by my meditation practice are designed to guide students through writer's block and open the field of invention strategies available to them. If we answer mind-distraction with mindfulness—if we understand that distraction is produced by the same mind that can quiet distraction—then we might begin to focus with greater lucidity on objects, feelings, and thoughts in and of themselves, without an "irritable reaching" for judgment and reason. As one of my first meditation teachers, Andrew Weiss, would remind me, "If you are distracted from your breath 100 times, just make sure you come back 101 times." In my creative writing classrooms, I have found that such an approach can help students recognize distractions when they threaten the writing process. Coming back to the page 101 times, students can confound distraction by incorporating it as part of the creative process.

More specifically, I have found that students must get to know their breath, as a way of involving the body in the writing process: the difference between long and short breath, where the breath touches the body and what this feels like, and the interconnection between the breath and the outer world. Because writer's block—my own and my students'—often comes from a temporary inability to incorporate external stimuli imaginatively into one's writing, I want students to practice responding to such stimuli while writing about something else. In this way, we are daring our distractions to meet us head-on. I periodically organize short freewriting exercises where students write about something else—a dream from the night before, an object in the room, an event they are anticipating later in the day—while writing simultaneously about the textures of their breaths. We begin with short, guided breathing meditation. Students get comfortable, and we silently count ten breaths. Students may be physically comfortable in their chairs, but the silence of a class of meditators is tense enough at first that it seems to invade the four walls of the classroom. But in the same way they respond when silences are deployed by instructors during discussions and workshops, students eventually make a tenuous peace with this silence as an invitation for self-reflection and patient thought. After ten breaths and uncanny silence, we write.

The third step in our guided breathing and in-class writing is to take notice of one particular image that recurs as we follow where the breath touches our individual bodies (usually, exhalations touching the tip of the upper lip). Of course, I place no boundaries on what this image can be, only that I want them to be comfortable enough with this image that in later steps they can manipulate and write about this image. Like all of us who teach creative writing, I have to trust in the image-making impulses of the human mind. The same trust is inevitable in meditation. As Buddhadasa Bhikkhu writes in *Mindfulness with Breathing*, "The mind merely inclines in a certain way and the image arises by itself."[2]

The final steps in this guided breathing and writing exercise invite students to become active observers while silent, much like we do in the silence of reading or writing. Perception cannot be a passive process when doing things in silence. I ask students to manipulate their image into something else, perhaps to change its shape or color or to change its range of motion, if any. I want students to feel comfortable changing the image, knowing that their minds can see sharp images, and that these images can be manipulated by the active imagination engaged (silently) in ordinary perception. Like all other aspects of this process, my invitation to manipulate the image might seem like pedagogical sleight of hand; after all, the objects these students see might not even be imported into their own writing. Instead these objects are tools by which to trick the mind into revivifying its imaginative skills. In this way, the mind can be redirected from passive, blocked silence into an active agent whose imagination makes a world—however harmonious, however discordant—from what is given. In the final stage of this process, students choose a version of this manipulated image and study it silently, in the mind, while always aware of the body as it is manifested in their breaths. I ask the students to write about one particularly vivid element of the object. Their writing can serve as an eventual reminder that if we confront distraction as one of many ordinary phenomena, then we can experience ordinary perception without pretending that the creative process occurs in passive silence, or that the creative process somehow operates independently of distraction and conflict.

Of course, I'm not the first to use meditation and body awareness in the creative writing classroom. Any student of John Cage might say all this more eloquently, and in fewer words. In his "Composition as Process" lectures, Cage asks, "Which is more musical, a truck passing by a factory or a truck passing by a music school?"[3] His question is more than a koan. It's a guide for how to experience the relationship between noise and music, language and poetry, silence and speech—a way of thinking about the silent, kinetic din of creative reading and creative writing.

NOTES

1. John Keats. "To George and Tom Keats." December 22, 1818. *Selected Letters of John Keats*. Ed. Grant F. Scott. Cambridge: Harvard University Press, 2005.

2. Buddhadasa Bhikku. *Mindfulness with Breathing*. Trans. Santikaro Bhikkhu. Boston: Wisdom, 1997. 62.

3. John Cage. "Composition as Process." *Silence: Lectures and Writings*. Wesleyan: Wesleyan University Press, 1961. 41.

It was evident that the man walking along deep
in thought was not from here; and if, when he was
at home, thoughts came to him in the open air,
it was always night. With astonishment he would
recall that entire nation—Jews, Indians, Moors—
had built their schools beneath a sun that seemed to
make all thinking impossible for him. The sun was
burning into his back. Resin and thyme impregnated
the air in which he felt he was struggling for breath.
A bumble-bee brushed his ear. Hardly had he
registered its presence than it was already sucked
away in a vortex of silence. —Walter Benjamin

Taking Poetry Out for an Essay

CHRISTINE HUME

Sun pulse, night open air, bee buzz—rhythm illuminates the intimate cor-respondences between people and world. The rhythm of walking repli-cates unwilled rhythms of the body—breathing, sucking, beating heart. The rhythm of walking paces a dialectic of being and doing, idling and vigilance, observing and participating. Walking drives you outward. A sentence might catch the rhythm and repeat itself as the sensorimotor connectivity of walking repeats. Each city block might be an imbrication of familiar terrain and unscreened encounters that the sentence strides through, shifting with minute perceptions. The unpunctuated country-side might extend a thought almost unbearably, sending language-as-you-know-it out for a hike. Try out observation and reflection within a context of "beginning again" (Stein), or "every end is also a beginning" (Emer-son). Try beginning with a generative sentence that abandons complete-ness; instead follow paratactic organization, using sound analogues, di-gressions, freak inspirations to keep opening up and keep it going. As a walker-writer, you might practice what Pauline Oliveros calls "deep listen-ing," a disciplined attention to inescapable, and intricately differentiated, sonic plentitude. Sounds pace through the body: the body paces through landscape. Walking organizes the multiple rhythms of mind-body-world. Language walks itself out of habitualized routes. A shortcut might short-circuit your reservoir of clichés; going for a walk, like good writing, is an invitation to surprise.

Experiment: Write an essay poem in your head while walking outside through a physical space—in the city or the country, with or without a des-tination, serendipitous or programmatic, at night or otherwise. Go alone across a sensorial peripherality. Let the syntax simulate the experience; let syntax become meaning and vice versa. The walk must be at least thirty minutes long, preferably an hour or two. Take no accompaniment (iPod, person, or companion animal), but enlist a choreographic attitude. Let the sentences mirror the walk; let the essay-poem reflect the way the mind works during the walk.

Ramble through a series of unexpected poetic neighborhoods—ethnography, ecology, geology, meteorology, and urban, architectural, and cultural studies. Become, in Baudelaire's words, "a botanist of the sidewalk." Walking is itself research if given a systematic frame. Walking spurs the active mind. Benjamin's peripatetic prose merges historic and scientific facts with their poetic counterparts to weave a "meandertale" (Joyce). Benjamin's technique of travel involves collecting and creating stories through a mix of thought figures governed by galloping sensitivities to mimesis. His signature idea of *colportage*, implying a unity between film montage and walking the city, becomes hallucinatory. It spills out—enjambed. *Enjamb* (from the French: to stride, walk, encroach) means the continuation of a sentence (sense) beyond the initial line.

Take a line out for a walk.—Paul Klee

Erik Satie composed music on his nocturnal homeward walks. Wallace Stevens famously transformed the rhythms of his walks to and from work into poetry. Guy Debord cultivated the practices of psychogeography, which sometimes included a "constrained walk," exploring the city on foot while following a restrictive logic such as tossing a coin at each intersection to determine the next direction or avoiding all trash cans. How might pursuing the *derive*, roaming the streets and being open to chance and diversion be updated? How might the literary tradition of walking be reinvigorated by taking physical—not simulated, virtual, or technologically mediated—paths? An essay means to try. A poem means to make. To open up the essayistic in your poem, prime yourself with reading: Henry Thoreau's "Walking," Lisa Robertson's *Occasional Work and Seven Walks from the Office of Soft Architecture*, W. G. Sebald's *Rings of Saturn*, Robert Smithson's "A Tour of the Monuments of Passaic, New Jersey," Anne Carson's "The Anthropology of Water," Virginia Woolf's "Street Haunting," Jean Baudrillard's *America*, Yoko Ono's "Walking Piece" and "Walk Piece," Charles Dickens's "Night Walks," Cris Cheek's *The Church—The School— The Beer*, Bruce Chatwin's *The Songlines*, Walter Benjamin's *The Arcades Project*, Jean-Jacques Rousseau's *Reveries of a Solitary Walker*, Robert Walser's "The Walk," and Andrew Fitch's *60 Walks*. Listen to Janet Cardiff's various audio "Walks," Christina Kubisch's "Electrical Walks," Erik

Satie's *Gymnopédies*, and Meredith Monk's "Duets: Walking Song" from *Volcano Songs*.

WORKS CITED

Baudelaire, Charles. "The Painter of Modern Life." *Charles Baudelaire: Selected Writings on Art and Literature.* Trans. P. E. Charvet. New York: Viking, 1972.

Benjamin, Walter. "In the Sun." *Walter Benjamin: Selected Writings, Vol 2, Pt 2, 1931–1934.* Trans. Rodney Livingstone. Eds. Michael W. Jenningss, Howard Eiland, Gary Smith. Cambridge: Harvard University Press, 2005.

Emerson, Ralph Waldo. "Circles." *The Essays of Ralph Waldo Emerson.* Cambridge: Belknap-Harvard University Press, 1987.

Joyce, James. *Finnegans Wake.* New York: Penguin, 1999.

Klee, Paul. *On Modern Art.* Trans. Paul Findlay. New York: Faber and Faber, 1937.

Oliveros, Pauline. *Deep Listening: A Composer's Sound Practice.* New York: iUniverse, 2005.

Stein, Gertrude. "Explanation as Composition." *Selected Writings of Gertude Stein.* Ed. Carl Van Vechten. New York: Vintage-Random House, 1990.

The Oddity of Point Roberts Mapping the Unknown

BRUCE BEASLEY

I have often asked classes to draw a map that makes visible what they think of as the relationship of the known (or potentially knowable) to the unknown or unknowable in the poems they write. It's an exercise that has always led to some of the most exciting discussions that get to the pith of what we think we're doing when we write poems, or what we're doing that we didn't know we meant to do. My own map is different depending on what I'm working on at the time, but one that makes sense to me is a map of Point Roberts. Point Roberts is a tiny community of thirteen hundred people in my county in Washington state. Wikipedia succinctly calls it a "geopolitical oddity" (I think of poems, anyway, as emotive-linguistic oddities) because it is south of the Forty-ninth Parallel and thus belongs to the United States although it is wholly surrounded by Canada. To get the thirty or so miles from Bellingham where I live to Point Roberts, you have to leave the United States, and then return to it: two border crossings to get back close to where you were. Or you have to cross a body of water that's wonderfully known as Boundary Bay.

What Point Roberts has to do with poetry for me is this: a poem is a small piece of the recognizable or familiar that you can get to, but to do it you've got to double-cross the boundaries. You've got to be willing to leave home intellectually, emotionally, even linguistically, to go to a place that's strange and unfamiliar and face down the guards of the border who are wont to ask you sometimes-unanswerable questions to destabilize you for a moment, to see what makes you sweat. You come back to where you started, as Eliot says in *Four Quartets*, and know the place for the first time. Know it because it's been estranged. Like Freud's *unheimlich*, the uncanny or unhomely, where the uncanny is uncanny because it's too much like home, but like a part of the familiar that's too close to be seen. And, in being seen nevertheless, chills us to the bone.

Every poem I read is like a trip across Boundary Bay through border and through border. The language is difficult, estranging, mysterious, intoxicating. I find out things I didn't know I knew by way of giving up for a while any expectation that I should know. The visceral fear of poetry many people harbor has to do, I think, with just that self-surrender. Poems that refuse to cross the border into the unknown in order to change how we see what we thought we knew all along are the poems that bore me. Poems that cross the linguistic, intellectual, or emotional border and don't come back are ones that thrill me for a while but finally bore me with their irresolvable not-knowings.

I ask students to display and explain their maps, which are wildly different from one another's and from mine, and we talk about whether the work of the poem is to represent or map out an experience that has already been had, or to exist in a contested territory between the empires of the Known and the Unknowable. I then sometimes ask students to exchange maps with another student and write a poem that embodies the poetic epistemology it suggests—to write, then, from a wholly other set of assumptions about the poem's relationship to what can be known. Sometimes I end by reading them one of Dickinson's poems in which the *speaker* doesn't know—much less the reader—what the overwhelmingly powerful thing being described (and named only as an antecedentless pronoun) is:

> 'Tis so appalling—it exhilarates—
> So over Horror, it half Captivates—
> The Soul stares after it, secure—
> To know the worst, leaves no dread more—
>
> To scan a Ghost, is faint—
> But grappling, conquers it—
> How easy, Torment, now—
> Suspense kept sawing so—
>
> The Truth, is Bald—and Cold—
> But that will hold—
> If any are not sure—
> We show them—prayer—
> But we, who know,
> Stop hoping, now—

WORK CITED

Dickinson, Emily. *The Poems of Emily Dickinson: Reading Edition.* Ed. R. W. Franklin. Cambridge: Harvard University Press, 1999. 153.

Competitive Poetry
Kukai

SAWAKO NAKAYASU

One thing I like to do in a writing workshop is a poetry competition, based on the Japanese *kukai* (a haiku-party or gathering—"ku" is short for "haiku"). I know that the idea of competition can sound potentially problematic in what is supposed to be a nurturing, supportive classroom environment, but really, it doesn't have to be bad in that high-school-PE-class kind of way. It can be just as harmless and fun—and encourage participants to improve—as any other kind of game or contest.

The first time I attended one of these events, which generally take place monthly in local community centers all over Japan, I remember reporting back to a friend that it was like "poetry-meets-bingo." What happens is that each participant shows up with the designated number of haiku, usually three or four. First the poems are recopied onto a separate form to ensure anonymity, then these poems are photocopied, distributed, and read (privately). Back in the day, and perhaps for some groups even today, all of this copying and recopying was done by hand, adding another element to the experience, I'm sure. Then, seated at tables in some kind of circular fashion, each person gets a turn reading five or so of their favorite poems. When you hear your own poem read aloud by someone, you're supposed to claim the poem as yours by shouting out your first name (this is the bingo-like part), and everyone keeps a tally on the poems selected. In a culture where most people refer to each other by their last names, it's unusual to use your first name, and just as unusual to shout your name out in front of a group—but it's part of the tradition. And, as with tradition, it's not uncommon for people to use pen names for poetry. There is always a leader or instructor present who will give comments on the poems at the end; otherwise the participants comment on the poems as they go.

One of the great things about this, naturally, is the communal aspect of poetry—the participants tend to vary quite a bit in age, and see it as an intellectually engaging, recreational activity. They enjoy having a regular audience for their work, and a regularly scheduled purpose for writing.

{ 131

There are also some participants who take it more seriously than others, and repeated success in a *kukai* can lead some poets to publication.

When I do this in class, it's not necessarily with haiku, but we usually use short poems, since otherwise it'd get unwieldy. We might set parameters, like a twenty-five-word limit, or some other kind of form or content prompt. Since we don't have time to recopy the poems or to make photocopies on the spot, everyone just brings in copies of their own poems, cut into strips and ready to distribute.

I like the fact that the means of voting for a poem is to read it aloud — it's valuable to hear your own poem read by others, and also to hear the same poem read by a variety of voices. And it's great simply to reinforce the physical, material way that a poem inhabits space and time, and to be actively forced into thinking why we prefer certain poems over others. The idea of a competitive game is pretty versatile, though. At other times I've experimented with doing a riff on the Iron Chef, with required ingredients and multiple courses and all — these can be done as team events. Or in another reincarnation of a traditional Japanese event, I've held a *mono-awase*, a "bringing together of things" — which is a contest of aesthetics, of natural and human-made objects. And in any case, at the end of the day, someone goes home a winner.

{ **Teaching Writing
without Writing**

BRIAN HENRY

Since I started teaching in 1998, I have encouraged my students to practice active reading (what Jed Rasula and others have called *wreading*, or what Steve McCaffery calls "tactical reading") as an avenue toward making poems.[1] Aside from being in itself a good thing, such reading demonstrates to students that they do not need to look only within to make something, that the ego and personal experience are not always necessary or sufficient for creating art.

More recently, I have designed courses to push this further and to unleash reading as a creative force. I designed and taught a course devoted entirely to working from sources and constraints: OULIPO, chance operations (John Cage, Jackson MacLow), erasures, homophonic and homolinguistic translation, censorship (Bob Brown's *Gems*), found texts, the terminal (John Tranter), conceptual writing (Kenneth Goldsmith), internet-sourced and computer-generated writing, hoaxes, parodies, etc. And more recently I have been focusing on writing without writing, particularly in mixed media formats. Erasures and treatments have been central—Ronald Johnson's *RADI OS*, Stephen Ratcliffe's *[where late the sweet] BIRDS SANG*, Jen Bervin's *Nets*, Mary Ruefle's *A Little White Shadow*, Travis MacDonald's *The O Mission Repo*, and the ever-astonishing Tom Phillips's *A Humument*—because they provide a concrete way to engage with the past, to create by destroying, to write without composing, to write by reading. They give us an opportunity to mine a text for hidden meanings or to reshape or remark upon an existing text; and they offer a formal challenge, a source-based constraint as well as new modes of expression and syntactical arrangements, particularly when the source text is not contemporary. And once complete, the work invites us to engage in an act of visual reading, an act more complicated than the usual left-to-right and down-the-page that we usually see. We are asked to *see* before we read— just as the work's maker had to see the new form within the original while reading.

NOTE

1. Steve McCaffery. *Prior to Meaning: The Protosemantic and Poets*. Evanston: Northwestern University Press, 2001. 11.

The Complaint

EMILY ROSKO

Students love complaining—but they don't do so in their poems often enough. In my poetry workshops, I have developed an assignment that pushes students to complain constructively. As a lyric mode, the complaint poem offers students a chance to expand the range of emotions that they might deem *poetic*. Because the complaint relies on the use of "negative affect" (i.e., those negative feelings, such as: jealousy, shame, anger, resentfulness, vulnerability, suspiciousness), the mode encourages the development of a strong voice and tonal dexterity in order to capture the subtleties of the poems' specific emotion.

A popular form throughout the Middle Ages and the Renaissance, the *complaint*—as a term—emerged from the vocabulary of the law. Historically, the complaint poem has been used to express objections or criticisms—to lament or to rail against injustice, social ills, and to voice stories of unrequited love, personal difficulties, and poverty. Traditionally, complaint poems were narrated by a woman's voice—even though the poet was, in most cases, a man. Early complaints told the story of the woman's mistreatment in love, and the poem detailed, in Katharine Craik's words, "the predicament of an abandoned female lover who laments her undoing at the hands of an unscrupulous male seducer."[1] Typically, the woman who narrates the complaint is already punished; sometimes she is dead already. The female speaker's story becomes one of a whistle-blower, but it is also a story of repentance for her own actions. In a literary culture where women's voices rarely were heard, the complaint offered a strange mix of sympathy for the female experience while also emphasizing a moral warning to women about chastity and fidelity.

By the nineteenth century and into the twentieth, the complaint poem had begun to lose its generic specificity as it came to blend with other lyric modes such as the elegiac lament, satire, the monologue, the confession, the insult poem, and even blues poetry. In a sense, the complaint is a mode that is everywhere, and yet we don't talk about it within its specific literary history often enough.

When presenting the complaint poem to my students, I select a range of historical examples from Shakespeare's "A Lover's Complaint" to George Moses Horton's "A Slave's Complaint." While Shakespeare follows the tradition of the female speaker confessing her fall, the 1829 poem by Horton (a former slave) emphasizes the high seriousness and direct social critique that the complaint can achieve. After this, we move on to twentieth-century poems. William Carlos Williams's "Complaint" offers a good example of how poets have revised the mode. How does the poem enact its complaint, I ask. And, how does the complaint change as the poem proceeds? Just as Williams's poem offers a chance to explore the subtle shifts in tone that syntax, punctuation, enjambment, and repetition can afford, Randall Jarrell's "The Woman at the Washington Zoo" and Louise Glück's "Labor Day" use such devices more explicitly to amp up the internal tension of their respective female speakers. With Jarrell's complaint, I ask students to pay attention to how the complaint is triggered, how the poem progresses into a deeper self-reflection, and how the poem manages to avoid sentimentality as the female speaker exclaims in the last line, "change me, change me!" Glück's "Labor Day" allows students to discuss how the poem moves from a clipped and condensed syntax that enhances the matter-of-fact tone to short sentences full of grotesque nature imagery to capture the speaker's mounting negative feelings.

Although Jarrell's and Glück's poems, narrated by distressed female speakers, are aligned more closely with the complaint tradition, the complaint poem has become its own forceful and often humorous mode open to any topic worth complaining about or commenting upon. To explore these two poles of the complaint—the humorous and the serious—I often end with Dean Young's "Chapped Lips" and Michael Palmer's "Your Diamond Shoe." While Young's poem launches a complaint at children and their perpetual state of innocence, Palmer's poem, in the face of contemporary tragedies, turns the complaint into one about, and against, poetry itself.

To get students to start thinking about the complaint, I ask them in class to generate a quick list of things they might complain about and then to freewrite. Students' results are always surprising—from complaint poems about that annoying person who talks too loudly on a cell phone to larger, politically informed complaints.

Even the best poetry textbooks that delve into form take form as a more rigid structure and, as a result, they tend to ignore the plethora of poetic modes that seem more fluid.

The complaint is one such mode: it offers a historical lesson, it's very adaptable to contemporary circumstances, and it offers a sense of freedom for students as they continue to experiment with persona, voice, and tone.

SAMPLE COMPLAINT POEMS
— "The Wife's Lament" (Anonymous, Old English poem)
— Geoffrey Chaucer, "Complaint to His Purse"
— Henry Howard, Earl of Surrey, "Complaint of the Absence of Her Lover Being Upon the Sea"
— Thomas Churchyard, "Shore's Wife"
— Samuel Daniel, *The Complaint of Rosamond*
— William Shakespeare, "A Lover's Complaint"
— Lady Mary Wroth, "Unseen, unknown, I here alone complaine"
— Andrew Marvell, "The Nymph Complaining for the Death of Her Faun"
— Abraham Cowley, "The Complaint"
— Aphra Behn, "The Reflection: A Song"
— Edward Young, "Complaint, or Night Thoughts on Life, Death, and Immortality"
— William Wordsworth, "A Complaint"
— Algernon Charles Swinburne, "The Complaint of Lisa"
— George Moses Horton, "The Slave's Complaint"
— William Carlos Williams, "Complaint"
— Randall Jarrell, "The Woman at the Washington Zoo"
— Donald Justice, "Nostalgia and Complaint of the Grandparents"
— Philip Whalen, "Complaint: To the Muse"
— David Ignatow, "Self-Employed"
— Louise Glück, "Labor Day"
— Dean Young, "Chapped Lips"
— Michael Palmer, "Your Diamond Shoe"

NOTE
1. Katharine A. Craik. "Shakespeare's *A Lover's Complaint* and Early Modern Criminal Confession." *Shakespeare Quarterly* 53:4 (Winter 2002): 436.

SUGGESTED READING
Kerrigan, John. *Motives of Woe: Shakespeare and 'Female Complaint': A Critical Anthology*. Oxford: Clarendon Press, 1991.

The Poetry of Superstition and Supposition

AIMEE NEZHUKUMATATHIL

Superstition continues to flourish around the earth even in the face of the most technologically advanced societies. Some may regard it as a curious relic dating from less scientifically advanced times when people sought explanations for the apparently random workings and spinnings of nature. To others, superstition is an integral and constantly shifting part of the richness of culture in an increasingly secular world. New technologies and new relationships to nature often breed new superstitions as we grapple with changes and advancements.

We now know that some superstitions originate from scientific fact, such as some that are related to animals, food, and weather, and yet—on other occasions, there seems to be no reason or rationale behind a notion at all. People *still* cross their fingers in a promise or become leery when a black cat crosses their path. Why do you think superstitions have such a hold on people? Imagine the spark (and sparkle) of incorporating *superstition* with *supposition* in a poem—it's a direct request of the reader to trust the speaker: *Trust me, have faith in me—just for a moment. First this stanza. Then one more. And if you like that so far, perhaps come along with me for just one more stanza* . . . Such intimacy for being total strangers, no? The intimacy can be as quiet and tender as if breaking bread together over a dimly lit table, or as fun and frolicking as if riding a tilt-a-whirl side by side. But there it is—at the end of a poem, it's as if the reader and speaker shared a knowing wink: a reader's loneliness solved, even if it is for just one moment.

Before you write, consider:

What does the word *superstition* conjure up for you? Any favorite superstitions come to mind? Do you actually believe in any? What does it mean to be superstitious? Is it harmful? Helpful?

Superstition = the poetic explanation / expression of a phenomenon that is otherwise logically unexplainable.

How does this function (if at all) in your writing of poems?

One connection between poetry and superstition that I see is *faith*—

i.e., What happens when something is believed and / or understood without explanation, or when you hold a belief and don't need physical proof in order to trust its existence.

Supposition is a way of drawing the reader into a moment of hypothesis. You can use, then, superstition to pose a question of "What if . . ." for the reader . . . a sort of welcoming (or nudging or shoving, even!) into the speaker's world of faith and imagination to present / explain a larger, more universal truth that is otherwise unexplainable. And to do this by choosing what Coleridge calls "the best words, in the best order."[1]

What happens when you take a superstition and try to connect it to a line or two of an actual belief that you hold, or an actual memory of yours? For example: What connections can be made between the belief, "There is no such thing as love at first sight," and the superstition that if you sleep with a yarrow herb underneath your pillow, you will see a vision of your future partner in your dreams?

PROMPTS FOR YOU TO TRY (FEEL FREE TO MIX AND MATCH)
1. Cover your mouth when you yawn or evil spirits will fly into your body.
2. If you sit by a fire with a group of friends and a person's shadow does not appear to have a head, that person will be the first to die.
3. If a bird frightens a pregnant woman, her child will be born with a wing instead of an arm.
4. "A mole on the arm can do you no harm, a mole on your lip—you are witty and flip. A mole on your neck brings money by the peck, but a mole on your back brings money by the sack."
5. If a hen runs into your house, you will receive important visitors.
6. If a person's eyebrows join at the nose, they are not to be trusted.
7. If you can catch a dragonfly, you will be married within the year.
8. Dimples are a sign that God has touched you with favor, but "a dimple on the chin means a devil within."

NOTE
1. Samuel Coleridge. *The Table Talk and Omniana of Samuel Taylor Coleridge.* Ed. Humphrey Milford. Oxford Edition. Oxford University Press, 1917. 73.

Obsession with Objects

MARTHA RONK

If you find yourself stuck, one obvious thing to do as a writer is form an obsession with objects.

The obvious has, as always, escaped me and would have continued fleetingly to do so, but for a phrase from Hegel's *The Phenomenology of Mind*: "A self having knowledge purely of itself in the absolute antithesis of itself."[1] It is also a line that is purportedly echoed in lines from the George Oppen poem "From a Phrase of Simone Weil's and Some Words of Hegel's":[2]

> We are the beaks of the ragged birds
> Tune of the ragged bird's beaks
> In the tune of the winds
> Ob via   the obvious
> Like a fire of straws
> Aflame in the world or else poor people hide
> Yourselves together   Place
> Place where desire
> Lust of the eyes the pride of life and foremost of the storm's
> Multitude moves the wave belly-lovely
> Glass of the glass sea shadow of water
> On the open water no other way
> To come here the outer
> Limit of the ego

In discussing the reference to Hegel and the Oppen poem Peter Nicholls comments that the poem seeks the "absolute antithesis" of the self in some pure exteriority which allows it to be seen as something bounded and limited in its recognition of what is not itself.[3] In an interview in *Contemporary Literature* (1969) Oppen speaks about the nature of reality and emphasizes the importance of the "apprehension of some thing, whether it is or not, whether one can make a thing of it or not"—the second thing here being a form, "the making an object of the poem."[4] Obsession with objects deflates solipsism. Even the object that is a poem written by someone else, or perhaps especially, since reading another's words seems to generate one's own. A rather round about path to the obvious all this.

Why am I so obsessed with objects I ask myself. These authors tell me that obsession with objects is obsession for the not-that-which-I-am, the relief and maddening bafflement that here is something I am not. Walking the world, touching whatever runs horizontally along with my hand, going along together with it until the wall runs out, the hedge stops, the ridged concrete blocks that can abrade and even tear the skin are no longer; one has turned left into the void. But then: there is a tree. It is a paper birch and the bark peels off in horizontal strips like paper. I can walk over and touch it. The papery bark is not the paper that is so often in front of me, entirely blank. As a child I spent hours among neighborhood trees collecting twigs of various sorts and peeling off the bark until pieces were caught under my fingernails and I carried them around with me pretending to be a tree walking. When I first read *Macbeth* in eighth grade, I was thrilled with the Birnam woods: people as things, things as people, the moving trees, the floating dagger, the excruciating sense of Macbeth's self-consciousness, the obliteration of consciousness in Lady Macbeth's sleep-walking madness.

The child had dirty fingernails. The tree is in you, you are in the tree, but where does one stop and the other begin. Objects are so silent; they never utter anything, but just sit there rooted in the ground, sitting on the tabletop, circled around one's wrist. Keep collecting the bowls you collect and what does it get you? There they are, lined up on the shelf, containers of rice for dinner on occasion, but mostly containers of air: potent, silent, charged with their own being, without any concern for the comings and goings of those who pick them up, dust them off, fill and empty them. What do they remind or not remind you of? what do they ask? what history lies in them and where can you find it? what new words might the Oxford English Dictionary definition provide?

Even objects that are not containers are "emptied out," but a bowl is a perfect example, and as your counterpart a reminder of being emptied out yourself. You touch the side of the celadon bowl. It is not you. The main part of the object is hollow, missing. Of course children imagine themselves as containers with a hollow middle underneath the navel and they draw human families as rounded circles, the skin clearly marked by the pencil, the inside mere white paper. Throughout life you keep looking for yourself in the that-which-you-are-not, but even the objects themselves have negated themselves before one has come to rely on them. Hence the obsession with objects before they disappear, Latin *objecta*: noun (from the verb *ob+jacēre*, to throw or place): a thing thrown before or presented: "Both Land and Water feasting varietie of senses with varietie of objects" (1613 Purchas, *Pilgrimage*).

NOTES

1. G. W. F. Hegel. *The Phenomenology of Mind*. Dover Philosophical Classics. Mineola, NY: Dover Publications, 2003. 14.

2. George Oppen. *Collected Poems*. New York: New Directions, 1975.

3. Peter Nicholls. "Modernizing Modernism: From Pound to Oppen." *Critical Quarterly* 44.2 (Summer 2002): 44–58. Nicholls provides the reference to Hegel, *The Phenomenology of Mind*. Trans. J. B. Baillie. New York: The Macmillan Company, 86.

4. "George Oppen." *Contemporary Literature* 10.2 (Spring 1969): 159.

{ **Taking Readings /**
To Take Time
MATTHEW COOPERMAN

In the introduction to *Broken English*, Heather McHugh opines, "Poems take place as time takes them; and they address their object as an attention does. The place of poetry is nothing less than the place of love for language; the place of shifting ground, for human song; the place of the made, for the moving" (1). In so adducing a poem's utility as a temporal "place taking," she gives it a particular kind of agency; the poem is a gathering of attentions—of memory, visual acuity, linguistics (love of language), the ecstasy and production of song. Space is cleared and Time is regained (bless her), and our homelessness (centrifugal or centripetal) is figured on a page.

There's something useful in this equation, something axiomatically environmental that is "a motion of attention, itself the consequence of attention" (Donald Revell, *The Art of Attention* 23). For it is motion that is a poem's evidence, to be moved *into* the world, our body's proprioceptive witness extruding daily a capillary line. And if the condition of the poem is something necessarily environmental, then there's something ethical in the "worlding" possibility it produces. Poems take place as an intersubjective part of a larger temporality (our atmospheric breathing, our cultural blink) such that the poem is always relational as a "planetary figure." Synechdoche Mundi (my stage name) . . . how often I've felt better, more spacious after writing a poem. Poems are then "answering forms" of places and times, and they address their lineaments to a living system that attempts a modest preservation of the energy in which it is found. Olson's "energy transferred from where the poet got it (he will have some several causations), by way of the poem itself to, all the way over to, the reader" ("Projective Verse," *Collected Prose* 240).

However inevitable the poem is as a functioning ecology, it is important to examine its assumptions (there are good and bad worlds, worlds of habit). As such, to take time to learn how to write a poem is to learn how to read a poem: your own, those of your peers, those comprising your cultural legacy. Attempt the large scroll. As Emerson reminds us, "There is then creative reading as well as creative writing" ("The American Scholar," *Essays* 471). What strains of English, from at least Shakespeare forward, are you heir to? How does your English filter across the pond? Cotton Mather or Walter Raleigh? Emily Dickinson or Walt Whitman? Are you, god forbid, Western? American assumptions all, or a colonial course only one strand of any poet's body. Where else (what else) are you from? What educations and books brought you to this shore? And whom of these fathers and mothers must you read *slowly*, again and again? Be as wide as you are deep in your lineal casting. Note that these affinities arise from places (and genres, and materials) as much as historical epochs. More environmental investigation: the poem as an environment of forms.

— Write a *mixed form* investigation—poetry and prose, fragment and image—that charts the course of your reading. Do it again charting the course of your physical environments. Be visual. How do these ecologies intersect? What qualities of speech or place animate the mix? What "daily" materials can you introduce? Read Clayton Eshleman's *Novices*.

— How do your poems *take time*? What are their durations, ripenings, excrutiations, sources, echoes? And how do they *partake* of time as a formal patterning of line lengths, breath increments, stanzaic imaginings, field wanderings, and picture takings? Read the essay "A Stranger's Way of Looking," from McHugh's *Broken English*; read Olson's "Maximus, to Himself," Nate Pritts's "Toward a Theory of Time in Olson" (*Jacket* 35).

— How do your poems *take reading*? How is it, like tea, or dope, something *taken*, an activity, an anodyne, an abduction, a time in a room? What is your citational practice? How do your poems "display" their reading? What streams of thought and efforts of confluence? And what swerves, what influences? Kill the father often? What books and propositions are you "at sea" with presently? How have those evolved? Dear Ephebe, read Harold Bloom's *The Anxiety of Influence*.

— How might you be in conversation with these *texts-as-places*? How might your imagining be complicated by an explicit address to place? Home and away? Nomad or hermit? How does this reveal a dialectical (or not) imagination? What procedures and invitations to chance might propel this activity? Read Brenda Coultas's

A Handmade Museum; Sina Queyras's *Lemon Hound*; C. S. Giscombe's *Giscome Road*.

— What is the *place of alterity in your work*? Where is the shock and the pleasure? The fear? Where do you allow yourself to be unraveled? What subjects do the raveling? Where is this felt in the body? How does this work as POV? What is beyond in your work? How does it figure as sound? If Zukofsky declares poetry an increment, "upper limit music, lower limit speech," ["A-12," "A" 138] what are the limits of your increment? Read Kristeva on chora; Khlebnikov on Zaum; read Amittai Aviram, *Telling Rhythm*; Christian Bök, *Eunoia*.

— What is the *presence of the world*? How is it cyclic? How is it sound? Where are its seasons, its tides? How does this figure as number and repetition? How is it a green thing with green imperatives? How is it gray? How might a neo or post-pastoralism be available, or be expressed in your work? What is the instruction? Read John Kinsella, *The New Arcadia*; Susan Stewart, *The Forest*; Geoffrey G. O'Brien's *Green and Gray*; Theodore Enslin's *Nine*.

— How might this all be expressed as *a series of opposites*? Time and your materials manifesting as respiratory praxis of forces: Reading / Writing, Speech / Writing, Home / Away, Kinetic / Mimetic, Arcadia / Utopia, I / Thou, Metaphor / Metonymy, Chance / Intention, Sobriety / Play, Centrifugal / Centripetal, Action / Reflection, Series / Sequence, Free Verse / Inherited Forms, Poetry / Criticism, Familiar / Exotic, Personal / Political, Male / Female, Literature / Life, Micro / Macro, Ma / Pa, Langue / Parole, Mind / Body, Peace / War, Ecstasy / Ethics, If / Then, Then / Now, Us / Them, Time / Space, Sea / Land, Line / Sentence, Here / There.

Love is form, and cannot be
without important substance,
the weight,
say, 50 carats, each one of us, perforce
a goldsmith's scale
—Charles Olson, "I, Maximus of Gloucester, to You," *The Maximus Poems*

{ **The Poetic Timeline**
Toward a New
Understanding
of Process

OLIVER DE LA PAZ

Students often view poetry workshops as opportunities to display disparate poems—pieces that usually do not have a dialogic relationship with each other. In this exercise, students explore an obsession of theirs by constructing a narrative framework. By introducing students to the notion of a timeline as a vehicle for a series of poems, they acquire a greater understanding of the poetic process as they engage in a sustained project.

The workshop begins with a brief discussion about what exactly an obsession is. There are varying opinions about the subject, of course, but sometimes it needs to be stressed that students will not be dealing with the subject as a compulsion, social disorder, or dysfunction. The poets then attempt to redefine the notion of obsession into that of meditation.

During this time, offer examples of poems like Lucille Clifton's "Kali" series from her book *i agree with the leaves* (also in *Good Woman: poems and a memoir 1969–1980*). Her poem, "the coming of Kali" initiates a timeline sequence as Clifton writes, "it is the black God, Kali, / a woman God and terrible / with her skulls and breasts." Soon after, Clifton's poem, "her love poem" seems to directly address the character of Kali as the speaker says "demon, demon, you have dumped me / in the middle of my imagination . . ." This particular poem is useful for students to see in the sequence because it suggests a freedom of movement—the poems of the sequence can drift slightly out of the immediate narrative into a larger, thematic narrative. Another Kali poem in the sequence, "calming Kali," has the speaker telling Kali to "be quiet awful woman, / lonely as hell, / and I will comfort you . . ." There are more Kali poems in the sequence, but only a few are really needed to give students the gist of what Clifton is up to.

A sample of Rick Noguchi's book *The Ocean Inside Kenji Takezo* is also useful. In one of the poems from the book, "The Breath-Holding Contest," the protagonist, Kenji Takezo had ". . . trained so hard, / It was the only real talent / He had. . . ." Later, in the poem "Kenji Takezo Learns to Keep

His Mouth Closed" we see his talents being put to use when "Kenji lay in the shorebreak / Waiting for the surf to smash / Him into a thousand tiny pieces." The poems demonstrate writing that attempts to examine all the angles of a given subject—in the case of this manuscript, surfing. "The Breath-Holding Contest" and "Kenji Takezo Learns to Keep His Mouth Closed" are good examples from this particular book because students can discern what's taking place within the narrative of the individual poem from the titles. The titles also suggest a chronology and indeed the theme of water and breath continues throughout the manuscript.

Both Clifton's work and Noguchi's work are great examples for "priming" the workshop because the titles of their poems denote a chronological trajectory. After students have read the examples, they are asked to think about an obsession that they would like to journal / freewrite about for the next few minutes. As in many things related to creative writing, have the students use concrete language—the more specific the subject, the better. A list of components for the poem is an option for instructors but not necessary.

Students open the session with a brief journaling exercise. Journaling is a way to open or initiate the poetic process for this idea. The writing exercise starts out harmlessly enough. The instructor offers several prompts centered around the students' obsessions. They are asked whether the obsession speaks a foreign language, is represented by a particular color, etc. Many of these questions come from a list of Surrealist parlor games and the spirit of the exercise shares the same level of playfulness. The instructor continues to supply journal prompts until many of the students have written a few pages' worth of journaling.

The next step of the early journaling process is essentially the most important step or moment of the class. It is when the student-writers make a commitment to their subject matter. Poets in the class must reread the journal entry they had just completed. They must then create a sentence, summarizing what they've written using only a five-word image. This five-word image becomes the base or center of the workshop. From the five-word image, students attempt all the poems that occur later on.

During the same class session, students are asked to construct a timeline, placing the five-word image at the center of the timeline. It is best if the students use a separate piece of paper. They are then asked to write two poems: a poem that takes place before the five-word image came into being and a poem that takes place after the five-word poem came into being. The image, when placed in this framework, offers many more avenues for creative exploration. It creates a visual sense of process, and it allows students to understand the idea of dialogic writing.

This is an ideal exercise for students who are preparing manuscripts, chapbooks, or students who claim to be suffering from writer's block. By giving the writers a way to envision the context of a single poem, they are often granted an avenue for the further definition of their subject or the subject of other poems.

WORKS CITED

Clifton, Lucille. *Good Woman: Poems and a Memoir 1969-1980*. Brockport: BOA, 1987.

Noguchi, Rick. *The Ocean Inside Kenji Takezo*. Pittsburgh: University of Pittsburgh Press, 1996.

Manipulative pressure and stretching are the most effective ways of modifying the energy potentials of abnormal tissues.
—R. B. Taylor, osteopathic physician

Nothing chemical or structural has been added to or subtracted from the connective tissue. Rather, by means of pressure and stretching, and the friction they generate, the temperature and therefore the energy level of the tissue has merely been raised slightly. This added energy in turn promotes a more fluid ground substance which is more sol and ductile, and in which nutrients and cellular wastes can conduct their exchanges more efficiently. In addition to this mechanical stimulation of pressure and stretching, a powerful thermodynamic effect can be produced upon the bioenergetic field of the patient by the stronger and healthier bioenergetic field of the therapist.—Deane Juhan, from *Job's Body*

Writing the Body
BHANU KAPIL

SMALL GROUP WORKSHOP

Question for the Writer:

Where is the abnormal tissue? Areas that lack "energy potential"—that don't exchange, discharge, recirculate, or feel in some way stagnant to you?

Questions for the Reader:

1. Can you suggest nutrients this piece might benefit from?
2. What needs to be discharged from the piece? Where is the cellular waste?
3. What is the potential of this piece? What does it reach towards?
4. Are there any areas that might benefit from "pressure" or "stretching"? Describe a formal modification / strategy / act of stimulation that does not involve adding anything or taking anything away.
5. Which parts of the structure are healthy and strong?

Writers, spend ten minutes responding to the "question for the writer," transfused from the opening quotes. Exchange your piece with the two other readers in your group. Share your notes with them. Readers, spend thirty minutes reading and then writing a response to return to the writer; then do the same for the next writer. Share your responses in a group.

REWRITING FOR ENVIRONMENT

1. Review your feedback. Select a course of reviving action. Which precursors to nerve / muscular activity will enter the pores of the delicate membrane that surrounds your work?
2. Allow your work to receive the necessary nutrients / bodywork. Hold your work as a different kind of witness to: asymmetry.
3. Introduce a new "line of stress" to bring your work into alignment with its movement goals: what it's reaching towards. This line is something of your own invention. It appears only after the space to see it at all has opened up.

REWRITING FOR SENSATION

1. Identify and describe "self-produced movement" in this piece, which is restricted, recursive movement—movement or gesture that doesn't extend. It just appears or repeats, but without a vibratory or territorial effect.
2. Suggest a "moving object" or "externally imposed body movement" that could be introduced into this piece.
3. What is the movement goal of this piece?
4. Suggest one area / image where sensation could be suppressed. Suggest a strategy for reducing intensity in this area.
5. Suggest one area / image where sensation could be amplified. Which sensation? Is it gesture or a pre-gesture that increases the intensity? In your text, what comes just before the radical sign, which is a disturbance on the page?

Writers, hi. What do you know about your piece that you weren't aware of before you began? Rewrite your piece based on the feedback you received, selecting from the domains above. Each decision results in a different movement goal. Describe a different future for your piece, whether that's the work you brought in today or your larger project. Perhaps there is just a subtle variation or perhaps a completely different set of "precise relationships" has arisen. I don't know.

NOTE

This essay duplicates my handout for a Fall 2008 MFA seminar, "Writing the Body," at Naropa University in Boulder, Colorado.

Trust the Turn
Focusing the Revision Process in Poetry

MICHAEL THEUNE

One of the very difficult aspects of teaching poetry writing is trying to encourage students to revise so that their poems begin to embody the power, mystery, seductiveness, and grace of great poetry without either becoming unclear and lapsing into disarray or else becoming overly clear by incorporating excessive explanations. One way to address this difficulty is to help students recognize the presence and importance of turns in poems, understand that the lyric poem (largely) is a linguistic unit the goal of which is the successful enactment of its turn(s), and then learn to trust the turns in their poems and revise with those turns in mind.

A poem rarely ends in the same place that it began—Randall Jarrell notes, "A successful poem starts from one position and ends at a very different one, often a contradictory or opposite one; yet there has been no break in the unity of the poem." Turns—rhetorical shifts in a poem's progress—are the places where a poem changes its position. Well known as a part of the tradition of the sonnet form, the turn actually is a vital part of all sorts of poems. In fact, just as many poems can be categorized by their forms, many poems can be categorized according to the kinds of turns they take. For example, to name just a few kinds of poems that employ a single turn, ironic poems turn from set-up to punch line, emblem poems turn from description to meditation, and retrospective-prospective poems turn from past to present or future. (A fuller list may be found in *Structure & Surprise: Engaging Poetic Turns* and at http://structureandsurprise.wordpress.com.)

A significant portion of the power and mystery of so many poems comes from the successful enactment of a turn. A good metaphor for this is the joke. Jokes work—that is, they please, thrill, and astound—largely by successfully enacting their turn from set-up to punch line. On the one hand, this means that jokes do not, on top of their setting up and delivering their punch lines, additionally feel the need to explain themselves. On the other hand, this also means that (good) jokes are not muddy / sloppy—that is, while working for the whole effect of the joke, the constituent parts of the joke each do their own separate, and even often sharply divided, tasks. The same is true of poems, and not just funny poems. If the poem is, as Wallace Stevens says, the "cry of its occasion," it is often best to simply and powerfully arrange the occasion and cry that emerges from it rather than messily mixing up such elements, or tacking on an explanation.

Thus, as a part of the revision process, it is important to:

Identify where and how a poem turns.

Identify and assess the specific work undertaken on either side of the turn(s)—is the turn clean? what needs to be moved, expanded, condensed, or excised to clarify the turn?

Identify and cut unnecessarily explanatory language.

Suggest how the impact of the turn might be modified to create a more powerful, surprising, and / or revealing poem.

Considering the poem an enactment of a turn acquaints students with a feature of a poem that T. S. Eliot calls "one of the most important means of poetic effect since Homer," and offers a concise way to encourage crafting sophisticated lyric experiences.

WORKS CITED

Eliot, T. S. "Andrew Marvell." *Selected Essays: New Edition*. New York: Harcourt, Brace and World, 1950. 251–263.

Jarrell, Randall. "Levels and Opposites: Structure in Poetry." *Georgia Review* 50.4 (1996): 697–713.

Stevens, Wallace. "An Ordinary Evening in New Haven." *Collected Poems*. London: Faber and Faber, 1954. 465–489.

Theune, Michael, ed. *Structure & Surprise: Engaging Poetic Turns*. New York: Teachers & Writers, 2007.

Impersonal Universe Deck (IUD)

K. SILEM MOHAMMAD

This is an exercise I assign to students in my introductory creative writing course. I used to use Michael McClure's original instructions for assembling a "Personal Universe Deck," based largely on the five senses of sight, touch, sound, taste, and smell. McClure describes his deck as a "word sculpture" for "creating spontaneous, subjective, stochastic imagery reflecting the personal self." I finally felt like the exercise needed updating in order to retain some cultural relevance at this advanced stage of globalized Spectacle, so I came up with my own variation. As with many of the other exercises I assign in this class, a primary objective is to get students to attune their sensibilities to the sonic and affective potential of language they might not ordinarily consider poetic, and to think about the role combinatory structures play in "expressive" logic.

■

The universe is a chaotic, hostile mass of mineral fragments, toxic vapor, and late-capitalist detritus that doesn't give a damn about you. Show it who's boss! Create your own Impersonal Universe Deck (with apologies to Michael McClure, creator of the *Personal* Universe Deck[1]).

You will need fifty unruled 3 × 5 cards and a black pen.

Compile a list of one hundred words (single or compound), divided into the categories described below.

Forty of the hundred words should be distributed evenly into groups of eight under these five headings (try not to think about it too hard):

FAST FOOD	SCARY ANIMALS	EMPTY SEX	BAD POLITICS	THE UNREAL
1.	1.	1.	1.	1.
2.	2.	2.	2.	2.
3.	3.	3.	3.	3.
4.	4.	4.	4.	4.
5.	5.	5.	5.	5.
6.	6.	6.	6.	6.
7.	7.	7.	7.	7.
8.	8.	8.	8.	8.

Choose twenty words by jamming your index finger twenty times at random into a dictionary or other arbitrary, alphabetized reference source.

1.	5.	9.	13.	17.
2.	6.	10.	14.	18.
3.	7.	11.	15.	19.
4.	8.	12.	16.	20.

Choose ten words by starting on page 23 of a book you dislike and selecting the twelfth word, then going on to page 24 and doing the same, and then page 25, and so on, until you have ten words. If a word repeats, or if a page doesn't have twelve words on it, just skip a page until you're done.

1.	3.	5.	7.	9.
2.	4.	6.	8.	10.

Choose ten words by turning a radio dial from station to station at a slow but steady pace and listening to the fragments of speech, song, etc., that you pick up in doing so. Pick the first ten words that jump out at you (only one word from each station).

1.	3.	5.	7.	9.
2.	4.	6.	8.	10.

Get ten words by approaching a friend, acquaintance, or total stranger and asking him or her to supply the following:

1. the name of a place he or she doesn't want to go to
2. the name of a famous dead person who was evil (besides Hitler— too obvious)
3. the name of a living celebrity who is evil, or at least very annoying
4. the name of a corporate product (brand name)
5. a boring word
6. a word that sounds good but has a negative meaning
7. a word that sounds bad but has a positive meaning
8. a word that's embarrassing to say
9. a word he or she has heard but doesn't know the meaning of
10. a word that's not in any dictionary

| 1. | 3. | 5. | 7. | 9. |
| 2. | 4. | 6. | 8. | 10. |

The last ten words should be your answers to the following questions:
1. What's the most disgusting thing you would put in your mouth for $25?
2. What's your favorite power tool?
3. Without looking, what would you guess the next word is in the dictionary after *abacus*?
4. If you had a spirit animal, what other kind of animal would it eat?
5. What's the worst band ever?
6. Imagine a six-foot-tall talking mosquito with an accordion. What's its name?
7. Suppose you walked out one day and the charred skeletons of angels were falling from the sky in slow motion, bursting into clouds of gray ash and bits of burnt feather as they hit the ground. What one word would you use to describe this experience?
8. You are in control of an army and a small nuclear arsenal. What country do you attack first?
9. What is the stupidest flower?
10. Name the last alcoholic beverage or other mind-altering substance that got you wasted (if none, just name the first one you can think of).

| 1. | 3. | 5. | 7. | 9. |
| 2. | 4. | 6. | 8. | 10. |

Mohammad { 155

Put the fifty 3 × 5 cards in a stack next to this completed sheet and go over the list at random, transferring two words at a time onto each of the cards until you are finished. Print the words neatly in bold, block capitals. Place the words on the cards playing-card-style, with one word on one end right side up, and the other word on the other end upside down (or vice versa, of course, depending on which way you're holding the card). The cards should look like this:

Once you've finished assembling your IUD, you're ready to use it as a tool for creating poetic texts. The possibilities for generating rules and procedures based on the deck are nearly limitless. Here are a few to get you started:

1. Shuffle the deck and deal three cards. Use the top three words in some combination as a title for a poem—for example: "Pituitary Nickelback Lube."
2. Shuffle the deck and deal fourteen cards. Write a sonnet using one of the fourteen top words from each card in each line, in the order they're drawn.
3. Write a series of sentences in which the first word is the top word on a card you draw from your deck, and the last word is the bottom word. Try to go through the entire deck.

Devise your own operations!

NOTE

1. Michael McClure. "Cinnamon Turquoise Leather: (A Personal Universe Deck)," in *Talking Poetics from Naropa Institute: Annals of the Jack Kerouac School of Disembodied Poetics Volume One*. Ed. Anne Waldman and Marilyn Webb. Boulder: Shambala, 1978. 97–109.

Five Steps to the Five-Minute Chapbook

SASHA STEENSEN

1. If you read the newspaper or watch television, you are likely convinced that the book is dying, if not dead. Journalists recount the decline of printed matter much in the way that they cover the extinction of an animal. A population of lemurs is dwindling, and scientists have been rushed to the scene, but it is too late. All they can do is gather genetic samples to relieve our collective guilt. In the extinction of books, this act of genetic collection is analogous to turning a text digital—its contents will be stored away for future generations in a digital archive. As Google is busy scanning every book ever published in order to install them on their searchable database, we are left empty-handed, with endless information. This is not to say, however, that the Internet hasn't done wonders for poetry; from digital poetry to online journals, the Internet has widened poetry's audience. But there is something irreplaceable, at least for this reader, about holding a book in one's hands. What does this digitization mean for our creative writing students, many who proclaim a burning desire to *publish* a book someday? What will this *published* thing look like? Who will read it, and in what ways will its material manifestation determine its reception? Now that the concept of the book is forever changed, what kind of a relationship will our students have with books, and how will this affect their writing lives?

2. There is nothing about writing or teaching poetry that is quick or instantaneous, easy or effortless, at least not in my experience. Even when the poem arrives quickly, there is a trail of thought leading up to it. Sometimes this looks like a tree trunk, with limbs and branches pointing in all directions, leaves dangling as thoughts unfurled. Sometimes this trail is more like a dotted line waiting for someone with scissors to cut along its edges. It's not so much the actual writing or even the revision of a poem that I focus on in my classes, but the work that comes before and after the writing of a poem. Preparing, which often entails reading, and then taking the made thing seriously are just as important to me as the writing itself. In my own writing life, this was not a lesson I learned quickly. In many

ways, it wasn't until I began to work as an editor, publisher, printer, and bookmaker that I began to see that what I was producing was in fact an object. We love to talk about the materiality of the poem; but what does this mean, especially to students who may or may not be familiar with Marshall McLuhan, textual studies, or notions of the embodied text? Is it important that they see their poems as things in the world, and if so, how do we as teachers encourage such an engagement?

3. The history of poets as publishers in American poetry goes as far back as Whitman and Dickinson. Whitman's 1855 *Leaves of Grass* was completely produced by his own hand—from manuscript, to printed book, and even to the first reviews which Whitman himself ghostwrote. Dickinson's carefully handwritten, sewn fascicles are an act of self-publishing. This carried over into the twentieth century, with figures like Gertrude Stein who, with the help of Alice B. Toklas, initially published her own work. Meanwhile, many of her contemporaries, like Pound and Williams, were publishing their work with small, noncommercial, often poet-run presses. By the 1940s, direct access to all sorts of printing technology—the letterpress, the mimeograph, offset printing—sparked "The Mimeo Revolution," the immediate precursor to today's small press movement. From Dickinson's unconventional experimentations to Ginsberg's controversial "Howl," much politically and aesthetically radical American poetry would never have been published if it weren't for poets acting as publishers. For the American poet, then, the composition and production of poetry have long been undivided acts. Is it important that our students are familiar with this history, and that they can see themselves as participating in this long-standing tradition? How can we as their teachers give them the opportunity to begin to see themselves as fully engaged with the material manifestation of their work?

4. Send them out of the classroom. Tell them to go in search of one $8\frac{1}{2}$ × 11 inch piece of paper with or without text, with or without image. Tell them it's best if there is some blank space somewhere on the page. Tell them that it's just as good if text fills the entire page. Tell them they can pull flyers off the wall, pick up a dropped piece of paper from another student's notebook, dig through the trash if they aren't afraid of such dirty business, tear out a page from a magazine, if there's one available. When they find their piece of paper and return to the classroom, tell them they are ready to make a book. Tell them all they will need to do now is fold the paper three times, make one simple cut or tear, grasp both sides of the page, pull apart, and fold one last time (see detailed instructions below).

You won't need to tell them that they've made a book; they will know by holding it. I like to do this activity on the first class of the semester because it's unexpected. Students expect the introduction to the class, the necessary but predictable recitation of the syllabus, perhaps the discussion of some exemplary poem that you happen to photocopy, read aloud, and then use as a jumping-off point for a wonderful discussion that you hope will continue, in some form or another, for the entire semester. Unlike writing and teaching, the five minute chapbook is quick and easy. It's an activity that instantaneously acknowledges that writing extends beyond the moment of composition. It is an activity that comes prior to writing, and it is a product that remains when the writing is done, especially if you ask students, as I do, to use their chapbooks to compose their first poem for the semester. I ask them to bring their books back to the second class, to read their poems, to tell us a bit about how the poem they wrote was determined by the activity of making the book. Students whose original 8½ × 11 page was filled with text often perform an erasure of that text, retaining words and phrases to form their poem. Students whose original page contained images often respond to those images in the composition of the poem. Other students find that the number of pages (six pages, plus cover and back), the size of the pages (approximately 2¾ inches × 4¼ inches), and the shape of the page (rectangular) allowed them to arrive at a form they would have otherwise resisted. The other benefit of the five-minute chapbook is that anyone can make one anywhere. Why not give our students something to do as they wait in line at the DMV, or dare I say it, as they endure a class that's not quite as anticipated as the creative writing classroom?

5. Ironically, though contemporary poets who are also teachers (myself included) seem to like to talk about materiality, they tend to avoid discussions of product. We valorize process over product, as if the product, the evidence of process, is an unfortunate outcome of writing. But there is a product, and it is important. There are books, and most of us like them. Sometimes I think students resent our continual emphasis on process at the expense of product. On some level, it must sound like we aren't taking their work seriously. When we refer them back to process, do they hear us saying, the product just isn't good enough to talk about yet? Meanwhile, we assign products in the form of books we expect them to read carefully. Even if we talk about process in relation to these assigned books, there is still the fixed object, the published book, the words on the page, the pages, the cover. This is a tangible object, and one that changes very little,

save the wear and tear any loved book suffers. Even if it's dynamic writing, writing that does not lend itself to one reading, one understanding, the primary makeup of the book remains more or less the same. If anything, it's the reader who changes, not the book. What we as readers hold in our hands is a product of the writer's efforts; though there are hints at the limb-like lines, the dotted lines of thought that precede and accompany the writing, it is the writing that remains for us to read. Rather than keeping the activity of producing books, objects, at arms' length, why not demystify this activity? Why not give students the permission and the responsibility to participate in all aspects of the production of their work? And, why not make it easy for once?

■

Instructions for the five-minute chapbook using an 8½ × 11 inch piece of paper.

1. Begin by putting the paper flat in front of you with the 8½ inch sides on the top and bottom. Fold the paper lengthwise. Open the paper back to its original 8½ × 11 size.

2. Keeping the 8½ inch sides on the top and bottom, fold the paper horizontally. Open the paper back to its original 8½ × 11 size.

3. Rotate the paper so that the 11 inch sides are on the top and bottom. Fold the 8½ inch ends so that they touch along the middle crease, and then open these folds. At this point, your 8½ × 11 piece of paper should have eight rectangular folds. These will eventually be the individual pages of your book.

4. Cut or tear along center from middle to fold (see image below—cut along dotted line).

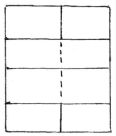

5. Pull torn edges away from one another and down. Refold the paper along the creases so that the paper forms a book with eight pages, including the front and back.

A Wicker Swimmer
Straying Home
PAUL HOOVER

In teaching poetry classes, I try to make no distinction regarding the supposed student level, advanced and beginning, graduate or undergraduate. To quote Kenneth Koch, we are all "fellow paddlers" in the art of poetry. I've always taught everyone at the level of my own interest.

In any poetry workshop course in which I am meeting students for the first time, from Beginning Poetry workshop (undergraduate) to MFA Poetry Workshop, I give two writing assignments, each to be written in class in fifteen to twenty minutes. After students have finished writing, we read all of them out loud and comment briefly. If someone writes an exemplary poem, I make note of it immediately. It's a far better teaching moment than the laborious negotiation of a poem's value in workshop mode. Everyone can hear the poem's greatness when read out loud. They can feel the intensity of listening in the room. By showing your immediate enthusiasm for the work, you make your standard for poetry clear and also the trustworthiness of your opinions.

The first exercise is based on Maxine Chernoff's book *Japan*. A proceduralist book-length series, it is an abecedarium; each poem has twenty-seven lines; each title is one word of five letters; no line has more than three words and usually only one or two, and there are few and sometimes no sentences in the poems. Emphasizing the music of the lines, I read three of the works out loud, in alphabetical order. Here's an example:

OVERT
Strand of
  me
   bright bearded
coast
   a middle distance
close
   a stuttered

semaphore
   conjured grace
in every
   never
fever strenuous
   forecast white
   so seer
implacable
   geese and offspring
faithless
   never mind
a wicker
   swimmer
brusque if courtly
   miles to empty
some tempter
   whitened
gauge
   last masque
a mote

So that students hear the rhythm and word relation, I repeat one of the musical passages two or three times, for example:

a wicker
   swimmer
brusque if courtly
   miles to empty
some tempter

The assignment is to write a poem that strictly follows Maxine's procedures, but of course to "use your own words." The results are usually very good. Students realize they are being given permission to write strangely and yet somehow "on note." They learn how to be complex and yet uncluttered; how to use received form like rhyme and enjambment and also to invent new forms; and how to make music, one of poetry's most enduring charms. But the most important lesson of this activity is difference and identity. You can begin virtually anywhere, in difference, and immediately arrive at word relations in lines like "never / fever" and "a wicker / swimmer." The range of possibility is greater when difference comes first, but finally it's the firm catches ("last masque / a mote") that we value and re-member.

Being terse, the *Japan* poems are models of compression and lyric. The second activity, writing middle to middle, demands extension. Using Zu-kofsky's "A-14," Gwendolyn Brooks's "I love those little booths at Bene-vuti's," part VII of "The Womanhood," and James Schuyler's "The Morn-ing of the Poem," I read three pages beginning and ending in the middle of a sentence. The Zukofsky model, especially, offers tonal shifts and quick changes of subject, a hinged progress of this, this, and this. "A-14" contains the famous "lower limit body / upper limit dance" passage. My selection begins six pages later. This is only an excerpt of it:

fly together: if
there are not

too many words.
Eloquence: self-laud.
My persistence reminds:

an escaped cat
ran down three
flights of stairs,

a little boy
after, he caught
it and climbed

back up the
three flights and
before closing the

door on it,
stroked it, 'you
pussy stay upstairs,

now *I'll* go
downstairs.' It became
the family joke—

'preventing an animal
errand.' They wash
the streets with

it in Poitiers.
Out of that
jakes my "Cats"

chaste—eyeing passionate
Italian lips two
thousand years near

to sharp them
and flat them
not in prurience—

of their voice—
eyes of Egyptian
deity that follow

each half step
blueing to translucent
Lunaria annua honesty

this side the
moon's.

The assignment is to fold a single sheet of typing paper lengthwise, creating four narrow panels. This page arrangement reminds students they are writing a poem. The extension is via the short line, down the page, not across as in prose. Working quickly and filling at least three panels, you must begin in mid-sentence (in *medias res*) and end in mid-sentence. Don't seek a conclusion. Don't prepare for your turns; take them cleanly and don't look back. Finally, get out when the getting is good; anywhere will do. This exercise has never failed to bring out wonders in the students. Because both extension and compression are basic principles of composition, the resulting works offer the open hand (narrative languor, like the cat story) and the closed ("blueing to translucent / *Lunaria annua honesty*").

Having created two strong and fairly sophisticated works in the first class session, the students are now ready for anything. Absorbed in the formal problem, they seem not to care at what level they are being addressed and proceed confidently.

To alter a phrase of Michel de Certeau, such writing is not "a polemological analysis of culture" (xvii) but a poemological analysis of poems. The greatest strengths often come of what may seem the greatest limits, just as the greatest errancy (course of error) can reveal what is most traditional and necessary. De Certeau refers to the "wandering lines (*'lignes d'erre'*) drawn by the autistic children studied by F. Deligny: 'indirect' or 'errant' trajectories obeying their own logic" (xviii). It is remarkable how often the so-called stray line embodies a house, mountain, bird in flight, or the joy of line-making itself.

WORKS CITED

Brooks, Gwendolyn. *Selected Poems*. New York: Harper & Row, 1963.

Chernoff, Maxine. *Japan*. Bolinas: Avenue B Press, 1987.

de Certeau, Michel. *The Practice of Everyday Life*. Trans. Steven Rendall. Berkeley: University of California Press, 1988.

Koch, Kenneth. "The Art of Poetry." *The Collected Poems of Kenneth Koch*. New York: Alfred A. Knopf, 2005. 256.

Schuyler, James. *The Morning of the Poem*. New York: Farrar Straus & Giroux, 1980.

Zukofsky, Louis. "A." Berkeley: University of California Press, 1978.

A Word Is a Thing
Teaching Poetry through Object-Based Learning and Felt Experience
DOROTHEA LASKY

To sum up what I am about to say about my own poetry teaching before I even start, a teacher of poetry teaches a student of poetry two important things:

1. That words and poems are things.
2. That these things are not precious.

In a poetry classroom, I try not to favor one school or one approach to poetry. I try to make a space for an expansive field in which my students can write / make from. Most importantly, I try to teach my students that no one poem is precious. Poems were made to be written and then thrown away. Or given away—chucked into the ether in a neverending act of generosity. In any poetry classroom of mine, no word (mine or my students) should be precious. For a student of poetry, preciousness is the death of all learning to be a great poet. The best thing a poetry teacher can do is to let her students play around with language and ideas in serious ways. As Emily Dickinson writes, "I believe and disbelieve a hundred times an hour, which keeps believing nimble." Teachers of poetry should always make a space in which their students can learn to simultaneously believe and disbelieve everything they have to say within a poem.

How this translates into actual curriculum always involves the connection of poetry with object-based learning. Poetry curriculum should involve objects, whether those objects are balls or paintings, the trees, the sun, our bodies, dirt, a piece of plastic, a television set, the wood of the dresser, feelings and emotions and events both personal and public, sculpture and all other objects of high art. These objects are the literal manifestation of the constant reconfiguration of elements in the mind, which happens in the creation of poetry. Despite the electrical luminosities of our technological age (in which our new technologies are they themselves objects if we dare to think of them as such), I believe that poets, more than any other artists besides dancers, are always engaged in the work of felt experience. By felt experience, I mean a connection between thought and the body, between the mind and the action of thinking and feeling simultaneously. A student of poetry needs to learn how to physically get into language, and no more so is this aided in the connection of words with objects. I encourage all my students to get into words by doing as much that has to do with poetry in their lives with as much as doesn't. For every poetry book they read or poetry reading they attend, I suggest that these acts always be balanced with some event non-poetry related, such as going to a museum, eating with a friend, taking a dance class, watching a science fiction movie, going on a date, and so on and so forth.

Laurence Buermeyer, a student of John Dewey, once wrote that "In mystical states of mind . . . we are conscious of an expansion of our personality thought union with something not ourselves, but this union is felt and not seen." John Dewey himself wrote much of the importance of materiality and felt experience when it comes to learning poetry. Both Buermeyer and Dewey knew, as all poetry teachers should, that words are objects and that to manipulate a word, in the quick change of syntax all poets engage in through acts of novel creation, is to manipulate a *thing*. I think sound is a set of objects and so it follows, that words are the symbolic things of the objects of sounds. These sound-things can be bounced around and smashed, but when things come together in the space of a poem, there is something spiritually and materially important to these connections. In *Art as Experience*, Dewey writes that the "formal relations" of words in a learner's imagination are not "empty containers" that "schools of philosophy have sometimes represented them to be" but "substantial" connections between words and ideas. The substance that makes a poem a poem is substance after all. To teach a poet to write poetry is to teach him or her that words and ideas are ultimately things, simultaneously real and imaginary, with a level of preciousness somewhere less than a china set and more than a brick.

How this looks in my classroom is that I try to get my students to create cabinets of curiosities of their own imaginations, with all these curiosities as a set of mental objects. In a cabinet of curiosity, in its traditional definition, objects were organized not according to historical relevance or genre, but by their aesthetic principles. I ask my students to aesthetically organize their experiences, images, and thoughts in their poems by seeing connections that are more felt than simply thought.

In your classroom, ask your students to involve themselves both deeply with actual objects and also to make objects within their poems of all their felt experiences. Try the following exercises, which I find work well:

A. Ask your students to consider: What is a word that you know that makes you most realize that words are things? When they all have a word, ask them to find a set of five objects in their houses that connect aesthetically to that word. Have them spend at least one day with each object, touching it in some way continuously, and as they see fit, and to write down one deep feeling-memory that object conjures up for them. Finally, ask them to write a poem after these five days.

B. Ask your students to think of their favorite animal. Have them imagine the daily routine of that animal for five minutes in class. Ask them to take notes on some of these activities. Have everyone leave the classroom and go into an open space, like a field outside or a hallway. Tell them to act through a behavior their animal might go through on a real day. For example, a student whose animal is a lion might stalk and hunt something. If you are not outside, go outside. Ask everyone to find a rock of some sort (rock may be defined loosely). Now have them write a poem where their animal spies this rock while doing the action they acted out.

C. Before the end of class one day, ask your students to think about a criminal act that fascinates them. Have them go home and find two individuals who have been found guilty of such an act on the Internet and read up on them. Advise them to go to sleep after finding as much information as they can on the lives of these two individuals both before and after the crime. Ask them to set their alarms for the early morning, like 5 A.M. (5 A.M. is a great time to write poems.) Now they should write a dialogue poem between the two individuals, in which the two individuals ask questions of each other about the act.

The poems your students write from these exercises may or may not show it, but I assure you that by doing exercises like these you will have done much to pave the way for creating a class of great poets. Hopefully, in their poems, as Flaubert suggests they should be, they will eventually be "everywhere felt, but never seen." And in due time, as we read the next great poetry books of felt experience, we will thank you for it.

WORKS CITED

Buermeyer, Laurence. "Mysticism and Art." Ed. John Dewey. *Art and Education: A Collection of Essays*. Third Edition. Merion, Pennsylvania: The Barnes Foundation Press, 1954.

Dewey, John. *Art as Experience*. New York City, New York: Capricorn Books, 1934.

Dickinson, Emily. Letter to Otis Phillips. 1882.

Flaubert, Gustave. Letter to Madame Louise Colet. December 9, 1852.

The Manifest An Idea with a Writing Prompt

JOHN GALLAHER

All writers write the same way: they put something down and then have to come up with a strategy to put something else down. Thus, all conversations of form and content can be distilled down to a conversation about how one decides to begin and to continue to set things down. One can remember things from one's past. One can imagine a story unfolding. One can cut things from books. One can randomize lines from one's notes.

No matter what one's strategy is, a lot rides on the moment before one is going to set things down, namely: how one's imagination is going to work, what one is ready for before the encounter (not just what one is listening to, but what one is listening for). You see some people on the street approaching, for instance. Say you want to write about that. You might think, "why are they coming?" And then it becomes a story of destinations. But what if you imagine them dancing—it could be a question of "why are they dancing," yes, but it could also be a question of "what is their dance like?" You see them and it's a question of unity and form and surprise.

So, what if the way one looks at an art object (the dance, the poem) were to be the way one looks at some aspect of the world (two people walking along a street)? It's a question of stance. It's a question of how one sets oneself up to receive language. Rendering into art from an art consciousness might be a nice way to conceptualize things. This might also be a good way of approaching the work of art before one, so that when experiencing that work, one's questions of who / what / where / when / why / how might be replaced by a less clinical and more playful environment of inquiry. Good, but how might one go about it?

Behind what I'm thinking here is my distrust of the New Critical readings and the modes and strategies approach of the usual creative writing workshop method. For one thing, and for me a very large thing, the workshop privileges the object (the poem, in this case). The object is not really the point. Much more important for the writer is what's possible to say around the object, and the possibility of more objects in the future.

Perhaps a useful workshop conversation could center on the stance, the place upon which the poem is standing. What does the world look like from that place? What suppositions is the language of the poem revealing about the world?

One cannot enact the world in art. There's already a world. What one enacts is a human relationship with the world (or with language itself, but that might be a little fussy and lead a conversation in unmanageable circles—but then again maybe not). That relation (or those relations), enacted in a work of art, can be as primary as any other thing in the world, though, as it will also exist in the world.

Description, then, is not the key to art. Nor is realism, as there is nothing inherently real about language. It's only noises the body makes. Nor are metaphors of form and content in the work of art. It all has to be something. Human relationships within the world are necessarily abstract and complicated, but they are only visible through specific events and images presented in language. They are composed of description, yes, narration, yes, but also with an awareness of themselves being composed, because to ignore the composed nature of a composition is to betray oneself to the fallacy that one is actually enacting the world (or the past or the authentic story). As the work of art is an event over time, the elements of word art: openings / endings / epiphany—are not so much in error as they are arbitrary and chance outcomes of how one is conceptualizing things. In the end they are beside the point (close, but no cigar). The point is the stance itself. The "What's possible to say?" The relationship of the world to the world that is us. The conceptualizations of craft are only to gain one access to a kind of forgetting that hopefully brings one into a more elemental position regarding the human relationship with the world, of which we are already always a part (and apart, as per the example of the brain thinking about the brain).

That said, there are stances and conceptualizations about the art act that do not help things along. Or perhaps to say it better, there are some ways of doing art that appear to be helping things, but in actuality bear false witness to the world by reducing the complexity of things and events, leaving the receiver to feel a sort of solace in the way things are, and a feeling that all connections are solid and meaningful. That has not been the case in my experience of the world. Most connections, in my experience, are delivered by chance operations and their meaning is situationally bounded. Therefore the art object itself can't really say things outside of itself, but it can participate in the reader saying things.

Anyway, the goal of the artist, I hope, is to get oneself to a position where whatever one does next in a work of art belongs. That one's method of propulsion down a poem equals the poem itself. What matters then, before the writing of the poem, seems to be of as much importance to the poem, as what happens during the writing of the poem.

A very basic writing class prompt along these lines of inquiry could be a formal poem that uses invisible form. Here's an example:

1. Visualize a scene for a minute or two without writing anything down (imagined or recalled, though at first it's better to imagine a recalled scene so that one doesn't have to work very hard). For a creative writing class (at any level) it's often good for a scene to be dictated. One I've used is camping, as it seems it's something nearly everyone has done. If camping doesn't seem interesting, one can choose any ritualized, social encounter.
2. Dictate the syntax of the title. Something like "The _____ of _____," where the writers, of course, fill in the blanks (An example: "The Importance of Monotony"). Unless they're feeling antic and write something like "The Blank of the Blank." In that case, it's fine as well. Now they're just writing an antic poem is all. The point to a prompt is never the rules of the prompt, but the action of distracting oneself from working one's imagination too hard on the surface of the poem.
3. The first sentence will be centering on an image of the natural world located in space. Something like "There are trees in the distance" or "One of the boys hid behind the others." It's important that one doesn't work on trying to sound poetic.
4. Try an action sentence now. Some movement across the landscape. Maybe a camper. Some birds.
5. "What are some things the people there have brought with them?" Answer this question in proper short-answer exam style, as in, "describe and discuss."
6. Quote something someone says. Attribute or don't, depending.
7. More scene. What might be happening that you're not aware of? Something to do with the engine, maybe, or the types of trees. Or the light through the trees.
8. Write a sentence starting with "All along."

9. Two sentence fragments. "The world at large." "We tell each other." "The spilling waterfall against the snow."
10. A sentence of desire. Desire something.

End there or repeat any of the above for as long as you feel like it. For number 8, if you're going to repeat it, you can change the "all along" to "just like" or "let me" or any other snippet from a title of a Bob Dylan song.

{ **Accessing Supra-Intelligence** Poetry and Intuition

CHRISTINA MENGERT

I think one of the more counterproductive assumptions that many new poets have when they begin to write is that they can wield a kind of hyper-rational control over their poems, and that their seeming conscious rational mind will, without recourse to other intelligences, carry them through to a sophisticated artistic realization. I say this not to denigrate their efforts, but because it provides a locus of intervention on my part as a teacher of writing.

What I perhaps value most as a poet—and what I most want to offer my students—is access to a creative supra-intelligence; and by that I mean the spontaneous creative faculty that expresses in us as we write, whether it be the unconscious intuitive mind or something more deeply metaphysical. So, for example, if I am writing an over-determined metaphor wherein a cow represents pastoral tranquility and suddenly I find myself writing that cow lit from the inside by a candle, and then suddenly the cow is on fire, I might not have immediate access to the reason behind such an image or maneuver (I think the same thing can work formally or syntactically, or any which way in a poem), but only later can see a creative logic in the image (the light as an image of illumination overwhelms the cow or the natural—or another possible reading).

So when I enter the classroom, I recognize that part of what I'm doing is disrupting comfortable or codified patterns of thinking, what Krishna-murti calls "thinking in grooves."[1] To that end, I've created an exercise that relies on a call and response structure between my students and myself. I usually begin by reading some ancient texts in which the "poem's" structure is one of question and answer or call and response. I also like to bring in musical examples of this, to show simply how much music and poetry have their roots in this kind of exchange. In this exercise, I pose questions that are unpredictable ("Are the children hungry?" "How do you speak a language of kingdoms?"), designed to invite unexpected logics, and give them thirty to forty-five seconds to respond on paper.

What I want to encourage in this exercise is a real-time reaction on the part of the student, in the hope that the exercise's constraints will urge them to rely more heavily on their intuitive faculties. Then, as a class, we can talk about the kind of creative logics and leaps their answers engage. And what freedom to realize that we are capable of new and unexpected thought! One of the secondary benefits is, of course, that they can see readers make meaning of their intuitions, which naturally loosens the vise of old thought and gives new reign to the imagination. So the first goal of the exercise, of the workshop generally, is to help them gain access to this supra-intelligence, the second goal is to encourage them to begin to trust it, and the third goal is to show them a readership capable of responding to their creative intelligence, which reinforces the first and second goals.

One final note: I think it is important in this exercise to have a discussion about and awareness of the force of our habitual thoughts upon our writing; this gives the exercise an important critical and theoretical dimension that students can reflect on over time. In a way, this is the important movement of reason in this exercise: the rational, critical reflection that liberates minds from habit and lets intuition and imagination breathe new air.

NOTE

1. Jiddu Krishnamurti. *Education and the Significance of Life.* New York: Harper and Row, 1981. 14.

Is a poem a way of *saying something*? Is a poem or poetry (not the same thing) *about* something?

About usually means wandering within the vicinity of something, as in "We walked about the park" or "We'll be there about seven o'clock."

There ought to be space in it for anarchy. So a poem for me, whether or not it is in verse lines, isn't a story or an essay. It's *about* something in a second sense. Or I should say the real gift of poetry is the giving of space, whether a line or stanza, or couplet or other form, to move around in this mystery.

To dream in sense plus sway.

I'm moderately interested in free verse poetry but only insofar as it knows what *free* is—what is it worth to the poem to be free from whatever the poet's notion of *form* is? A line of poetry that *really frees* itself into space can be magnificent. But the merely *formless*? A recitation of a line that may as well be the opening of a story or an essay only makes me wish the writer had surrendered the line break and finished the thought.

It's not the fragment of thought that makes a poem, in other words, but the belief in unknowableness. Cast a thought adrift on the surface of what you see.

One of my favorite exercises, which I adapted from a curious reading habit described by Olga Broumas, involves asking students to write about an intense experience with an individual. They must write this paragraph in prose. Once a page of prose has been written another page is laid over the top of the prose cutting it in half vertically. The student then transcribes what remains. The sentences thus broken create stunning effect, both sonically and in content.

A random scrap of my own journal is thus rendered:

I've gotten to
rope and I have
rare form

to reign it in
last day of
be nothing

(Even by chance operation, even cut to pieces, I'm still the same melodramatic drama club kid I've always been!)

In another exercise that came into my head after reading the strange novels of Fanny Howe, collected in *Radical Love*, is to try to combine observance with environment: the students divide a page in four sections. In section one, they write a little bit about their current state of mind, how they are feeling. In section two, they write about the weather outside and about the landscape, either traveling to school or out the window. In section three, they try to write a few sentences about a narrative moment that is affecting their emotional view from section one. And in section four, they write down anything they have overheard, scraps of conversation in the coffee shop, a headline from a newspaper, a sign they saw, something that might have been playing on the television in the background. The assignment is to then create a piece of prose or verse utilizing language from each of the four squares.

To me, most obsessively in my own work, the form of the couplet scratches my itch. Usually the first line introduces a mood or a moment and the second line answers it back, riffs on it or erases it some way. I think there ought to be a psychic connection in any formal choice. The sonnet *does* something; you have to find what possibilities it gives you. Otherwise there is nothing fundamentally interesting writing in any particular form, received or invented.

(In order not to be attached to a particular phrase or way of something students can read their poems out loud to a peer.) Once recitation is complete, the peer tries to reconstruct the poem as close as possible as she remembers it. The writer is then able to see what pieces of language seem to stick or resonate, what pieces of language or images forget themselves. An alternative version has the peer reading the piece to the writer and the writer trying to reconstruct her own piece.

If you've written four or five drafts of something, go back to the earliest drafts, find some language you revised away, and work it back in.

My writing life was changed utterly when I heard Kathleen Fraser explaining her belief in typographical errors. In her case it was typing the word "boundayr" when she meant *boundary*. Ever since I have respected utterly the possibilities of typographical errors and word muta-

metimes an error is an errancy. Once a student wrote to me in an
ntire my life" when she meant *My entire life*. My job description
l I correct the phrase but what a crime against language it was.

re my life I
wanted to speak
myself   smoke

Finally, I think one should know that you never know anything. A poem
is whatever it wants to be and nobody knows how language really works. I
think it is healthy when you fight with your teachers and even better if you
really dislike what some poets do. But what is it you are reacting against
so strongly? What is it you believe about poetry? Being a heretic as much
as possible means reading what you yourself think is heresy.

To me language can begin again in all the terrifying ways with a line of
poem or within the shape of it entire.

When I thought I understood what I thought about writing I read seven
books: *At Passages* by Michael Palmer; *Swarm* by Jorie Graham; *Unlock*
by Bei Dao; *Selected Poems* by Fanny Howe; *Home. Deep. Blue.* by Jean
Valentine; *Sappho's Gymnasium* by Olga Broumas and T. Begley; and
Arcady by Donald Revell.

It all changes so quickly. What do I know about writing or about poetry?
Nothing really. Really nothing.

{ **New Approaches
to Poetry Courses
and Methodology**

Why I Hate MFA Programs, or an Argument to Prove That the Abolishing of the MFA Program in American Universities May, as Things Now Stand, Be Attended with Very Few Inconveniences

LISA JARNOT

for Evan Kennedy

I received an MFA (Brown University, 1994) and have been a visiting writer / adjunct professor in various MFA Programs since 1998. In 2008 I resigned from a teaching post in Brooklyn College's MFA Program where I had been employed for four years. This resignation came as part of a decision to stop contributing to a system that seems to do more harm than good. Here are some of my thoughts on this matter:

MFA programs increasingly tend to emphasize "professional development" which leads to a "career over craft" attitude. Students become much more interested in attending the annual AWP conference than in visiting Charles Olson's Gloucester or Emily Dickinson's Amherst.

MFA programs highlight the idea that poetry is a commodity that will allow the poet an academic position, high-visibility magazine publications, a book contract, and the skills to negotiate through a social world of academic conferences and publishing house circles. These are all antithetical to the craft of poetry.

MFA programs in their emphasis on career discourage young poets from acting in a socially responsible manner. Poetry becomes a track toward financial security and fame (if such a thing exists in the world of poetry). Poets groom themselves, their poems, and their public statements away from controversy and toward bland neo-liberal, middle-class values that will lead to acceptance among AWP and MLA colleagues.

MFA programs cause economic harm. Many programs are prohibitively expensive, putting young people into debt in exchange for a degree that will give little in return (except the chance to teach entry-level English classes for low wages).

MFA programs encourage and require "workshopping." Workshops in their very structure encourage mediocre poets to compliment or criticize each other without an attention to the vital traditions of poetry that surround them. Workshops also tend to run on the useless discourse of "I really like your poem."

MFA programs are a breeding ground for a cult of personality. Students flock to high-priced MFAs where they may be able to study with the high-profile poet of the season whose work they may or may not be familiar with. The emphasis is not on what the teacher knows but on how well-known the teacher is, regardless of his or her talent or teaching skills.

In a perfect world, were MFA programs to exist, here is a potential curriculum:

	FALL	SPRING	SUMMER
Year One	MWF 9–12 Basic Elements of English Grammar	MWF 9–12 Basic Elements of Prosody	M–F 10–4 Bunting's Books: Homer, Ferdosi, Manuchehri, Dante, Hafez, Malherbe, Aneurin, Heledd, Wyatt, Spenser, Sidney, Wordsworth
	TTH 10–6 Historical Overview of Western and Eastern Poetry	TTH 10–6 Historical Overview of Western and Eastern Poetry II	
Year Two	MWF 9–5 Western Language (Siesta and Lunch 12–3)	MWF 9–5 Eastern Language (Siesta and Lunch 12–3)	Travel abroad
	TTH 12–5 Modern Masters	TTH 12–5 Objectivists	
Year Three			
	MW 9–12 American Poetry 1950–1970	MW 9–12 American Poetry 1970–Present	Community service

M–F 3–6	M–F 3–6
Vocational Training	Vocational Training
(non-poetry field)	(non-poetry field)
TTH	TTH
Workshop	Workshop
9–12	9–12

The 95¢ Skool
JULIANA SPAHR and
JOSHUA CLOVER

Twelve people sitting around a table talking about poems is not going to ruin poetry.

This isn't an endorsement of the writing workshop as it is currently taught; but in imagining how it might be done better, it seems important to understand exactly what the flattening or engaging possibilities of the thing might be. So it bears repeating, as we struggle to vomit up the Kool-Aid of heroic individualism: of itself, a dozen people puzzling over a poem at a shared table is not a problem. And it even has the possibility of possibility.

The problems though are obvious and have been inventoried again and again by those other than us. They include boredom, the pedantry of professionalization, the policing of group norms, a pedagogy of proofreading and minor revision, an unacknowledged aesthetic elitism and narrowmindedness, anxiety about outcomes other than the outcome of the poem. You will note that these are different names for one linked problematic, and that the all-too-familiar complaints that litter this debate (competition, traditionalism, obeisance to the professor, regression to the aesthetic mean, etc.) are also aspects of that problematic.

We have attempted to imagine another school. We have attempted to imagine this while walking to meet friends for drinks in a bar. Attempted again in an empty classroom right after teaching our pay-to-play workshops, the week's poems still in our hands; in the middle of the night, resting our heads on the soft pillows that we keep on our beds, and again, at our desks in the midafternoon, staring out the window at the rain that always falls from the poetry magazine skies. In our trances, the best option we have come up with is a Poetry Skool that costs no more than 95¢.

By which we mean, no one should go into debt to study poetry. This is not proposed as panacea but possibility: a possible unwinding of the dynamic pushing poems and students and professors to succeed according to the contemporary whims of the art economy. Our reverie: to allow poems their own logics of production.

Which doesn't mean we're against the more successful capitalists paying the less successful capitalists to allow the sitting-around-a-table.

But we do mean that any Poetry Skool committed to more than niche marketing of the well-made object with its minor telltale difference (a.k.a. its logo) must begin by refusing the pay-to-play of the current tuition system, refusing the credit-baiting of the federal government student loan program, refusing a star system of highly paid professors. Those who want cachet and connections and career, those who conceive of Skool as an investment, will go elsewhere.

This is not because poetry is pure and should float above the economic systems that currently wreck the lives of so many. It is because poetry needs all the brains it can get. Our double faith is simple: one, that decreasing both barriers to entry and compulsions toward reward will get a dozen people around a table who are more committed to the particulars of that collective work. And two, that this dynamic of poetry for its own sake will not be insular and aestheticized—will be as a result not less but *more* open to the visible and invisible social contexts of poetry, not having had to harden itself to endure the marketplace.

Individual skools might do this in various ways. The models are out there, Mondragon, LETS (Local Exchange Trading System). If you are talking about two weeks, two facilitators, two guests, twenty other participants, one seasonal administrator—the model that currently floats through minds—it can follow any number of informal methods: passing the hat, everyone contributing 10 percent gross of two weeks' income, barter and exchange. The details bear discussion but at this scale present in no way an insoluble problem.

Once everyone has ponied up according to their means, what do they, and we, do at that table?

Say poetry is understood as a specific mode of engaging the same set of problems that everything else means to engage. And the desire of poetry is not to represent the world but to change it and be changed by it; to be adequate to its time, of its time, part of the constellation. Say poetry is understood as being a way of grasping things that otherwise would escape, or grasping things in a way that understands them otherwise: a kind of counter-cognition.

If this is true, and we hope it is, this sets some terms for the workshop's discussions, procedures, assignments, and / or lectures. Our first thought experiment is to have facilitators invite guests to discuss what they know, not necessarily poetry in the specific. That is, each week or fortnight has a context or two. The project of the workshop becomes neither poetry nor context but the potential relation of the two. This is the work of the work. We take this to be fundamental to workshop: no separation of poetry as an independent or personal activity. And we recognize the need for variable ways of recognizing and realizing this.

This fundamental hope must shoulder aside lesser tasks of the very kind for which workshops currently pride themselves. For example: no reading for revision! This is not to argue for the superficies of *first thought best thought* (which cannot compete in the war of slogans with *measure twice cut once*). Rather it is a guiding logic: craft is not what's at stake. So, no endless condensing. No polishing bannisters. No lapidary work at all. We are not sure what the goal is, desperately and hopefully not sure, but we are certain that it is not the incontestable object with the slack removed and the jointures hidden.

So we add, no tolerance for the distinction between thoughts and feelings! This is merely the division of labor in the academic factory, with the inevitable consequence of separation, alienation, reification. Poetry should be at least as thoughtful as scholarship; they should be warp and weft. Neither the beautiful nor the true, insofar as each idea suggests the object which succeeds by its own measure, an object able to escape its process. We elect Heraclitus over Parmenides, political economy over money, sewing over sewn. We take all of this to be not utopian but the beginning of realism.

{
The Anxious C
Translation ar
Disabled Peda
JOYELLE McSW
JOHANNES GÖl

1. We have made the point that the translated text—the "disabled text"—causes a great deal of anxiety in people (readers, writers, reviewers, publishers, teachers, thesis committees, students, etc.), and that those anxieties are really the manifestation of anxieties about texts in general: that we cannot master them, that we cannot objectively evaluate them. We have made the point that this anxiety should not be covered up or whited-out. We are for an anxious text, an anxious classroom.

2. The Creative Writing Classroom may be seen to be the source of much anxiety as well. Some people claim that art cannot be taught, that the Creative Writing Classroom is a way of administering and controlling the spontaneous expressions of people. Others have expressed the anxiety that art cannot be taught because the students are unable to learn the nuances of advanced reading and writing. Others argue that the Creative Writing Classroom is a crypto-religious refuge, a contemplative space providing the student a safe zone from the onslaught of mass culture.

3. Correlated to anxiety about the Creative Writing Classroom is anxiety about the Creative Writing Student: Teachers and would-be pedagogues want to save the students, but the students are generally found lacking. Since the institution of Literature / Poetry is so highly intertwined with the Creative Writing Classroom, these poets are anxious that they produce the right kind of students (pro- or anti-language poetry, pro- or anti-confessional poetry, pro- or anti-Surrealism, in any case with the proper etiquette and restraint), the right kind of Next Generation of American Poetry.

4. We welcome the Anxiety of the Creative Writing Class.

5. We don't want to provide a sanctuary. We don't want to provide an enclosed, well-wrought classroom that will produce well-wrought urns, but an anxious, wrinkled space where students can interact with other students and writers, readers, and artists, nonwriters, nonreaders, nonartists, inside and outside of that classroom. We want to urge

students not to overcome but to explore their anxieties about living, about writing. Not to inhibit but to inhabit.

6. Aside from anxiety over the Student, there is the anxiety of the Teacher qua Teacher. The fear that, at heart, Creative Writing cannot be "taught," and that, at all costs, something must be "taught." The fear that Creative Writing can't be graded, and that, at all costs, something must be graded. Revisions must be required. Work must be shown. Work must be work. Workshops must be forums of correction, and the students must practice correcting each other. A discipline is being communicated. Results must be replicated. Each student must collect his or her work in a portfolio complete with a reflective essay demonstrating that something Has Been Learned.

7. While many of these prerogatives are requirements of an academic administration itself anxious about creative writing, it's also true that these concerns reflect anxieties at the heart of the teaching writer him or herself. Why am I the teacher? What am I teaching? Am I merely replicating the way in which I was taught? Is that a problem, or is that the point? Why is creative writing pedagogy based around critiques rather than creation? Why is creative writing pedagogy based around critiques rather than reading? Why must the workshop student sit in silence? To find out what it's like to be read-when-dead? The ultimate fantasy! What would happen if the student spoke? What would happen if the student spoke in tongues? What would happen if there was no critique? Would the classroom literally fall apart? What would happen to the discipline?

8. These are the right questions and should be in the mind of the creative writing teacher contemplating the Creative Writing Classroom. This is the anxiety that should not be extinguished. Instead, the classroom *should* fall apart. The walls should fall open. Boxcars, boxcars, boxcars, whatever they were. The students should work together. They should work in whatever media or genre or pet language or permutation represents an electrification for them. A digitization. Articulate the questions and keep them open on pain of expiration. Approach the expiration date. Sail past the expiration date. Sell it anyway, cut-rate. Increase the price and everyone will want it. Rotten goods! Today's assignment: a patter. A bill of goods. A colonial gazetteer. What's arriving at the harbor (Guillén). A dirty anthem, a samizdat hymnbook (Dickinson), a black market slang (everyone in the world). A new code for ships at sea. What one microchip said to the other (Tomorrow

I'll be smaller). Try on the roles of sideshow barker, treasonous orator, persuader, dissuader, sociopathic CEO, devil's advocate, shaman, showman, snakeoil salesman, juke joint singer, murderer, superloser, hypocrite reader, double, friend. I'm talking to you, teachers. But you can try it on your students, too.

9. Just as in Poetry in General, the Translated Text provides a nexus for a lot of the anxieties in the Creative Writing Classroom. Va fan pratar vi om? The Translated Text asks us to read a text in a literature we have not "mastered." In the process it shows that we are not "masters" of Our Own Literature. It shows that we don't have Our Own Literature. It shows that our language is bursting with various languages that have been kept out of literature. It shows that there is no central language, no true language, no "natural" poetry. We become traffickers of the unnatural, artificers and transvestites. Poetry is what is lost in translation; therefore we must constantly translate like mad. Translation is the Underworld. Eurydice is Poetry. Orpheus is the most boring part of that story, until he gets ripped to pieces. Hades gets the girl. Hades, the Translator and Hades, Translation.

10. Some think it was the electroshock but we think it was the translation cure Artaud never came back from. He wrote from there the rest of his life.

11. If there is no central aesthetic, true language, no one lineage, no right way, then what are we teaching the students? We must abolish the Teacher as Authority, a figure meant to block the anxiety of the classroom. Poetry is not a set of rules and requirements to be imparted to students, a downloadable instruction sheet, a read-only pdf. But we must also not fall back on the Classroom as Students are Always Right. That leads to nothing. Surprise, we're not nihilists. The teacher must challenge the students, must create obstacles and imbalances. The teacher should assign a virtually intolerable amount of reading, viewing, listening. The Student should have to take action. The Classroom should still be a site for learning and in order for learning to take place, the students' assumptions must be questioned. Their anxieties must be laid bare—including their anxiety of not having a master, and not working toward mastery. What then are we working toward? How did I get out on this tightrope? This is not my beautiful wife! Privately, densely, defensively, generatively: new triaged strategies, strange new dances, new lisps become the lingo. Poetry-in-the-classroom, a dynamic of interaction—a translation.

Thinking, Practice
STEPHANIE YOUNG

SOME THINKING

Five hundred to one thousand words, more or less, to say something about teaching poetry, feels like an appropriate restriction—not unlike the restriction of semester and quarter units, class meeting times, the space of a classroom, institutions. Which is to say something about the context I'm speaking from: I teach one undergraduate poetry workshop a semester ("beginning" and "advanced," in rotation) at an institution where I also work full-time as an administrator for a large (one hundred student) graduate creative writing program. And so I think a lot about the workshop model across various and fairly specific contexts: the problems and possibilities of the workshop as a space for thinking in groups. What is a workshop for? And what can it do?

I've become increasingly interested in the ways a workshop may function as a provisional, immediate community, where some relationships dissolve when the container of the class dissolves, and others persist. This feels both like and unlike the poetry communities I'm a member of. I tend to work with other people, and often come into brief but intense relationships within the frame of collaboration around a performance or event. Some of those projects grow into long-term creative partnerships. But there are also several less easily categorized ways wherein almost everything I write is in some way responding or thinking through the conversations and relationships of local, national, online, and international poetry communities as I experience them.

I don't have room here to sufficiently problematize some of the terms I'm using, "community" in particular, which in the Bay Area, a location central to my thinking and experience, is decidedly plural, overlapping, contestatory. And while there exist all kinds of bridges and pipes and paths between poetry classrooms and poetry communities (a permeability that comes with its own set of problems and possibilities), finally the space of the classroom isn't equivalent to that of the writing community, the latter of which so often plays out at public and private readings, in galleries, bars, homes. The possibilities to compare and contrast here are many: the poetry scene with its messy, deeply engaged friendships, and sex (I'm thinking of a lyric from Penelope Houston: "where everyone in the room must be once or future lovers"); the shared, usually volunteer labor that produces everything from chapbooks to reading series; but also the poetry scene's confusing, uninvestigated social relations and power differentials, administered by a multitude of institutions yet often claiming noninstitutional status. In contrast, the classroom comes equipped with an entire exoskeleton of visible hierarchies (teacher / student, beginning / advanced, etc.) and calcified taxonomies, policing and further producing everything from genre to market to canon.

Still, the writing workshop can do some things a writing community can't, namely, it can require things of its members: that they show up regularly, read, write, and commit to speaking together about one another's writing for a predetermined set of time. Sometimes these requirements, a certain model for community, do actually generate networks of response and engagement in the class. Sometimes they don't. Classes don't always *work*.

Other things the workshop can do: actively think about things like genre and markets, make some arguments around these things visible, maybe even denaturalize the trajectory of undergraduate creative writing major to MFA to contest submissions. Thus, part of what I try to do in the workshop is make many kinds of contemporary writing visible, especially conversations between contemporary writers (whether framed as such or those which unfold in the space of poetry) but also the means of production that generate and make that work available, the gift economies and often relational milieu which contemporary work emerges out of, and into.

I also try to construct a set of conditions that foster thinking through a field of questions or concerns together as a class. In constructing a class (the texts we'll read together, the order in which we'll read them, and some usually formal prompts that might be paired with reading), I try to maintain tension between a field of inquiry constrained enough to focus the group's conversation, and wide enough that individuals can continue whatever it is they came into class working on. (I should say that I'm talking here about the advanced workshop I teach, which I have so far taken apart and reconstructed every time I teach it.)

I put a lot of work into constructing the container, and in the best cases it's something I hand off to the group at the beginning of the semester. And then I'm a member of the group and we mess around with this container together, and in this way I learn a lot about the structure I've made, the questions or concerns I was trying to surface.

SOME PRACTICE

Last summer Amber di Pietra, a Bay Area poet and Kelsey St. Press editor / member, posted a proposal / project on the Kelsey St. Blog: "Send Us Your Vertical Answers."

The premise: "In the years since *Vertical Interrogation for Strangers* was published, Bhanu Kapil has received dozens of letters and emails from readers who have taken the questions that foreground the book's structure and answered them in their own way . . . Kelsey Street Press invites you to send us your answers to the Vertical questions."[1]

Amber's post sent me back to the book. I wanted to respond to the call but wasn't sure how or when I'd have time. At the same time I was trying to figure out the structure for a workshop in the fall. In past workshops, I'd paired two texts and asked writers to respond in some way to the combined pressures of the combinations (i.e., Gaston Bachelard and Mei-mei Berssenbrugge, Brenda Coultas and Mark Nowak, David Antin and Tracie Morris), and it struck me that it might be interesting to shift modes and answer the twelve questions from the *Vertical Interrogation for Strangers* in workshop. I was also thinking through some problems of earlier classes where I'd assigned more outside reading than people were willing to read for a workshop, which negatively impacted our conversations and limited the emergence of a field of concern or inquiry.

In constructing the class, I paired each question with a single reading. From the syllabus:

> Our basic procedure will be to read and discuss, in conjunction with each question, a poem or other piece of writing that in some way addresses, upends, interrogates, or comes alongside the question . . .

> At the next class session, you will each bring in a poem that in some way answers, rejects, upends, interrogates or otherwise addresses the question, and / or the reading we've discussed, if the reading takes you in a useful direction.

The questions and paired readings are as follows:

Who are you and whom do you love?
No reading; for the first poem, please answer from whatever place your poetry is currently engaged.

What do you remember about the earth?
Reading: *Gentle Now, Don't Add to Heartache*, Juliana Spahr

How will you begin?
Reading: "VIA (48 Dante Variations)," Dante and Caroline Bergvall

Describe a morning you woke without fear.
Reading: "G-9," Tim Dlugos

Tell me what you know about dismemberment.
Reading: "The Cherry Pickers," Yedda Morrison

Where did you come from / how did you arrive?
Reading: selections from *Dictée*, Theresa Hak Kyung Cha

Who was responsible for the suffering of your mother?
Reading: poems from *She Tries Her Tongue, Her Silence Softly Breaks*, M. Nourbese Philip

What is the shape of your body?
Reading: poems from *The Cow*, Ariana Reines

How will you live now?
Reading: "To be in a time of war," Etel Adnan

What are the consequences of silence?
Reading: "Lecture on Nothing," John Cage

How will you / have you prepare(d) for your death?
Reading: "punk half panther," Juan Felipe Herrera

And what would you say if you could?
No reading. The final project, a chapbook, will serve as your answer to the last question.

Writing now, I'm thinking about everything that shows up in the negative space of this syllabus, particularly how the inclusion of certain readings was thanks to various conversations and encounters: Dana Ward pointed me towards Tim Dlugos's devastating long poem "G-9" in the on-line journal *EOAGH*, Tyrone Williams played some sound recordings of M. Nourbese Philip at a talk he gave in the Bay Area, and then the work of Ariana Reines was being feverishly discussed at various blogs when I was putting this syllabus together. I could go on.

What emerged over the fall semester were a number of things I hadn't seen, particularly the way that many of these poems work with framing devices and upset various reader expectations, how many of these poems ask questions about language acquisition and use, all the complicated ways speech and writing intersect with history, economics, location, migration, war. Some of those concerns are embedded in the questions themselves (and certainly in Bhanu's book, which we read and looked at about half-way through the semester), and I'm unclear now which preceded which. Something else that emerged over the semester was the way that several readings and questions could easily have been switched; some readings could have been paired with four or five of the questions. I'm curious how another person might have constructed a syllabus from the same questions—what would happen if the questions were reordered, paired with different readings, or no outside reading at all? What if the questions were answered more than once—twice, three times? What if each student in a twelve-person workshop answered only one of the questions, for the entire semester? What about teaching twelve workshops in a row, each centered around one of the questions? What else?

I'm still thinking about and am not sure how successful this construction was. So many questions / readings made for a breakneck speed, with little space for meaningful revision, rewriting, or staying with a particular question longer than another. I'm also thinking about how difficult some of those questions are to answer, finally. In terms of community building, something about the difficulty of the questions seemed most operative—being together in the questions, the surprise of how one writer might find a way to reject the terms another writer in the class might build an entire project from.

NOTE
1. www.kelseyst.com/news/2008/07/25/your_vertical_answers

Varieties of Poetic Experience

JED RASULA

The title of my course plays on William James's *The Varieties of Religious Experience*. By emphasizing poetic experience, and above all its varieties, I try to take some of the stress off the poem, that wretchedly segregated *thing*. Experience gives us a continuum between words on page or screen and words on lips or even deep in the cranium, resounding—and potentially beyond words altogether.

Even before reading any poetry, then, I begin with an episode from the history of surrealism: the quest for the "surrealist object." Buñuel's film *Andalusian Dog*, the photographs of Raoul Ubac and others, the speculations of Salvador Dalí on "psychoatmospheric-anamorphic" objects, and Hans Bellmer's doll. All this to get to the point of putting the reader under scrutiny by the thing.

From the surrealist object, then, passing through Michael Palmer's *The Promises of Glass* like the liquid mirror-door in Cocteau's *Orphée*, we venture into the domain theorized as "deep image" in the 1960s (Jerome Rothenberg, Robert Kelly, Robert Bly, James Wright), at once a belated American encounter with surrealism and a moment (via David Antin: "Black Plague") anticipating language poetry. The collective oneiric idiom emblematic of that moment (e.g., Merwin, Kinnell, Strand) has been most persistent and influential in the work of Swedish poet Tomas Tranströmer, which raises the issue of translation. (This segment of the course fueled the chapter "Medusa's Gaze" in my latest book.)[1]

Poetry in translation is poetry in flux, on the move, submitted to the agitation of *metaphora* (the Greek word for moving, as in Allied Van Lines). A convenient Heraclitean river is classical Chinese lyric, so I put into play poems we can read in as many as a dozen renderings. We also look at some of Rilke's Sonnets to Orpheus in a half-dozen English versions, as well as the conveniently short war poems by Giuseppe Ungaretti in the four or five available translations. (A recent and bewildering cascade of Cavafy translations offers a plausible alternative.)

Translation is not only about words, but can extend to intermedia and *mediation* any way it comes. "The Waste Land" is a convenient case, not only because it slips collage into the practical poetic arsenal, but because of its treatment as online hypertext (to say nothing of its reception history). Eliot's theme conveniently opens out on what I call *poiesis in extremis* in the work of Paul Celan and Emily Dickinson, in which Pound's principle, dichten = condensare, really has teeth.

At a certain limit, where condensation is most fully in play, we come up against the old problem of abstraction, particularly when put in the form of a question: abstract or concrete? The "obscure" or "unreadable" poem nonetheless persists as material lump, blob, excrement. I like to turn at this point to film as offering another variety of poetic experience, particularly the early pioneering work in abstract (or concrete) cinema: Viking Eggeling's *Diagonal Symphony*; shorts by Hans Richter, Oskar Fischinger, Mary Ellen Bute; and Ralph Steiner's bewitching *H²O*. Maya Deren's *Meshes of the Afternoon* and Chris Marker's *La Jetée* add a narrative twist.

Having sundered poetic experience from text-dependency, a good place to return to the word is via the refractory personalities set in motion by Fernando Pessoa's heteronyms. Heteronymy splits the reader up too, asking what you want and how you want it. It's not a big step from there to the vast domain of procedural writing. Ronald Johnson's *RADI OS* serves it up straight, and a smattering of approaches documented in Steve McCaffery's work fleshes it out. Ron Silliman's primer in poetics, "Sunset Debris," is a *locus classicus* of pertinent questions.

From there we move on to documentation, extraction, assemblage: Muriel Rukeyser's "Book of the Dead," Charles Reznikoff's *Testimony*, and Marianne Moore's laminations rubbing up against Joseph Cornell's boxes.

The end approaching, runway visible, a theme announces the rudiments: sight and sound. El Lissitzky's typographic design for Mayakovsky's book *For the Voice* opens the eye, along with some Italian futurist *parole in libertà*. Kurt Schwitters and Raoul Hausmann sound it out. The whole itinerary settles on the wobbling pivot of song in the end: in this case, Éluard and Plath in the spellbinding settings of Finnish composer Kaija Saariaho ("The Grammar of Dreams"). We're done, though it feels like just begun, as it should be. Poetry is adamant: *experience* the varieties.

As words etched on the glass of an exit, I offer these by Hans Bellmer:

The essential point taught us by the monstrous dictionary of analogies and antagonisms that is the dictionary of the image, is that every detail, every leg, is only perceived and stored in the memory (and thus made available for use), in short, is only *real* if desire does not insist on regarding it as just a leg. An object that is simply identical to itself lacks any reality.[2]

NOTES

1. Jed Rasula. *Modernism and Poetic Inspiration: The Shadow Mouth.* New York: Palgrave, 2009.

2. Hans Bellmer. *The Doll.* Trans. Malcolm Green. London: Atlas, 2005. 127.

{ **Poundian Poetic
Ambition on the
Semester System**
JENNIFER MOXLEY

Early in the course of my own (self) education, Michael Palmer's talk "Counter-Poetics and Current Practice" was a touchstone.[1] I first read it in the early nineties, when I was just beginning to take the question of poetics seriously. I had a poorly photocopied version from *Pavement*, the Iowa magazine where the talk first appeared. I was hungry for stories of how one "found" the map of the poetry that mattered, and Palmer's was a compelling one. He movingly describes his longing for an alternative to the "Frost-Eliot-Auden" core of official modernism offered to him at Harvard. There is the *de rigueur* narrative of discovering Pound, and before you know it the young Palmer is heading off to the Vancouver Poetry Conference to hear Olson, Creeley, Duncan, Ginsberg, and Levertov. There he discovers that these writers are all friends, and that an exciting living poetry community coming out of the *other* modernism (Williams, Zukofsky, Stein, etc.) is alive and well, even though places like Harvard don't want you to know about it. Duncan, a generation older than Palmer, tells a similar story. As an editor of his college literary magazine, the young Duncan finds he likes all of the submissions his coeditors reject. One day, he returns a rejected poem personally, so he can meet the writer. It turns out to be a young woman. She suggests he read Ezra Pound. He buys *A Draft of XXX Cantos* and reads the opening line "And then went down to the ship . . ." A world opens up.[2]

Two, maybe even three generations of poets in the counter-poetic tradition (to stick with Palmer's term) went to school at the "Ezuversity." This is no longer the case. Pound has not fared well in the post-sixties era. Though both Palmer and Duncan are openly critical of Pound's "views," they acknowledge the centrality of his influence. In addition, in both Palmer and Duncan's origin stories the university is a conservative force, which they have the seemingly innate sense to resist. Neither story mentions wanting to go further in school, or to get published in major magazines, or to win prizes, or to cultivate a readership. The concern is to find a poetry that matters and enter into a dialogue with it. What sets a poetry that matters apart from everyday verse? It engages your *whole being* and *changes every-thing*.

Though I could have used other examples of what I will call the "con-version narrative" of counter-poetics, I picked Palmer and Duncan be-cause they stood in my development where Pound stood in theirs. They are central figures in my own conversion narrative with a difference: I was introduced to their work at the university, and I had no innate sense of re-sistance to what was offered there. By the time I was in school "literature" with a capital "L" (Frost-Eliot-Auden) was no longer on offer. That is no doubt because of where I went to school (UCSD). Perhaps if I had gone to Harvard I would have faced that dinosaur. Instead of teaching me radi-cal modernism and the New American Poetry as alternatives to conser-vative modernism and its blue-blood Ivy League inheritors, my teachers offered it as an alternative to the harmless workshop poetry of the Iowa-school—personal, narrative, self-righteously liberal—that glutted the na-tional magazines at the time. I realize now that, by doing this, they also unintentionally undermined all of the poetry written out of the identity movements of the 1970s, much of it by women. And yet, reading figures like Duncan and Palmer somehow felt grander, as though I had stumbled upon a continuation of the greatness of poets like Rimbaud and Baude-laire. It was partly because these poets partook in the romantic drama of the "rejected artist"—which I now know to be mostly false and much overplayed in the counter-poetic tradition—and partly because they pro-posed poetry as an all-encompassing vocation. I fell in love with the idea that poetry could be an act of resistance, and that it was an intellectual and artistic vocation that could engage your *whole being* and *change every-thing*. It is a tall order, and, according to many of my students, unrealis-tic and elitist.

I recently realized this after assigning Palmer's "Counter-Poetics and Current Practice" to a graduate class. The essay had clarified so much for me when a young writer, I thought it might do the same for them. Palmer's collected essays *Active Boundaries*, recently published by New Directions, included it, so I was able to make a clean photocopy from a freshly typeset version. Rereading the talk in preparation for class, I was flabbergasted at just how much of Palmer's thought I had incorporated into my own. I was also surprised at how the world it described was no longer mysteri-ous and seemingly inaccessible to me, but was *my* world. Palmer's essay had helped me to see its borders and values. It had also provided a read-ing list. Though the "conversion narrative" and the us / them division he writes about had already started to become untenable by the time I encountered it, it was meaningful to me. It helped me begin to draw a map through the contemporary and justified my desire to define my ambition on a Poundian scale. But what I found in teaching the essay is that everything seems to have switched around. In the first place, it makes no sense to reject Auden or Eliot when you've never read either (strangely most *have* read Frost). Secondly, the notion of one cohesive alternative tradition neatly packaged in one convenient anthology is no longer viable. And finally, there is no getting around the fact that Poundian-scale ambition is unrealistic on the semester system.

When I teach as though poetry should engage your *whole being* and *change everything* my students look miserable. So I try and meet them where they are. This is a good method for me because, in addition to my own ambivalence toward my tradition (and my odd place in it), I have a constitutional aversion to proselytizing. I have zero interest in convincing them to write the way I do or to like the writers I value. If they want to know my personal map, there is a healthy print record to consult. On occasion I have a student who asks, in which case I am perfectly happy to share my list of favorites. But I have found that most of my students don't read my work, and some are even surprised to learn that I have published books. To them authors are "out there." I used to be bothered by this, but over the years I have found that it is actually a very common phenomenon. And perhaps it is for the better. On the semester system I am not a chosen mentor sought out by a young acolyte, I am the teacher of the workshop they signed up for, nothing more or less.

In that capacity I have found that students often claim to love poets they know almost nothing about. In fact they may have only read a poem or two in an anthology. The following is one method I have used—with fairly good success—to address this situation. On the first day of a workshop I will ask the students to list the names of up to three poets they have read a little, and liked, but don't yet know much about. I then suggest they pick one name from the list and spend the first half of the semester reading everything they can find by and about that poet (they must also memorize a poem by their chosen poet). A sample of the questions I suggest they seek to answer is: When and how did your poet live? How did your poet start writing and get published? Did certain writers influence your poet? Is he or she associated with a particular movement or magazine? Where is your poet placed in the history of poetry? What kind of poetry does your poet write? Did you find any discrepancy between the ideas you had about this writer before this assignment and after? Did you learn anything about your own poetry through the extensive reading of another poet? Mid-semester I meet with students individually for an hour-long conference during which they teach me all they know about their chosen poet and perform a memorized recitation.

I find this to be a successful strategy for introducing, in a very small way, both poetic tradition and Poundian ambition. Really learning about one poet inevitably leads students to learn about that poet's education and influences. It also impresses upon them the work involved in being serious about poetry. Sadly, students all too often also learn that most poets lead miserable lives. They learn that being a poet can be, to use Duncan's phrase, an "appalling destiny." And yet, by the end of this project, they have placed at least one pin in the complex map of poetry from which they may begin to determine their own location. The desire *to know* originates in the student, and they determine the *depth* of that knowledge. Of course some students treat the mandate like an onerous assignment, and do little more than hurriedly Google their poet the night before our one-on-one conference. This doesn't bother me. I just figure they aren't ready to take their own desire for knowledge seriously (and as a result may never be poets). But mostly I have found that students get very caught up in their poet of choice, reading deeply and discovering much. It is also notable that students don't always end this assignment liking the poet they chose. In such cases I assure them that their time was not wasted, for they are now in the stronger position of rejecting a certain poetic path from a position of knowledge. Whichever way students end up feeling, both they and their poetry are inevitably changed by the process. I should also mention that because my students rarely pick poets that I would, they become my teachers, and I the beneficiary of their newly found knowledge.

In the latter half of the semester, when I know my students a little better, I pick a second poet for each of them to read. I attempt aesthetic matchmaking. This is the part of the assignment that I enjoy the most, though it is a prickly business. My choices for them are inevitably over read, and can sometimes prove disastrous. Because I am in essence saying: "I have thought carefully about your particular case and have determined that this is the poet for you," students take it very seriously. I make my matches based on a complex of questions that include: What sort of poems is the student writing? Which poet did he or she choose to learn about during the first half of the semester? What ideas about poetry does the student seem to be carrying around? In which psychological or intellectual direction is he or she veering? Though I am aware of the prohibition of bringing psychology into the workshop (and I try not to meddle), I can't help but learn something about the dimensions of my students' emotional and psychological lives when reading their poems. So this information comes into play in my matchmaking as well. Using a pastiche of past experience, I will give two examples of a successful match, and one that failed.

First example: A student picks Allen Ginsberg as his first poet. He is attracted to the idea of Beat counterculture and poets who challenge power. He feels his generation has a responsibility to scream its head off. He is frustrated because poetry is not politically efficacious. He has only a dim sense of history—literary or otherwise—and is sure no one has ever felt as he does. His own poems are a tad self-indulgent and filled with unfocused anger, and yet he refuses to own up to the subjective voice in them. He has a tendency to use end-rhyme (though poorly), and write poems of about two pages in length. Taking in all this information, I give him Mayakovsky for his second poet. The match takes. The student identifies with Mayakovsky's tone, feels envious of his historical moment, and broadens his idea about what it means to be "countercultural."

Second example: A student chooses Theodore Roethke as her first poet. She writes short poems with a rolling rhythm and delicate imagery from nature to describe psychological states. She is a lesbian, but is not interested in writing explicitly about her sexuality. She is drawn toward mysticism, but is not quite sure how these feelings relate to poetry. She has a keen historical consciousness. Taking in all this information, I assign H. D. as her second poet. The match takes. H. D.'s book-length poems set an example for the student of how she might go beyond the short lyric. She also sees in this work another way to use nature imagery (connected to, but distinct from Roethke). The student becomes fascinated by H. D.'s relationship to Freud, as well as her rethinking of classical figures.

My third example is of a match that did *not* take. A student picks Sara Teasdale as her first poet. She is drawn to Teasdale's handling of love. She herself writes of nothing but, often using figures from Greek mythology. She likes traditional form, but writes in poorly executed ballad meter with half-realized end-rhymes. Taking all this in, I choose Duncan for her second poet. To my mind Duncan's measures echo traditional meter, he writes beautifully about love, and he is constantly evoking mythology. But the match fails miserably. The student rejects the complex literacy Duncan's work proposes, as well as his use of organic form. She is not comfortable outside the borders of heterosexual romance. She can see no continuity between her work, that of Teasdale, and Duncan's. Did I fail to read this student correctly? Or was she too closed, refusing to try and see what Duncan might offer her? Sometimes I try to match students with poets on a continuum with what they are doing, other times with poets who might serve to expand their poetic outlook. In retrospect, I realize that the Duncan choice was an instance of the latter, which is always the riskier course.

I realize that because this method requires that the teacher commit to a substantial amount of one-on-one time with each student, it will only work in a small class. In order to handle my workload, I balance that commitment by spending less time writing out extensive comments on student poems. In my experience students rarely revise poems based on teacher comments, and are more likely to take in what is being said on a more general level in workshop. Another benefit to this method is that it frees students from having to spend a lot of money on books. This is critical when you teach at a place like the University of Maine, where many of the students are cash strapped. Though my hope is that they can do all their research at the library, I have discovered that even well-known poets may not be well represented in the stacks. I have tried to address this problem by letting my students know that if they *can't* find work by the poet I give them, I can loan them copies from my personal library (I am always picking up extra copies of poets I like at used bookstores for this purpose as well).

Though hardly on the scale of Pound's mandates (Learn Provençal! Start a press!), my small directive to "go forth and learn more" fits into the confines of the semester system. What it keeps of the spirit of Poundian ambition is the quest and the independence of mind, with a slight touch of mentoring. Through my matchmaking the only "conversion narrative" I hope to author is that of a young poet's move to a more animated engagement with those who have said before, "I want to be a poet."

NOTES

1. Michael Palmer. *Active Boundaries*. New York: New Directions, 2008. 237–266.

2. Robert Duncan. *Lecture on Ezra Pound*. n.d. MP3. PennSound. http://writing.upenn.edu/pennsound/x/Duncan.php.

{

The Contract Model
of Workshop

ARIELLE GREENBERG

When I began to teach graduate poetry workshops, I thought back to my own experiences as an MFA student and about how much more constructive I found feedback that addressed the larger aesthetic concerns and issues raised by my poems than line edits. My own revision process is such that, while line edits can certainly be helpful, I'm more likely to produce a totally new poem based on a workshop discussion that addresses global concerns than substantially improve the one I brought to class through small changes. Also, I'd been frustrated in graduate school at what I saw as the lack of attention to the human context behind the poems—not in a group therapy sense, but in the sense that it seemed ridiculous not to be able to bring all of the class's outside knowledge of a particular poet (e.g., their other poems, their stated goals, their life story, their literary influences, etc.) to bear on a poem. So I came up with a way to bring this kind of discussion to the table, literally, of an advanced workshop class.

I call it "the contract model" of workshop. The name comes from something one of my graduate professors, the poet and essayist Mary Karr, once said, which is that every poem forges a sort of three-way contract with the writer, the reader, and the poem, and that the process of writing the poem is that of making good on this contract, while the process of reading a poem is that of meeting the poem on its own "contractual" terms. As a workshop technique, the contract model asks students to step back and think about this metaphoric contract and then talk about the poem only in terms of how successfully it fulfills it, or where it breaks it. This avoids talking about a poem in ways that are irrelevant to the poem's own world or aspirations, and focuses instead on understanding the aims of the poem / poet in the context of an aesthetic. The results of this technique have students thinking seriously about why they write the way they do, something which, to my mind, workshops are often not as rigorous about as they ought to be.

We start by trying to identify what we see in the poem before us—a simple step, but one too frequently skipped in advanced workshops, I think, where students tend to rush headlong into minutiae. Typical questions I ask in a contract model workshop include the following: What *kind* of poem is this—is it an epistle, a portrait, a sonnet, a collage, a sound experiment? What seems to be influencing the poem, either through poetic forbearance or other, nonliterary sources? What does this poem require its reader to know? How does the poem's beginning, or title, or even end, teach us how to read it? What expectations are set up by seeing how this poem looks on the page? What is the engine (emotional, philosophical, narrative, language-based, or otherwise) that seems to be driving this poem? How does the poem move from moment to moment? If the poem has multiple voices or characters in it, to whom does the poem seem to belong? I know none of these are groundbreaking questions or ideas, but positioning the conversation this way seems to genuinely change the workshop experience.

I typically hand out a sheet of such questions and talk through the model at the beginning of the semester, and do a lot of moderating to help folks get used to the discourse. I guide students to talk about problems with a poem as places where the contract has fallen through or been neglected or to identify where the terms of the contract seem to shift (though we also acknowledge that such shifts and breaks can make a poem exciting or better, too). Depending on how quickly a class latches on, they may need very little prompting, or I may continue to pose a "contract"-style question at the beginning of each poem's workshop time. Students who try to jump in with overly prescriptive comments are asked to reframe their point, so that if someone says, "I don't like the ending; it's weak and would be stronger if the last two lines were cut," I ask them to talk about what it is about the last two lines that seems to break the contract of the poem. (As an aside, I will say that I've often found there to be one student who remains resistant to the model throughout the semester and tries to go straight for the prescriptive suggestion every time. I just keep asking them to reframe their comments to suit the model.)

This model has two big advantages, in my view. The first is that poets get to hear about how their work is coming off overall, as well as about any across-the-board problems (ethical, aesthetic, or otherwise) that may be marring the work, and that this, more than line edits, helps guide poets toward making substantial leaps in improving their work. The second is that it helps the other poets in the class, the readers, be more open-minded and nimble in their ability to read poems different than their own, and requires them to take a more complex, holistic view of the poem and poetry in general, rather than zeroing in on tiny details in a poem that has larger problems, or wonderments, than comma usages or word choices. Besides, as I tell students who are disappointed to hear that they won't be getting much line editing in my workshop, there are *plenty* of workshops that revolve around line edits, and one can always ask for that kind of feedback during office hours or from a trusted peer. Most students have reported finding the contract model refreshing and extremely useful.

I've found that while the contract model works particularly well for graduate and advanced undergraduate students, who are far enough along in their own work that their poems tend to be cleaner and their aesthetic sensibilities more defined, and who, like me, may be ready for a break from more traditional workshop modes, it can also be used for intermediate-level students as a way to foster a better conversation about what poems can do and be. I don't, however, recommend its use with beginning students, whose poems often need help simply forging a contract to begin with, or understanding that such a contract exists at all.

Obstructions

JOEL BROUWER

A few years ago, my colleague Joyelle McSweeney recommended I see *The Five Obstructions*, a 2003 film by Lars von Trier, the rigorous and depressive co-founder of the Dogme 95 movement and director of such masterpieces (or angsty swamps of affectation, depending on your point of view) as *Breaking the Waves* and *Dancer in the Dark*. In *The Five Obstructions*, von Trier challenges his friend and mentor Jørgen Leth to revisit *The Perfect Human*, a twelve-minute film Leth directed in 1967, and to remake the film five times under certain constraints—"obstructions"—to be provided by von Trier.

For the first assignment, von Trier directs Leth to use no shot more than twelve frames long, build no set, travel to an unfamiliar place, and answer all the questions posed in the original film's dialogue. Such constraints, we assume, are intended to back Leth into corners he'll only be able to escape by inventing fresh structures. As a poetry teacher, I've often used similar tactics with students, urging terse writers to ramble, gluttons for metaphor to diet, prose poets to lineate, and so on. Not, I tell them, because what you're doing is bad or wrong, but because when you work with unfamiliar tools you both discover new muscles and come to understand the familiar ones more fully.

Leth makes the first film and shows it to von Trier. Over caviar and vodka, von Trier admits that it meets the given requirements, but he doesn't hide his frustration. Leth is by temperament, reputation, and his own assertion an aesthete, an observer, a formalist for whom style is all. In his film, he has treated the obstructions as formal problems, and devised formal solutions for them. Von Trier had been after something more fundamental. His intention, he says, is to "banalize" Leth. "The highly affected distance you maintain from the things you observe: That's what I want to get rid of."

This is where the film really begins to grip me, because suddenly it's not just an exercise. It's *personal*. Over the course of von Trier's subsequent obstructions and Leth's filmed responses, von Trier tries to claw his way into Leth's deepest assumptions not only as an artist but as a human being, and Leth works to maintain his air of elegant nonchalance. The uncomfortable candor of their conversations reminds me of my acting days in college, where a director once told me and a fellow actor that our performances as onstage lovers would never succeed unless we became off-stage lovers. Let me be clear: the director wasn't simply suggesting my colleague and I have sex (though she was suggesting that too). She wanted us to *love each other*. I'm pretty sure she also had a friend of hers assault me at a party because I was "lousy at rage" and needed practice.

I've always taught poetry writing in much the way von Trier believes Leth makes films: impersonally, and with formal considerations paramount. In class I talk a lot about tools and effects and almost never about content or ethics. I know I'm not alone in this. The notion of the poem as a machine to be built, inspected, tuned, and repaired goes mostly unquestioned in the academic discipline known as "creative writing," and we pointedly call our courses "workshops," not "sessions," "encounters," or "treatments." *The Five Obstructions* led me to wonder about these assumptions and habits and to consider alternatives. I wouldn't recommend my students shack up or punch each other, but perhaps instead of just tinkering with the sound, shape, and rhetoric of their poems I could do something a bit more . . . visceral? Basic? Intense? I wasn't even sure how to explain to myself what I was after.

For the next graduate poetry workshop I taught, I chose a reading list of texts which seemed to me the product of their authors' self-imposed obstructions, including A. R. Ammons's *Sphere*, Ted Berrigan's *The Sonnets*, Thylias Moss's *Last Chance for the Tarzan Holler*, Barbara Jane Reyes's *Poeta en San Francisco*, and others. I showed my students *The Five Obstructions* and discussed it with them. I asked them to bring to our first class meeting three poems they felt best represented the writing they were doing at the moment. From each student's submission, I chose one poem which the student would be required to rewrite five times over the course of the semester, under the burden of obstructions I would supply. After each revision was completed, we would meet to discuss it, and at the end of the term, each student would submit a portfolio including the original poem, the five obstructed rewrites of it, and a note describing his or her experience of the process and what he or she had learned from it, if anything. The most important element of my vision for the class I kept to myself. I would try to engage students in ways that I hadn't before, to have conversations with them which would sound like von Trier's with Leth. I would try to make it personal.

That was the plan. The results were mixed. The failures are easily generalized. Either the student balked when asked an essentially disconcerting question, or—more often—I lacked the acumen to discover and pose one. Each success was unique and usually serendipitous. I would point out a habit or assumption in the poem and ask after its basis, the student would be generous and vulnerable enough to admit he or she had no good answer to my question, and together we would use the obstruction assignments to disclose and often, to some degree, transform the way the student thought about making poems.

I'm purposely avoiding specific case-study examples of the journeys I took with these students, in part because they were private affairs between each student and myself, and in part because I want to obstruct you a bit here too, reader. What assumptions are you making about the interactions I had with these students? Are you eager to challenge me to explain the dichotomy between *formal* and *personal* creative writing pedagogy that I seem to have proposed? Do you cringe when I use terms like *case-study*, *journey*, and *private affair* to describe relationships with students?

When a student writes a story about feeling suicidal, send him to the counseling center, because if you fail to get him help you could be held responsible, and if you try to help him yourself despite your lack of official qualifications, you could be held responsible. When a student invites you out for dinner to talk about her poems, politely refuse, lest it appear that your relationship with her is inappropriately intimate. When a student sets forth a poem in class that contains political ideas you abhor, focus the class discussion on the poem's sonic patterns or line breaks and keep your opinions to yourself. The short history of "creative writing" is chock-full of obvious and indisputable reasons why teachers should follow (often unwritten) rules like these. But it's also obvious and indisputable that teachers and students alike are diminished and degraded when they must stop to check their personalities at the workshop door.

I haven't taught the obstructions course a second time. Not because it was taxing and sometimes uncomfortable, but because I've come to realize that it wasn't taxing or uncomfortable *enough*. Leth was von Trier's professor at the Danish Film Institute, not the other way around. Next time it will have to be the students who give me the obstructions.

{ # Creative Writing
Midterms

ELIZABETH ROBINSON

When I am teaching a poetry workshop, one of my principal aims is to get students to recognize that reading and writing are continuous activities, and that they will be stronger and more interesting as poets if they can read well and creatively. I am also, always, eager to create a sense of community in the classroom. The demons of vulnerability and, sometimes, narcissism can make the class an alienating space and that is not useful for anyone's writing. I also prefer to approach the workshop as just that: a place to work, a laboratory, and not a place to show work that is already polished and complete. To that end, I like the students to write a lot of poems and share them on a regular basis. My hope is that the requirement to write a great deal compels students to write even when the result is a bit sloppy or outside their comfort zone, so that little apertures open in their writing that lead to new possibilities. Also, in this scenario everyone is equally exposed and, eventually, comfortable together as they practice reading and sharing work.

In an ideal world, the workshop is small and intimate enough that every student gets to share their work every week or, at least, every other week. We obviously don't live in an ideal world. To remediate this situation, I've tried various strategies with varying success. In a small class, I just ask students to copy a writing sample for me and for everyone in the class *every* week. In the usual gigantic university "workshop," I split the class in two and have the groups alternate: each group copies a writing sample for the entire class *every other* week, and thus each student has a growing file of poems from every other student. (There are typically complaints that this leads to paper waste, and I acknowledge this problem. Perhaps using an online resource like Blackboard would work well here.) The students are then supposed to read all the submissions from their classmates closely week by week.

There is evidence that students do not read each other's work closely each week. So I've worked up some tactics to facilitate this. For example,

I hardly ever have a student workshop a single poem: I prefer to ask her / him to select two or three poems we can look at. This helps to make clear, fairly quickly, what that writer's proclivities, gifts, and weaknesses are. It's pretty fun too. A student who hammers down her prosody with prepositions will get called on it. I once had a student who put a maternal figure in every single poem; he didn't realize this until a classmate lined up a row of pages submitted to the class over the course of a month, the mother underlined in each poem.

The ability to read patterns into each other's poems has not resulted in untoward criticism. I've found that it enhances the workshop in two ways: first, the writer tends to be gratified that there are in fact discernible patterns to their work, that they actually have a style and skills to match; second, the readers become more lively because they gain more authority as readers and they can share their insights with the author.

One semester, I thought it would be fun to deepen the reading / writing exercise and try to bring more personal attention to each student from a peer. So I decided to assign a two-part midterm.

PART ONE

Each student is given the name of another student in the class. That student then has to go back to his or her class archives and read, with scrupulous attention, the work of the student they have been assigned. Example: Matt reads all of Kelsey's work and takes notes on everything he notices. He notices what she is good at and likes to do (she has a terrific eye for imagery), and he notices what she does too often, less often, or less effectively (she has a tendency to lard her work with adjectives). He looks for things that she altogether avoids (Kelsey has never made a rhyme in her life). On the basis of his observations, Matt will now make a midterm writing assignment for Kelsey. I always warn students, lest they make nasty, unwritable assignments, that they will also be receiving an assignment for themselves. The assignment is supposed to take into account the author's particular gifts and make room for them. At the same time, the assignment is supposed to offer a challenge that will invite / beguile / force the poet to try something new.

PART TWO

After a week, the students all come to class grinning and exchange assignments. They have written these with relish. The assignments are supposed to come, by the way, with some explanation and rationale that is based on concrete observations of student poems. The recipients are given a week to make a poem that follows the mandates of the assignment.

About halfway through the week, I usually begin receiving distraught emails from students who are certain that they cannot complete the horrible, impossible, insufferably stupid assignment they have been given. (I just want to warn other teachers who may undertake this.) I try to be somewhat unsympathetic; I will remind people that there are ways to cheat ("You are supposed to write a poem in iambic pentameter? How about writing every other line in iambic pentameter? The first and last lines? The title?") It's true that sometimes people write brutally difficult assignments. More often, people write surprisingly astute assignments that legitimately honor and challenge the author.

PART THREE

By the time students turn in their finished midterms, the sense of community in the classroom is measurably enhanced. They sometimes compare notes with each other as they study their assignee's work in order to create the writing prompt. They often call each other, later, to clarify or argue the terms of the assignment. For me, this is frequently the most entertaining and enjoyable class of the semester. It's revelatory to see what happens in the work of a poet who prefers to write short three-word lines when he is made to write lines of ten words or more. A student who writes poems that are wonders of Oulipo technicality is told to write a poem that focuses on content, specifically an emotion: love. Students have been required to do any number of things: frame the poem carefully with a title, make use of the entire page, add or subtract syllables, add or remove pronouns, adjectives, verbs, rhyme, alliteration, etc., or interpolate narrative. Certain words or images may be put off limits or prescribed for inclusion. The results are often hilarious or gorgeous or both. They almost always bring a startling new dimension to the author's work.

I will admit that the authors are often those least able to see the sharpness and value of their new writing. The upside to this is that the class then becomes a cheering section for people who are trying out things that seem foreign and uncomfortable. A most powerful result of this exercise is that in completing the assignment, the author will commonly come to a point at which he or she is overtaken by exasperation and simply loses control. That's when the really terrific, unanticipated writing erupts. It's like id on paper.

I can't promise that poets reliably come away from this process willing to employ their newfound skills. Still, my experience has definitely been that they become both more avid and forgiving as readers, and more supple and curious as writers. In our culture, there aren't many venues where vulnerability and loss of control (within certain parameters!) are welcome. If this is made possible in the workshop, then the vital trust that makes for good art can start creeping into our conversation about, and practice of, writing.

Exploring Bias in the Writing Workshop

PRAGEETA SHARMA

Entering the classroom, I am a short—4′10″—South Asian woman. I am a child of immigrants, a first-generation American. But I am also a poet, a calling that has given me a voice and the opportunity for a kind of freedom that would not otherwise be possible. Sometimes, as a teacher, I am forced to conflate both identities, and thus I am and have always been set on empowering and supporting both the study of poetry and the power for students of poetry to transform their own histories, identities, and difficulties into forms of resilience.

Because of who I am and what I look like, I have often found myself, over the years, attuned to difference, bias, and racism in the classroom. In response, I have thought a lot about ways to not perpetuate cultural hierarchies in the workshop setting in order to have some practical pedagogical models to connect to the act of creative writing—a writing practice inherently caught up in voice, perspective, stamina, perseverance, and, sometimes, talent.

Race and culture come up directly in the workshop setting, but often in odd and seemingly innocuous ways. I had a student once comment: "We're all white here." No, indeed we were not. I'm not and there was also another student who appeared white, but who was not. Another student said to me affectionately: "I don't think about your ethnicity." I thought to myself: "I know." I know this student didn't intend this comment as a kind of erasure; neither student understood that their whiteness historically positions them to tell others what they are and are not. I can also recall a class where the students earnestly said, "Isn't it better that we couldn't identify the poet as black?" The notion that it was a good thing that this poet was being read outside of his (in this case it was a he) race, that he was therefore not limited to being defined in terms of race and consequently more accessible, does not sit well with me. What is at the heart of this tendency to universalize, and from poets who should know better than to universalize? Could this desire to move *beyond* race be an unconscious effort to keep it at a distance? And could this mark a disengagement because there is no personal connection?

In fact, I often find such a lack of personal connection to race and culture arising indirectly in a workshop setting, in the guise of disinterest, as in: "This poem was not interesting to me," or "I can't relate to it so I'm not sure how to respond." When the poem being read and workshopped is intact and does not exhibit unintentional grammatical errors of any sort, but is, to some degree, exhibiting the imaginative and experiential space of the student, it is often, at this point, a place to reckon with the content. The poem enacts or is trying to do something unknown; it does not constitute a readily shared personal or literary experience. When students reading the poem cannot put certain cultural symbols in place as signposts, the poem becomes unrecognizable in their peer's sense of the world. Responses are guarded, with students unwilling to explore what, at the first or a second reading, makes the poem *unknown*, or disengaging. While this also happens when teaching established poets in a classroom setting, then the students do have an innate sense of the *authority* of the poet being taught. This is not necessarily the case for peer critique and response in the workshop environment.

Expectation (as in tokenism or reductive representations of identity) also inhibits engagement. In the words of poet Charles Bernstein:

> My problem is not the introduction of radical alternatives to parochial and racist reading habits engendered by the educational system and the media, but that alternatives are often ameliorative rather than politically or aesthetically exploratory . . . I see too great a continuum from "diversity" back to New Critical and liberal-democratic concepts of common readership that often—certainly not always—have the effect of transforming unresolved ideological divisions and antagonisms into packaged tours of the local color of gender, race, sexuality, ethnicity, region, nation, class, even historical period: where each group or community or period is expected to come up with—or have appointed for them—representative figures we all can know about.[1]

Expectations and a willingness to engage in someone else's identity are important for an individual to deepen her understanding of her own identity. More so than ever, poets are consciously and unconsciously connecting their aesthetics to ideas about their environment, socialization, and identity. Discussions about aesthetic range and inclusion are particularly valuable when students are able to discern the motivations behind what their *tastes* look like in relation to their schooling or aesthetic bents. It's important to think about classroom pedagogy in relation to aesthetics so that false hierarchies are not made to disengage students from their ideas about aesthetics or poetry. Furthermore, I think it's important to establish a set of outcomes for students as well—that they don't seek to dismiss each other out of a kind of intolerance of cultural diversity in the name of aesthetic diversity. I've seen workshops divide around aesthetic biases, and I've also seen them come together because of them.

When bias in the classroom arises, I try to use the workshop as a place to explore ways that we as poets and thinkers are inclusive (as a way of forming our styles, nurturing our voices) and also exclusionary (as a way of protecting ourselves from what is unknown and potentially threatening). Because what I've found is that students need to say something about where they come from and who they are; it is damaging to their psyche when they cannot. Oftentimes if the individuals in the group do not find a way to represent their cultural places—to talk about how culture informs their aesthetic—and if a majority of the group is privileged in some way, those outside the majority may not be granted a certain essential credence to the direction of their art.

Which leads me to strategies in the workshop. Some years after I began teaching, I encountered Peggy McIntosh's *White Privilege: Unpacking the Invisible Knapsack*.[2] In it she creates a list of biases based on the daily effects of white privilege in order to discuss how "invisible" forms of dominance play out in academic environments. Here are some examples from the McIntosh article:

1. I can if I wish arrange to be in the company of people of my race most of the time.
2. I can avoid spending time with people whom I was trained to mistrust and who have learned to mistrust my kind or me.
3. If I should need to move, I can be pretty sure of renting or purchasing housing in an area which I can afford and in which I would want to live.
4. I can be pretty sure that my neighbors in such a location will be neutral or pleasant to me.
5. I can go shopping alone most of the time, pretty well assured that I will not be followed or harassed.

6. I can turn on the television or open to the front page of the paper and see people of my race widely represented.
7. When I am told about our national heritage or about "civilization," I am shown that people of my color made it what it is.

We, like McIntosh, are able to create a list of the kinds of biases we bring to the classroom based on our perceived notions of race, class, and gender in relation to aesthetic. With Bernstein in mind to ask: what are students seeing as "packaged tours"?

I have seen McIntosh's list work successfully in a variety of academic settings and in community meetings to improve understanding of our cultural differences. I am just starting to explore this approach in the classroom, by brainstorming a list of daily effects for my students in order that we can explore what in their content and their form relates back to particular socialization(s), biases, or even a (positive or negative) resistance to their own socialization. I am also finding that it can serve to combat what we have all observed as an all-too-common phenomenon of dismissal and disinterest among students in a workshop setting. And in doing so, it can create a forum in the workshop to discuss aesthetic and intention in relation to our own experience of race, class, and gender in order to immerse ourselves within it, enjoy it, or redefine it, if we so wish.

NOTES

1. Charles Bernstein. *A Poetics*. Cambridge: Harvard University Press, 1992.

2. Peggy McIntosh. "White Privilege and Male Privilege: A Personal Account of Coming to see Correspondences through Work in Women's Studies." *Race, Class and Gender: An Anthology*. Ed. Margaret Andersen and Patricia Collins. Florence, KY: Wadsworth Publishing, 1988. 94–105.

Teaching Writing Through the Sonnet Tradition

KARLA KELSEY

The sheer variety of form and mode renders poetry a Sisyphean genre to teach, for the poetry instructor necessarily confronts the opposite attractions towards mastery and multiplicity. How do we encourage a student to entrench deeply enough in a mode of writing to cross the threshold towards mastery while, at the same time, remaining open to other aesthetic modes? The ever-occurring challenge, then, becomes the development of techniques for compelling students to stand back from what they think they know about poetry, and to look at the genre with new vision.

At first glance the sonnet may seem to be the *least* apt vehicle for such a practice of opening. However, tracing the form through literary history invites students to see the sonnet as a form born in translation and powered by innovation. The first English-language sonnets, authored by Wyatt and Surrey in the sixteenth century, were translations of Petrarch's Italian. Our English-language tradition begins there and continues with vigor, as is evident in contemporary work such as Karen Volkman's *Nomina* and Ed Allen's *67 Mixed Messages*—just two recent examples of book-length sonnet sequences exploring both tradition and innovation. If students can see the interlocking of tradition and innovation illustrated by the sonnet form, they can then find similar patterns in other aspects of the craft, thus thinking of tradition as dialogue and conversation rather than as mandate and dictation.

In pursuit of such dialogue, I developed a workshop course called "The Sonnet as a Form of Tradition and Innovation." The goals of this course were to engage students in formal aspects of their craft and to introduce them to the idea that any aspect of poetic tradition(s) includes both adhering to, and breaking with, established precedents. The course involved reading widely in the English-language sonnet: we studied *The Penguin Book of the Sonnet*, which covers five hundred years of the tradition. In addition, we read individual volumes of sonnets that push at the limits of the form such as Ted Berrigan's *Sonnets*, Jen Bervin's *Nets*, and Aaron Shurin's *Involuntary Lyrics*.

For the first seven weeks of the course students wrote poems fulfilling all aspects of the form. In the second seven weeks students could take liberties with the form, provided that they were able to speak to the ways in which their variations were in conversation with the fundaments of the structure. The course was geared toward undergraduates, so we spent a fair amount of time learning the rules. A similar class geared toward graduate students would have extended reading lists and focus on the ways in which a literary tradition can be plumbed in our contemporary context.

Once students begin to engage with sonnet texts, models and exercises abound. Along with writing sonnets that adhere to the various architectures of rhyme, some of my favorite prompts include the following:

Homophonic translation: translating a sonnet from another language using sound rather than sense á la Louis Zukofsky's translation of Catullus's Latin into English

Writing around rhyme: using the end-rhymes of an already made sonnet, writing into, out of, and around these words á la Aaron Shurin and Steve McCaffery's "Dark Ladies"

Reconsidering the turn: turn as rhetorical moment, as change in speaker, as change in perceptual attention, as change in visual register

Patterning translation: translate the pattern of rhyme into another aspect of craft (*a* lines might become exterior description, *b* lines philosophical, *c* lines description of interior landscape, etc.)

The prose poem sonnet: see the wonders of Emmanuel Hocquard's *A Test of Solitude* translated from the French by Rosmarie Waldrop

As you might expect, students' initial reaction to a workshop course based around the sonnet ranged from apprehension to hostility ("she wants us to spend the semester writing *what*?"), but students quickly warmed to the form and to the constraints of our investigation. Focusing on this specific structure not only allowed students to develop their poetic vocabularies, but also brought discussions of form's relation to content to the fore of workshop sessions. While not all students became passionate about the sonnet by the end of the course, our fourteen weeks with the form taught us all to revise our relationships to poetic structures, innovations, and traditions.

WORKS CITED

Allen, Ed. *67 Mixed Messages*. Boise: Ahsahta Press, 2006.

Berrigan, Ted. *Sonnets*. New York: Penguin, 2003.

Bervin, Jen. *Nets*. New York: Ugly Duckling Presse, 2003.

Hocquard, Emmanuel. *A Test of Solitude*. Trans. Rosmarie Waldrop. Providence: Burning Deck, 1999.

Levin, Phillis. *The Penguin Book of the Sonnet*. New York: Penguin, 2001.

McCaffery, Steve. "Dark Ladies." *Fence* 7, no. 2. 61–63.

Shurin, Aaron. *Involuntary Lyrics*. Richmond: Omnidawn, 2005.

Volkman, Karen. *Nomina*. Rochester: BOA, 2008.

Zukofsky, Louis. *Complete Short Poetry*. Baltimore: Johns Hopkins University Press, 1997.

Readings

JENA OSMAN

For me, teaching poetry workshops is about reading. First, there are the *outside* readings, which I try to make as various, thought-provoking, and perhaps overwhelming, as possible. I know that I can't really teach my students how to write, but I can suggest things for them to read that will broaden their sense of what's possible. When I was in college, and then later working towards my MA in Creative Writing, I took a lot of poetry workshops. Sadly, I don't remember much that was said in those sessions; however, I have distinct memories of the readings we were assigned (as well as those suggested to me by my peers) and the sensation of the aesthetic ground shifting under me. Those books clarified for me the kind of conversation I wanted to have through writing. I have a theory that people are most open to the light bulbs of accidental textual affinities when they are younger (or maybe they just have more time to actually notice them), so I try to stack my syllabi with as much electric current as possible.

Lately I've been asking my students to think a lot about visual art analogs. Last semester I taught a graduate workshop around the rubric of "poetry as conversation." I proposed that by thinking about how conversation works, the default of the poem as a structure reflecting one's own concerns and private procedures could shift to one that privileges contact with an other. I asked my students to think about obvious things like intertextuality, literary allusion, and reader response—but also about relational aesthetics, community art projects, and visual art collectives that were engaged in conversational acts. We looked at groups like Temporary Services, WochenKlausur, and Group Material[1] alongside collaborations between poets and artists, interviews between poets (available at Pennsound), and Nourbese Philip's dialogue with an eighteenth-century law document in her recent book *Zong!* I'm not sure if the visual art analogs changed the actual poetic practices of the workshop participants, but perhaps they broadened conceptions of how a poetics of relation can function inside and outside of a textual world.

This semester I'm continuing the interdisciplinary focus by teaching an undergraduate workshop around the theme of psychogeography and investigations of place. We're looking at Land Arts and experimental geography as well as Ecopoetics and work (both visual and textual) that takes its materials from various archives. Although these assigned readings are thematic, they are meant to suggest possibilities in form and structure rather than content. For example, students are asked to think about Land Arts and the various ways that artists (ranging from Andy Goldworthy to Gordon Matta-Clark) work with the environment as they find it. They are then asked to make a series of poems constructed from language found in their own environment.

Just as important as the outside readings in my workshops are the *inside* readings of the texts the students are producing themselves. Rather than asking students to position themselves as observers or evaluators gently poking and prodding the pieces written by their peers, I set up systems for a more active engagement. Here, I end up using strategies that I first learned while teaching composition as a graduate student, primarily those used by Peter Elbow and Pat Belanoff in *A Community of Writers* and those used by Bard College's Language and Thinking program.[2] The response methods range from simple underlining and freewriting around lines that stand out for the reader, to performing reading experiments suggested by the text itself.

A hypothetical example of such an experiment might go as follows: A poet writes a long piece that is shaped in dense text blocks with each line requiring a paratactic leap in order to get to the next. A reader is overwhelmed by the poem, but senses a particular thematic hidden in the textual weave and decides to uncover it by erasing everything outside of that thematic. At the beginning of the poem, the reader notes that the lines that remain have to do with natural landscape, and those that are erased belong to the category of the "man-made." But as the experiment progresses, the reader realizes that separating the natural from the "man-made" becomes more and more difficult. As a result, her interpretation of the poem begins to shift—the text blocks aren't a random assortment of disjunctive materials; rather they chart the course of a recognizable language being replaced by a hybrid of natural and material discourses. Such an experiment allows the reader to learn the work from the inside-out rather than the outside-in, and in turn allows the poet to see how a reader's mind actually engages with the materials set in play.

NOTES

1. The Chicago-based artists' collective Temporary Services (http://www.temporaryservices.org/) focuses on particular engagements with place, people, and public phenomena. The Austrian group WochenKlausur (http://www.wochenklausur.at/) has staged conversations between groups who would normally never talk to each other. From 1987 to 1989, the New York collective Group Material held a series of "town meetings" on the topic of democracy.

2. Joan Retallack has been the director of Bard's Language and Thinking program for a number of years. The book she coedited with Juliana Spahr, *Poetry and Pedagogy*, is another very useful teaching resource. An essay called "Deformance and Interpretation," by Jerome McGann and Lisa Samuels, outlines a system of response related to the experiment method I've described above.

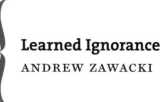

Learned Ignorance

ANDREW ZAWACKI

I'm constantly aware of the specter of knowledge haunting the class-room. In certain fields—hard sciences—this would not be a problem but a horizon, for what is a university if not where knowledge is pursued, passed on, intermittently achieved. Anyone who teaches literature, certainly, is sensitive to the misconception that reading poetry—to say nothing of writing—is somehow easier, less rigorous or serious than other disciplines, where knowledge is the aim. Hence the insistence, from most of us, on no writing without substantial reading—the topics course, say, that gathers materials into an historical, generic, or sociopolitical frame. There's my tendency to spend two hours discussing the "outside" reading—as though anything could be outside the poem, as though the poem were not itself the outside—leaving only an hour to workshop student pages. Hence the demand that participants in my writing seminars offer a major essay or a pair of slightly shorter critical papers during semester, privileging meat-and-potatoes analysis over appreciation. Hence the requirement, too, to preface a final portfolio of "creative" exercises with an aesthetic statement, including an exploration of what one was trying and a candid evaluation of which projects worked out and, more crucially, which failed and why. I frequently default, for better or worse, to organizing my workshops along lines associated with "straight lit" courses, in no small part out of a desire to prove that writing is hard work and, because it's impossible without critical engagement, harder than criticism. I don't govern the weekly exer-cises, except insofar as they're meant to participate in the textual rhizome of the class at large.

A case in point, from the annals of my short four years of teaching: a workshop—one for undergraduates, another for graduate students—in "Ruin / Erosion / Erasure," in which we engaged various strategies for treating source material, especially methods that courted the deleterious. Among those formal gambits, despite satisfactory terms for their respec-tive methods: erasure or carving (Rauschenberg's effaced—or defaced— de Kooning drawing, Brian Dettmer's book autopsies, The Reverse Graffiti

Project), homophonic and oblique translation (the Zukofskys' Catullus, James Wagner's *Trilce*, Susan Landers's *Covers*, Chris Edwards's "A Fluke"), writing through or "thorow" (Thoreau by Cage and by Susan Howe), writing over or crossing out (*A Humument*, Bernadette Mayer's "X ON PAGE 50 at half-inch intervals," a dozen shorts by Brakhage); re / arrangement (Harry Mathews's "Preverbs," Brian Eno's "Three Variations on the Canon in D Major by Johann Pachelbel," Aram Saroyan's *Gertrude Stein*), in / filtration (Kristin Prevallet's "Lyric Infiltration"), curating decay (Peter Delpeut's found films, John Wolseley's in- and exhumed notebook entries, Bill Morrison and Michael Gordon's *Decasia*), fabricating arcana and the archive (Ossian, Armand Schwerner's *The Tablets*, Nabokov's *Pale Fire*), and other forays into Oulipean, constraint driven, or "uncreative" writing. These varieties of appropriation, of creation via damage and forgery, involve at minimum a source each and are therefore already inter-textual, implying an initial act of interpretation; the class collective labor adds yet further layers onto the critical palimpsest. Looking back (or, as it were, below), these texts can't be legitimately approached without understanding at least the rudiments of precursors' ideas and ideals. Take Michelangelo's imperative to cut away "everything that is not David," for instance, just as negative theology removed the predicates for God, to approximate Him; or think satanically instead: Blake's infernal method, the counterfeiters in circle eight of the *Inferno*. In the eighteenth century there's the Atheneum group's obsession with manufacturing ruins and, in the nineteenth, Mallarmé's association of the muse with destruction, in turn not far from the Hegelian premium on sublating opposition as the means to securing self-consciousness. More recently, we can summon psychoanalytical accounts of repression, Simone Weil's "decreation," the sampling within modern music, and the poststructuralist death of the author. Indeed, each of these "contexts" could equally serve as a central concern, not least because the syllabus's so-called "primary sources" are already adamantly secondary.

In addition to evacuating students from the subjectivities they spend so much energy mutually reinforcing, such a course demands a confrontation with intellectual history. Even those who sign on only half-heartedly supersede the journal-entry, response-paper, I-spy dynamics on which their high school creative writing modules (and some of their college writing seminars) had been premised. Maybe because my training has been more academic than fine arts oriented, I'm attracted to devising classes of this kind, because they coax students to recalibrate their judgmental scales on the fly, position student exercises within an exciting, fluctuating, alternative tradition, and engender conversations less driven by what might make a better poem than by how a given text or site is working, whether it fulfills the scope it sketches for itself, and how worthwhile that objective is. How do Jen Bervin's erasures of Shakespeare, which allow the original sonnets in grayscale behind the overt, remaindered poem, differ from Stephen Ratcliffe's, which present few, usually minor words on an otherwise wholly blank space? What are the effects of whiting out words, à la Mary Ruefle's *A Little White Shadow*, as opposed to ridding them cleanly, digitally? How is erasure distinct from the strike-throughs Anne Carson employs in "Appendix in Ordinary Time," which leave the wording intact but signal its cancellation, as if a jury were told to disregard the opinion it has nonetheless just heard. What's at stake in knowing that Clark Coolidge devised his *Bond Sonnets* according to an operation, but that he doesn't remember how aleatory, how rule-bound it was? Conversely, is Jackson MacLow's "Ridiculous in Piccadilly" somehow superfluous because he gives away the procedure up front? Can we tackle the Coolidge without starting at Ian Fleming's *Thunderball* (will the movie do?), or enjoy the MacLow—or the Carson—without knowing Woolf? Is an uncreated text stronger, or weaker, if to *get it* we need to know the antecedent it's ripping off or riffing on? Are *stronger* and *weaker* appropriate terms, and is there any *thing* to *get*? Does it matter that *Beryl of the Biplane* might not be an actual book although Ashbery swears it's behind "Europe"? Why do so many of these works, e.g., *X* and *M*, advertise their impetus if not their m.o.—shouldn't a poem be able to stand on its own? To what degree can a poem ever be said to stand *alone*? Does the inverted theology (no longer the correct term) of Johnson's *Radi os* possess the same visionary, or revisionary, power if we're unsure about Milton's? And how might we translate *Radi os* into another language—by translating *Paradise Lost*, before clipping the *same* words Johnson did, thereby messing with the *mise en page*; or else by translating the constellations according to their spacing on the page, presumably dismantling the semantic *meaning* in the process? Or, how would you translate Johnson from English *into English*? That will instruct you not in the unfamiliarity of a foreign language, but rather in how you are a stranger in the language you mistakenly call your own. Eventually it becomes apparent that all writing, even the supposedly discrete, transparent type, is what *eroded* work can make visible: a rumor momentarily stilled by decision, a principle of economy in a system of proliferating signs, what Adorno might call an it-could-have-been-otherwise.

I like such courses, but not because I believe poetry is a species of knowledge. Quite to the contrary: poetry is the refusal of concept and category, of positivism. However, the workshop, like university tout court, is an artificial setting, and for quite pragmatic reasons we should take advantage of the paradigm. Unfortunately, it comes down to fitting a square peg into a round hole: the institution has protocols of structure, logic, progress, development, the teleological narrative, whereas poetry is surfeit, excess and exasperation, anarchy. They're exigencies of divergent orders. So I try to convene a relatively coherent set of problems and texts, internally diverse but nevertheless restricted, so we have a domain to focus our energies on. To spite the expectation, on the part of some students, that my course will offer determinate knowledge, I try to ensure that we retain, rather than feint toward resolving, the radical undecidabilities that all texts contain—or that, properly speaking, they cannot contain. Poems maintain themselves in their impossible tensions, contradictions, paradoxes; they are passages suggested by the very impasses and aporias they articulate or suppress (which is an important mode of articulation). With such ambiguity and ambivalence at issue, it's important that I refrain from playing the first or final arbiter: I set the parameters, pace, and tenor of the course, can usually provide background material, avenues to interpretation, point to related reading, or play devil's advocate when someone is too sure of herself, cheerleader when she's shy—but I haven't got *answers* and shouldn't be solicited for them: poetry has a rapport only with questions. It's not merely that poems should resist the intelligence almost successfully. It's about setting an example for students about my own "learned ignorance," to borrow Nicholas of Cusa's phrase. Notwithstanding experience, publications, and a piece of chalk to write with, I am no more *expert* than they: the poem eludes me, if it's working and I'm doing my work, for it's comprised of elements I do not and cannot *know*: it's an alterity that, greater than the sum of its parts (though often most fascinating on the smallest, local scale), only masquerades as familiar because it's made of words. My relation to it is asymptotic, since it's without a fixed point—though not without prompts. Our task as readers, within this experience of distance that keeps throwing us outward (the pleasure and unease that attends that), is to narrow into increasingly accurate, but never complete, characterizations.

My conception of the poem is faintly informed by vestiges, say, of *The Cloud of Unknowing*: poetry forces us, through its discipline, to break the habits we conjure and find our comfort in, to undo received patterns of understanding, to innovate or expand how we look, hear, feel, figure—as well as by postmodern thinking of interruption and event. Although my students are never illiterate and rarely disadvantaged, my aspirations as a teacher follow Rancière's *Le maître ignorant* and Freire's *The Pedagogy of the Oppressed.* These studies are committed, each in its radical manner, to ensuring that the dialectics of learning are firmly centered in the subject who undertakes—and deserves—to know. One way I've occasionally tried to put the ball in my students' court—a provocation, but also the most responsible move I can make—is by announcing that the book we'll discuss next week is not one I've read yet myself. If graduate students aren't necessarily alarmed at the revelation, undergraduates find it incredible, or shocking that someone would admit that—but I'm not *admitting* anything, if admission implies guilt. Instead, it's an invitation, excitement about embarking with them along path that this work will open—and obscure—for each, for all of us. There's an extreme to be avoided here, sure: a slip into anti-intellectualism (which would sit all too well with the lazier students, who thought they were going to write in this class, not read), or the appearance of basic unpreparedness. At its most productive, though, students come to suspect that an approach to poetry, however informed and well researched (the book ain't on the syllabus by accident), cannot be one of conquest or mastery, of foreclosure or even closure: poetry frustrates the effort to sew it into seamlessness. By and large, intro students are frightened by indecision or equivocation, and saying that a book is new to me, too—that a book can never *not* be "new"—is a palpable way of promising I won't make their minds up, as well as showing them a vulnerability that is less my insufficiency than poetry's general bequest. If this seems counterintuitive, so much the better: poetry is the "counter, original, spare, strange" par excellence, except that nothing so other can ever be called exemplary.

Continuing Poetry
HOA NGUYEN

For the last twelve years, I have led private, weekly poetry workshops. My students have included teenagers, MFA graduate students, painters, musicians, and English professors. I charge very little for the classes that I hold in my home on Sundays. You can't earn credit or a grade. I do not take attendance. You have to buy one book of poems (assigned) and bring a notebook and a pen so that you can read for an hour and then write for an hour. Classes are small and intimate. Sometimes we drink beer.

One student of mine likened the workshop to sitting meditation where you are chanting in Japanese, and you don't know why you are doing it, but when you are done you are centered and energized.

It begins with a book of contemporary poetry. I like choosing epic poems or large collections of poems so that we can get in deep with the selected poet. In 2006 we read all of Charles Olson's *The Maximus Poems*, and after that was Alice Notley's *Alma, or The Dead Women*. Other books that we have engaged include the collected poems of Lorine Niedecker, Ted Berrigan, Joanne Kyger, and Philip Whalen. Sometimes we don't make it through the whole book. Sometimes we go forward and circle back to revisit poems we read the week before and discuss how they feel different that second time.

The workshop's first hour: read poems aloud.

When I begin a new workshop (a big new book), I start by contextualizing the poet's history and literary engagement. I might mention with whom they are linked, describe their place in lineage (influence), and identify the poets with whom they were in correspondence. Other than that, there is very little discussion or explication. We read the book of poems in turn. The poems are vocalized, bouncing all around us in the room, one after the other.

Second hour: we write. We read what we just wrote in our notebooks (optional).

For the writing portion, we respond to two writing exercises of my design: these are inspired by and drawn from the text we just read. I challenge the class to adopt similar writing approaches and offer prompts, rhetorical strategies, and ways to tune one's attention to sound and the specificity of naming. Below is an example of a poet's challenge.

> Try to INCLUDE as many of the following elements as possible:
> A color
> A body of water
> Something you ate recently
> Chiasmus ("placing crosswise"—ABBA words repeated in reverse)
> Select ten verbs at random and then half rhyme them to produce ten
>   additional words for a total of twenty words at your sonic disposal.

The intention here is to apprehend different elements operating within poems, to be fed by the poems, and to produce poems. It's a way to give concentrated attention to poems and enact some by engaging the elements, newly. We read a poet's work collectively, we write, and then we read what we just wrote—if we want. Then we go home. For the last class we create mini-manuscripts by formalizing the work from our notebooks: we arrange words on a page, give it a title, and call it a poem.

In the final class, we share these groups of poems with each other. The poet is given an opportunity to read her poems aloud and ask specific questions of her audience. In turn, the readers can speak to the poet's intent and ask questions or offer readings and suggestions. Collected during weeks of our engagement, the poems are given a context as a body of work. This allows us to see our poems in conversation with themselves—and with others—with our readers, with poets living, and poets dead. It's as Joanne Kyger once wrote (in a poem): "Poetry is about continuing poetry."[1]

NOTE

1. Joanne Kyger. *ABOUT NOW: Collected Poems*. Orono, Maine: National Poetry Foundation. 1997. 631.

{ Teaching Asian
American Women's
Poetry Subjectivity and
the Politics of Language
SUEYEUN JULIETTE LEE

Poetry provides a rich location for Asian American women to voice and create a "new language" that can speak to the realities and possibilities for their lives as well as conceptualize and critique the forces that have shaped them. Poetry also serves as one means for beginning and framing inquiry from the standpoint of the marginalized. Asian American women's experiences and subject positions can highlight various aspects of patriarchy, globalization, capitalism, racism, and heteronormativity that other positions may not render as richly. By engaging a variety of stances regarding these forces, we can better understand their multiple, shifting forms and better strategize to neutralize and disperse their power.

Despite the rich opportunities for understanding and critique that poetry offers, scholar Juliana Chang has noted, "the vast majority of [. . .] critical writing within the field of Asian American literary studies analyzes works of prose fiction and nonfiction, and, to a lesser extent, drama." Chang points out two contradictory tendencies in how we read and recognize poetry. First, that "the poetic, narrowly conceived, is generally considered lyric and therefore the real, or the private, as opposed to the public or social." Alongside this "privatization" of poetry, Chang charts how poetry, and indeed most art, is simultaneously conceived as "heavily social" via its burden to represent for the collective when produced by colored bodies.

Due to these contradictory stances towards poetry, *what* gets included is also frequently limited. For example, Ben Huang, in an article describing his experience teaching Asian American poetry, chose not to include work by John Yau and Myung Mi Kim, two noted Asian American experimentalists, in favor of work by "contemporary poets representing a range of ethnicities [. . .] Their subject matter was similarly diverse: Hawaiian volcanoes, roses, breast-feeding, basketball, high school proms, Chinatown sweatshops, etc." He chose work that he thought "students would find fairly accessible," over work that he believed "the class would find too obscure." I question what gets lost in this move towards "accessibility." What happens to work that seeks to challenge the very grounds of intelligibility? Work by scholars Laura Hyun Yi Kang and Zhou Xiaojing seeks to bring into the purview of Literary Studies "experimental" and "difficult" Asian American female poets whose writing challenges disciplinary notions of legibility. I see my teaching project in accord with such efforts.

I taught several courses on Asian American women's poetry utilizing a creative writing approach under various guises at the University of Massachusetts from the fall of 2003 to the spring of 2005. UMass Amherst is a large research university that enrolls approximately twenty thousand undergraduate students. Since 1987, the number of self-identified Asian American students enrolled at UMass rose from 335 to 1,381 in 2005.[1] Most of these students are in-state, with most living in the urban centers of Boston, Lowell, and Worcester. By teaching Asian American women's poetry in a workshop setting, I hoped to introduce students to various Asian American women authors, many of whom are never taught. A class devoted solely to their work recognized their agency and authority while also acknowledging the literary merit of their writing by making it a model for production—a privilege too often associated only with white writers. Furthermore, I wanted to tackle assumptions regarding poetry as a genre by encouraging students to engage both as readers and producers. Lastly, I wanted students to develop a stronger critical awareness of their subject positions and their identities.

I juggled the various demands of the course goals and how best to fulfill them through the class's structure. I settled on a format in which there were writing workshops four times over the semester after the class had read several authors. Students also wrote self-reflection papers documenting how the readings informed their writing practices, as well as student-to-student response letters regarding their poetry. I held individual conferences twice over the course of the semester to discuss their final writing projects—a chapbook manuscript.

I erred on the side of incorporating poets that are typically considered *difficult*, such as Theresa Hak Kyung Cha, Myung Mi Kim, and Mei-mei Berssenbrugge, and contemporary—some had only one book out, and one had only a chapbook. We read poetry by Kimiko Hahn, Wang Ping, Pamela Lu, Eileen Tabios, Summi Kaipa, Hoa Nguyen, Cathy Park Hong, Prageeta Sharma, and fiction by Bharati Mukherjee, Jhumpa Lahiri, Monica Lane, and Mary Yukari Waters.

I expected the class to primarily constitute Asian Americans. In fact, recruiting Asian American students for such a course proved to be quite difficult. Though UMass Amherst hosts an Asian American Studies certificate program, it was at a fairly young stage, and only two of my students came from this program. One of the most frequently asked questions I received was if this class fulfilled any requirements. Many students, being the first in their families to attend college, felt pressure to do well and finish quickly, which meant little exploration outside their majors. I was especially invested in recruiting Asian American students because so few of them are encouraged to express themselves in writing: many of them told me they were poor writers, though the majority of them were receiving honors.

To begin discussion and to foster a sense of community in the class, I used an "I Come From" exercise, which I modeled after a poem by artist and writer Joe Brainard. I asked each student to write several statements, each beginning with the phrase "I Come From." Everyone then shared a single statement by means of introducing themselves to the class. Students then selected one statement that they wanted to include in a class poem.[2]

I come from a family of five and I was the only one lucky enough to
    be born in a refugee camp. Everyone else lived through the war.
    We struggled constantly since the day we came to America. [. . .]
    All I know are stories, stories of my parents working day and night
    in horrible factories when minimum wage was four dollars and a
    quarter.
I come from . . . a car accident and a girl in the fourth grade. An
    introduction to the frustration, confusion and inevitable isolation
    that death leaves in its footprints.
[. . .]
I remembered the first time my father hit me. My father did not hit
    me with his hands but with his wrist for he lost his hands in the
    Vietnam War.
I come from a home that had a room decorated in pastels. A room
    that smelled of milk and baby powder.
I come from
encouragement,
a place where as the shouts increase,
my heart flutters,
filling with condensed joy.

From the student writing, many of the same themes and considerations that informed the poets we would be reading were very much at work: immigration, loss, family, location, sexuality, and generational differences. This exercise also served to raise questions concerning authorship—what one chooses to write about, in what manner, and why—which structured students' readings of the poetry throughout the semester.

One Hmong American female, Tam, who rarely spoke in class handed in a long poem exploring her family's displacement via war and the consequent fracturing and confusion of identity that followed. She begins her poem with a pastoral, highly visual, nostalgic description of her homeland. She articulates this sense of peace being tied to a national identity.

THE "I" AS BEING A HMONG ASIAN AMERICAN
Laos_
Peaceful, deep soil and quietness of the mountainous highlands, we
    created our villages.
    The rich fertile soil of the Laotian hills grew our hearty stalks
    which fed us.
Farmers blade cutters whistled in the air like chirping birds on a high
    tree.
Never ending brooks glistened and silently brushed against the rocks.

                Our self sufficiency made us felt strong.
                    We were like a nation.
                    A nation of our own.
            Not civilized, yet able to survive in peace and happiness.
Where Was I?

BOOM! BOOM! BOOM!

The idyllic tranquility is suddenly ruptured by "the roaring of B-52 American airplanes" that raided the skies. The narrative and syntactical structure of her poem slowly starts to fragment:

He swam the Mekong river. Some drowned.
    She ran into the mysterious jungles of Laos at the break of sunset.
    Some shot.

            They got into a ferry and sailed to Thiland. Some made it.
                Babies cried. Some were left behind.
                    Grandmas and Grandpas died. Some were too old.

Hunger?
Families?
Home / Villages?
Life?
   American Soldiers gone_SILENCE_
[. . .]
Homeland is G.O.N.E!
Culture, life and families all D.E.S.T.R.O.Y.E.D!
Can't S.P.E.A.K., R.E.L.A.T.E., but_

Her use of periods echoes the earlier military violence in her poem, acting like visual bullet holes that puncture her words. The words are still legible and maintain some integrity—"G.O.N.E."—but now, as acronyms, they point to a distant—and now lost—greater meaning.

Tam related her work strongly to Catalina Cariaga's poem "No Stone" because "she also speaks about a person in her family's history and how her people survived." Tam was also inspired by the structure of Cariaga's poem:

Also the way she wrote her poem: they were complete sentences and non-connecting sentences, and diagonally. [. . .] This had an impact on me when I was writing my poem, I was able to stress my experiences as well as my parents and put it together to show the relationships of two different lives that had the same cultural and social struggles.

The fragmentation of voices in Cariaga's piece led Tam to consider and see a similar dynamic in effect in her own writing, leading her to a critical use of language.

I will let the students' work testify to the advantages of teaching poetry in this manner, but wanted to also acknowledge that there were pitfalls. Foremost was my concern that students might simply appropriate these Asian American women's language or experiences without any actual consideration of the forces the authors sought to respond to. I tried my best to keep discussions focused not just on the craft, but on what claims these women were making about identity, the United States, gender, power, and difference. In the end, however, I believe that teaching Asian American women's poetry in this context has great value in not only addressing and shifting student anxieties around poetry, but also encouraging generous and reflexive reading practices.

A word of special thanks to my dear mentor Prof. Miliann Kang at the

University of Massachusetts at Amherst, who allowed me to work with her students and ultimately teach this course. It was also with her encouragement that an earlier version of this paper was written and presented at the Association for Asian American Studies Conference in 2005.

NOTES

1. This study only includes students that were U.S. citizens, so the actual number of Asian American students is higher.

2. All excerpts from student work are included with permission by the authors.

WORKS CITED

Chang, Juliana. "Reading Asian American Poetry." *Melus* 21.1. 1996. 81–98.

Huang, Ben. "Teaching Texts: Teaching Asian American Poetry." *Journal of Asian American Studies* 8.1. 2005. 81–92.

Office of Institutional Research. "Race / Ethnicity of Undergraduate Students (US Citizens)." University of Massachusetts Amherst, 2005.

Seminar Craft, Career, and Dead Giant

BOYER RICKEL

I called my first graduate poetry seminar "20th-Century American Originals" (though I cheated by slipping in two foreign favorites, C. P. Cavafy and Gloria Fuertes). In chronological order from date of birth we read week to week (in addition to Cavafy and Fuertes) such poets as W. C. Williams, Marianne Moore, Delmore Schwartz, Frank O'Hara, Lucille Clifton, Susan Howe, etc. I wanted poets of consequence, and contrasts of voice and temperament; contrasts that would force us to create new vocabulary for describing and discussing each poet's work. We met once a week for two and a half hours to discuss the work of a new poet. After introductory remarks by one or two student discussion leaders, attention to issues raised in the craft papers and creative responses class members had brought to the table, somewhere in the last fifteen minutes, if we were lucky, we sometimes began to scratch through to a number of substantive observations. What I had hoped would be a series of weighty explorations, building week to week through the conflicts of aesthetic sensibilities of the seminar poets, felt more like labor in unlit mines with toy picks.

I learned from that to trust—and teach from—my own process as reader and writer. It takes me a long time to know how to talk about / describe the work of a genuinely original poet. I have to invent a new language for myself, try it out on others, see if I'm making any sense. And I love nothing more, when I discover a new poet, than reading chronologically through her books, observing the shifts, intensifications, and occasional leaps of craft and thematic development. I wanted a seminar that would make possible the process of thinking through such an unfolding over the course (to date) of a career.

For my next seminar I employed a structure I've found rewarding ever since: instead of twelve to fifteen poets, we read four in depth, each at a roughly different point in his or her career—one early-, one mid-, and one late-career poet, ending with a Dead Giant. All I retained from the first seminar was a desire to have such contrasts poet to poet we'd have to reinvent our critical terms as we entered the work of each new poet. The terms early-, mid-, late-career are a convenience, of course; they are suggestive, more about the number of books a poet has published and the trajectory of her aesthetic travel than place in a career. Poets publish books at such different rates (and some die young, some old), that the early-, late-, etc. designations I treat with great flexibility. But spending two and a half weeks on one poet's work gives us the time for larger, more meaningful observations.

I like to start with someone who has published perhaps two book-length collections (Marie Howe after *What the Living Do*, and Barbara Cully after *Desire Reclining* are two recent choices); followed by someone who might have published four or five books, possibly a selected (my last in 2006 placed Harryette Mullen in this position a few years after *Sleeping with the Dictionary*; in a seminar some years before that we read Heather McHugh after publication of *Hinge & Sign*); followed by a widely recognized older (what does that mean?) poet, such as Frank Bidart, my most recent choice, whose collected poems, *In the Western Night*, and *Star Dust* gave us a great deal to work with. Dead Giants have included George Oppen, Elizabeth Bishop, and Hart Crane.

Perhaps the most exciting element for me in these classes has been the extraordinarily intelligent, challenging, and creative assignments the students have come up for each other as they prepare, in groups of three or four, to introduce and lead classes on their poet.

I try to model class structure (two-and-a-half-hour classes require some stage managing) and assignment questions that will lead to brief craft papers and creative responses in the first few weeks before we start in with the seminar poets. Students take over at that point, writing questions, collecting the work, studying what they get from their classmates in advance of seminars so that they can plan and shape the period. I am always, always delightfully humbled by the rich and varied angles small groups have taken in their assignments for classmates—and by the papers, poems, and other creative work (responses in other media are often an option) produced by seminar members. With thanks to Mary Marbourg, Todd Balazic, Toby Goostree, and Paul Longo, who led our Crane discussions a few years ago, I offer just a few of the terrific analytical and creative questions they came up with (their classmates wrote alternately on an analytical question one week, a creative question the next—and again, the terms analytical and creative are conveniences to my mind, the *creative* responses in particular often beginning and ending in substantive analysis):

Harold Bloom has said of Crane: "his logic of metaphor characteristically gives us the sensation of an impacted density, sometimes resistant to un-raveling." Through close reading of one or more poems from *White Build-ings*, analyze "the logic of metaphor" Bloom refers to. Things you might consider: is "logic" the appropriate word for it, or do you have some other term that makes more sense to you? Is there an underlying principle? Are there patterns or regularities that are uniquely "Cranean"?

Allen Tate once wrote: "Crane's poems are a fresh vision of the world, so intensely personalized in a new creative language that only the strict-est and most unprepossessed effort of attention can take it in." Discuss the challenge of hermeticism in Crane's writing. Look closely at one or more poems from *White Buildings*, and describe how you make meaning out of, or simply experience, the work. Do you think Crane's work justifies your "effort of attention," or is his vision too "intensely personalized"?

CREATIVE

Crane is unusually fond of the prefix "un-" (and its cognates, "ir-," "im-," "in-"). Likewise, he makes telling use of the suffix "-less." Crane frequently uses negation to assert the *contrary* of a property, rather than simply as-serting the property directly. His uncanny use of modifiers creates a meta-physical space in which he invites us to experience the *positive absence* of things. Try writing a poem in which you imitate Crane's use of affixes in order to open a similar metaphysical space.

For the contemporary reader, one of the most striking aspects of "To Brooklyn Bridge" is the poet's adoration of his subject. Today, such a dis-play of feeling might not be permitted and irony would certainly be used to undercut a similar apostrophe. Write a poem addressed to something inanimate and keep a close eye on how soon you turn to irony. Be prepared to describe to the class how this process worked for you.

{ ## The Ambition of
Rhetoric Finding
Poetry in Composition
KRISTIN PREVALLET

Like many poets struggling to bridge creativity and academia, I've spent many years teaching freshman composition. And like many poets, I sometimes feel that this level of teaching diminishes my textual calling. After all, students come into the class reluctantly and most haven't embraced creative inquiry and bookish curiosity. Although most universities view composition as central to their core curriculum, they hire adjuncts at substandard rates to do the work that most of the full-time faculty try and avoid. And although the directors of almost every composition program I've taught in are passionate and devoted to student writing, it is rare for there to be any sense of continuity between composition and the more "serious" classes being taught in the English department. Yet, there is a pressure placed on composition classes, as if we can determine a student's academic success for the next four years.

Nevertheless, for a variety of reasons, I've changed my attitude about teaching composition. In part this is because I've taken a full-time job at St. John's University, teaching three courses of composition per semester. To make this commitment, it was essential that I find both meaning in relation to my students, and relevance to my work as a poet.

I know many poets who introduce their first-year writing students to the wonderful possibilities for inquiry within experimental writing. Every semester they move through weeks and weeks of bewilderment, resistance, and confusion until finally a few of them (or more, depending on the class) achieve the great eureka moment where they are activated as both readers and writers, participants in the barrage of language they are confronted by in college, able to see themselves not as passive recipients of knowledge but central to its construction.

For a few semesters I taught experimental writing in my composition courses, and of course I loved the moment when students got what I was doing and took ownership of their writing. But I soon grew weary. I realized that too many students were being left in the dark because they were simply not ready—or to be fair, not interested—in my passion for assembled meanings and complicated truths.

So, I had to switch gears and figure out other ways for poetry to be incorporated into first-year writing. It was clear to me that part of my job was to give students the practical skills for writing in the dialect of academia (thesis, research, argument, analysis). But the soullessness of academic writing, divorced as it so often is from a student's genuine inquiry into a passionate thesis, is painful to teach.

Rosanne Gatto, a colleague of mine at St John's University, has designed her course in a way that seems to circumnavigate "academese" and yet, allows students to discover it in their own way. In her syllabus she writes:

> You will be writing a book this semester. It should begin with *one specific event*, located in *one specific place* and then be explored from there. This book will also be a memoir of sorts, for it will chronicle your personal investment in your topic. The format, style, and feel of the book will be up to you. The length of your manuscript must be <u>10 typed single-spaced pages</u>. Don't be nervous. This is your book, researched on your terms. The page length will not be a problem to meet. What are you burning to tell the world? This is the question I would like for you to think about over the next couple of weeks.[1]

When I read this I thought about myself as a young writer taking freshman composition at the University of Colorado many years ago. We studied Machiavelli's *The Prince*, and I remember the well-meaning graduate student was having a hard time convincing anyone to participate in the discussion. The paper I wrote was dismal because I had no idea why I should care about power in the Western World. All I cared about was boys, my hair, and hanging out with this cool group of kids who were attending Stan Brakhage salons and helping Ed and Jenny Dorn publish *Rolling Stock*. And all I wanted to write about was my mother—she had died of cancer the previous year.

When I read Rosanne's syllabus I realized that perhaps my work as a poet doesn't have to be just about teaching poetry. Perhaps it's actually about introducing students to context, reflection, and perspective—in short, giving them the rhetorical tools to write the stories they want to tell. Perhaps students could use this dreaded composition course as a means of bridging their personal story to the larger forces that shape and construct their lives (social, political, economic, moral, psychological). My own goal was that this story be used as a vehicle in which to experiment with and practice academic dialect—in other words, they have to analyze an external source and reflect on how the source informs their story and how research gives them insight that they did not previously have.

My goal is to show them how to access the fruits of academic discipline: the satisfaction that comes from researching the context of an inquiry that blows perception wide open. Perception means shifting assumptions and breaking down walls.

As my student Louis Romero wrote in a process letter after he finished his book about his parents' struggle with AIDS: "I think the best way, really, was developing my life by writing it down and finally destroying the stone wall I had been hitting all my life, that was stopping me from stating the truth about my life. The wall has come down and I am ecstatic to let go of my secret."[2]

When I read Louis's reflection I thought about why I had become a poet, and how Robert Duncan's *Fictive Certainties* resounded with my ambitions as an idealistic young writer:

> We are no more than ourselves, members of the human community at once hopeful and despairing, if not at war with the threat of foreign tyranny, at war with the threat of our own inner tyranny . . . at war for the totality of our human nature against the polemics of a character-forming rigor mortis; and yet, we are envisioning the greatest commonality, seeing as if with "God's" eye a release of Man's fullest nature from its bonds.[3]

Release students' fullest natures from their bonds in my freshman composition course? It sounds overly pretentious, and ambitious. But why not. After doing this work now for three semesters, I'm continually amazed by the intensity of the wars most of my students are fighting and the gratefulness many of them have expressed in having the opportunity to share them. And I must admit—although teaching poetry is intellectually satisfying, teaching composition has been a revelation.

NOTES

1. Syllabus, used with permission of Rosanne Gatto.

2. Process letter, used with permission of Louis Romero.

3. Robert Duncan. "Man's Fulfillment in Order and Strife." *Fictive Certainties*. New York: New Directions, 1983. 120.

Now I Will Do Nothing but Listen, to Accrue What I Hear into This Song, to Let Sounds Contribute toward It; or, a Pedagogy

JAKE ADAM YORK

HOW DO YOU TEACH POETRY?

Incredulous citizen, desperate colleague, you suppose no answer, or only one. Teaching committee, you want curriculum, want rule, want way.

Here is a syllabus.

Thoreau:

> So thoroughly and sincerely are we compelled to live, reverencing our life, and denying the possibility of change. This is the only way, we say; but there are as many ways as there can be drawn radii from one centre. All change is a miracle to contemplate; but it is a miracle which is taking place every instant.

Here is a syllabus.

Students, let us not compel. Let us not reverence anything that does not justify itself.

I am less interested in your writing a *finished* or *perfect* poem than I am in your seeing *some* way toward a poem.

You want rules?

Insert Tab A into Slot B. Write a sonnet: fourteen lines, a volta, some application of syntax or sound to announce or witness the poem's turns of thought.

Now: ask not how this poem satisfies the idea of the sonnet, but where it forgets the sonnet. Where is this poem thinking of something else?

Thelonious Monk (via Steve Lacy):

> A genius is the one *most like himself.*

Where does the poem become most like itself?

So, the poem: a thing (think, thought) most like itself.

I have done it, too. Here, this is the moment when I forgot the assignment.

When I began to improvise.

Improvise. Begin with a plan, but know the plan will change, that it will *have* to change.

Improvise, from Latin *improvisus,* "unforeseen," adding *in-* to *provisus,* past participle of *providere* "to see ahead—more at PROVIDE" (*Webster's Ninth New Collegiate Dictionary*).

The poem will require what you cannot see. It is what you cannot see.

You improvise because something is not provided. You answer the lack of something: material, plan, rule. You work with what arrives, what's provided later, what was unforeseen.

So, you improve what was given and what is given.

So: false, folk, improvised etymology: *improvise*: to improve what's given, what arrives, emerges.

So: the poem provides itself.

The rule got us started. Now let us reverence this. Not what could be compelled.

Whitman:

> is not so impatient as has been supposed that the slough still sticks to opinions and manners and literature while the life which served its requirements has passed into the new life of the new forms . . . perceives that the corpse is slowly borne from the eating and sleeping rooms of the house . . . perceives that it waits a little while in the door . . . that it was fittest for its days . . . that its action has descended to the stalwart and wellshaped heir who approaches . . . and that he shall be fittest for his days.

Pay attention.

The syllabus is borne from the writing rooms. It was fittest for its days. Now.

When you write, you allow something that did not exist, that could not be asked for exactly, to come into the world. You help that, which could not be provided or be provided for, to provide itself and to provide for itself. You help this language emerge.

You could get in the way if you're not paying attention.

Attend, from Latin, *attendere,* literally "to stretch to" (*Webster's*).

Quiet now.[1]

1. This is to say that in my twelve years of teaching poetry, I've used every exercise I could find, every approach.

My goal is not so much to find a *right* exercise, but to create an environment, through a variety of engagements, in which a student can find his or her way.

My students ask for rules. They want laundry lists and step-by-step do-it-yourself directions. So I give them a new prompt each week. Whether a form, like the sonnet, a mode, such as invective or elegy, or a nonce, like "write a love poem using the tone of an infomercial"—I try to be as descriptive and enumerative as possible—e.g., "your poem must have fourteen lines" or "you must use five exact phrases from the infomercial of your choice."

They think *workshop* will be simply a matter of seeing whether the poem followed the rules. Instead, workshop works to identify the rule the poem has discovered for itself that will enable it to be unique, that will allow it to transcend rule and exceed, without fully resisting, description. This is to say that workshop is basically a process of reading the poem and then rereading the poem more deeply, which is a process of imagining the poem that has yet to arrive.

I participate as well, not just in the workshop, but in the work: if I assign a walking poem, I write a walking poem, and I occasionally show the students my process, so I can point out the moment in the work when I discovered my poem in the midst of answering the prompt.

To put this simply, I am teaching improvisation by putting the students, as best and as consistently as I can, in the midst of that negotiation, trying to determine what's on hand, what's changing, how quickly the change is happening, what's about to happen, and how to participate in that change.

Workshop, each week's discussion, is the micro-level, but I play this out on the level of the course as well.

This is to say, I plan a course, and then I plan a secret course.

The course is a linked series of fourteen exercises: one a week. This will please the rule-hungry student on the first day of class as well as the teaching committee several weeks later.

But, the secret course must emerge, in response to what the students provide, namely themselves. Invariably, the day arrives when the program begins to overwhelm their investment, and on that day (usually just before midterm), I destroy the syllabus. Each week, we decide what we want to do the following week, and then we have a syllabus-in-process that's revised weekly.

This is a practical consideration. After eight years on a commuter campus, I've found that this is a necessary step to get my students to take the work seriously. My students are all returning to school and to discipline. They left their first school because it was too programmed: they were working full-time or nursing a dying parent, and they saw how nonprogrammed the rest of the world was, and they rejected the artificial situation of the academy. I have to do the same. I have to take the scholasticism, the curriculum, out of the school.

What I offer, in a different way each term, is a better curriculum: the curriculum each poem demands.

Each poem is a radius, and a radical. It must reach at its own angle. It must grow its way through its soil. It must attend to its environment, and we must attend to its growth, allowing it to reach for us, to show us how to perceive change, and how to change with it.

WORKS CITED

Lacy, Steve. "Foreword." In *Thelonious Monk: His Life and Music*. Ed. Thomas Fitterling. Berkeley: Berkeley Hills Books, 1997. 14.

———. "T. Monk's Advice (1960)." *Do The Math*. 31 Mar 2009. http://thebadplus.typepad.com/dothemath/2008/12/stave-lacy-on-monk.html.

Thoreau, Henry David. *Walden. Walden and Civil Disobedience*. Penguin Classics Edition. New York: Penguin, 1986. 53.

Whitman, Walt. "Preface 1855—*Leaves of Grass*, First Edition." *Leaves of Grass: Comprehensive Reader's Edition*. Eds. Harold W. Blodgett and Sculley Bradley. New York: New York University Press, 1965. 709.

———. "Song of Myself." *Leaves of Grass: Comprehensive Reader's Edition*. Eds. Harold W. Blodgett and Sculley Bradley. New York: New York University Press, 1965. Lines 582–583 (section 26). 55.

Talks / Directives

My Next Great Poem

TRACY K. SMITH

How, as writers, do we motivate ourselves to move forward into new terrain? How do we wean ourselves from what we've already attempted and grown adept at? What do we move toward when the tools and themes that have led us forward seem suddenly to have lost their appeal, their urgency? These are the questions that inevitably arise from time to time in our writing lives.

Larry Levis's broad, ambitious, meandering poem, "Elegy for Everything that Had a Pattern in It," ends with these lines:

> As if we're put on the earth to forget the ending, & wander.
> And walk alone. And walk in the midst of great crowds,
>
> And never come back.[1]

These days, I'm hearing those lines as a kind of admonition to venture past what I have learned and wander into a space that makes a stranger out of me. And to keep going with no particular sense of what kind of an ending or resolution ought to be anticipated or moved toward. Indeed, if every already-encountered ending is something one truly manages to forget, there is no precedent in the mind for arrival, no sense that the journey itself—the wandering and the solitary seeking—ought to lead to any particular rewards, let alone any particular *what* or *where*.

When I try to think about those lines as something I might heed in my literal life (not just the intellectual life, the side of the mind that exists chiefly to parse or account for experience rather than to actually participate in it), I think a little bit about the appeal that travel holds for me as a person. The thrill of landing in a place characterized by different smells and sounds, different rules for navigation, a place beholden to a different history and set of customs, a place—most importantly—in which there is no particular space or group to which I belong. That freedom. The paradox of being a visible outsider one moment and virtually invisible the next. The space and manner in which you begin to exist under such conditions is very different from what it is at home, or near to home, or with people who constitute home for you. You begin to hear things that only a ghost might hear; things intended for no one arrive at the nonperson you are and hit home, and awaken something that isn't usually active in you. You're aware of yourself in a different way. Or, rather, you are aware of the different self you've become, and you take note of what she has to say, and she makes a surprising kind of sense, and she teaches you something you didn't think you or she knew. And you take all of that home with you and look at it under a familiar light, and you try to describe it to others, and some of it stays with you, and much of it doesn't. You've gone and returned.

But Levis says, to the writer, or the reader—who, I believe, inevitably begins to elide with the speaker of any given poem—"never come back." Never set this newly discovered side of the self down on a shelf of curios and knick-knacks and back away as it begins to gather dust. Surrender the original self to this new one, and then another new one, and another. As much as that would be a powerful and passionate way to live life, most of us choose not to follow it. But it's a choice possible for the side of our lives lived in and through the writing of poems. All we need is the courage to choose it. It doesn't mean turning against what we've already done, so much as moving beyond it, with the tools or skills or insights or desires the previous work has imparted.

Take a moment to remember the last good—or, go ahead, admit it, great—poem you wrote. Be honest. How does it work, what does it look and sound like, what strategies does it employ, what revelation does it contain?

Now play devil's advocate with yourself and make a list of things your last great poem *did not* do. And go all out. Don't fall back on things you've already done in other poems. Get creative, ambitious, hyperbolic: *"My last great poem was not funny. It did not incorporate references to seismology. It didn't do anything technological. It did not frighten me. It did not frighten anyone. It did not contain any out-and-out lies. There was no woman in it wearing something green. No one famous made a cameo. There was no sex. There was no sorcery. No one stood up in the middle and demanded their money back."*

Your assignment is to look at the types of things your last great poem failed to do—failed, frankly, to even consider—and to write your Next Great Poem, which does, or attempts, each of those things in earnest. Furthermore, your ongoing assignment is to come up with your own version of an exercise like this that knocks you into some other, unfamiliar creative space every time you feel the need to pick up and start wandering all over again.

NOTE

1. Larry Levis. *Elegy*. Pittsburgh: University of Pittsburgh Press, 1997.

What I Usually Say to My Students

LINH DINH

Hoard your time, since you'll need it to be alone to think and to write.

Be frugal, since it'll allow you to work less and have more time to think and to write.

Try, as best you can, to have an overview of what's possible in writing, the various strategies attempted throughout history, throughout the world.

Identify the writers or works you admire the most, and read them very slowly, as many times as necessary.

Have faith that you will get better at thinking and writing, and that people will notice it, even if stingily and reluctantly, since you're not entitled to any attention.

Be prepared to be disappointed over and over.

For the sake of experimentation, it's OK to write badly, even foolishly, but don't try to pass off crap you yourself are disinterested in.

Even if you'll end up a mediocre writer, there's an outside chance you will become an excellent reader, so this pursuit will still be worthwhile, sort of, even as you lie there, unheated, loveless, and clutching your last packet of Ramen Pride.

Don't be afraid to be as weird—meaning as PECULIARLY YOU—as possible. Try to say it all. Be shameless. Don't hesitate to revisit a piece over and over to follow and capture everything that it really wants to say. Use each draft as a lead and a springboard into revealing something truly astounding, even if the actual changes (a revised noun here, an added adjective there) may be minimal.

Be as crazy and as perverse as possible, be inspired to the point of madness, but don't be glib.

Poetry should astound and frighten, not make you giggle for two seconds.

The Poem as Animal
or Machine

TERRANCE HAYES

I am walking the streets of an industrial northeastern city with a great writer. She is a year younger than my mother, a fellow Southerner, but Texan where I am South Carolinian, white where I am black. I have given a reading at her university and now on our way to dinner, she is telling me, in her way, what she thought of it: "The poems are not for you, they're for your readers," she says. "Forget that navel gazing, ain't-I-clever shit people like Ashbery write," she says, her high-heel boots wounding the sidewalk. When I say, "I like some of Ashbery's stuff," she snaps: "Quote some lines of your favorite poem!" I can't and she says that's the first sign of bullshit in the midst.

Does it sound like she's giving me a hard time? She is, but it's during this conversation that I know / decide we'll be true friends. I am listening. *The reader is there to have dinner with you, not to watch you eat, not to watch you play with your vegetables and shit it out*—she doesn't say this exactly, but it's what she means. We reach the restaurant. Our talk will have to end and to end it I ask what I believe will settle the dispute:

"Do you believe the poem is an animal or a machine?"

"It's a machine, she says without even having to think about it. "A thing finely wrought in language."

"That means you think a perfect poem can be written? You believe there's such a thing as a perfect poem?"

"Yes!"

"That wrought finely enough, everyone, anyone will recognize its beauty?"

"Yes, my father had a sixth-grade education. I write poems he can read. I write them slowly, labor over them, because Hell, if you're not playing with the big dogs, the ones who have written the perfect works, why play at all?"

There is a great deal of validity in arguing for the poem as a machine, a vehicle, built to transport the reader. A machine can be *perfected*. The automobile, the pacemaker, the iPod—those are fine machines. They are continuously improved because the dream of perfection is a feasible one.

Poetry workshops, poetry conferences, how-to poetry books suggest the poem has an engine that can be repaired if not improved. But for me the poem is an animal. It's imperfect, asymmetrical. Rules and laws are probably good for it, but it has a mind of its own. It can get across the room even when one leg is shorter than the other, even when it has no legs.

My belief has to do with the very nature of language. It's that no one owns language. No one owns the word *blue*. A writer can only borrow the word. Only add or detract from it. But the very nature of writing pretends one can tie down a word like *blue*. Fix it to the page, fix it to do the writer's will. I don't mind this. I love the rodeo, the wrestling to tie it down: the attempt to tame it.

But can you see that fighting with a word implies it fights back, that it's alive? It has to be alive and fighting if it's to be tamed. Be a color, we say to *blue*, and it wants to be a mood.

The poem is an animal. The words are its cells and teeth and bones. It can be tamed, taught not to piss on the carpet, taught to roll over, but it has a *self* of its own. A self born of history, epistemology. And as an animal, as language, it is far from perfect, far from being perfected, mastered.

Our nation of course has a long history of aspiring to Mastery. We dreamed and still dream we can master the wilds of nature, the principles of democracy, of business and industry, of technology. Some call this the dream of Progress. Of course, tied up in our narratives of mastery are the narratives of oppression, of colonization; the mastery of people, of countries and cultures. Even knowledge is thought of as something one can master. Isn't that why we give Masters degrees?

The belief in the poem as a machine is rooted in a belief that you can *know*, can *learn*, can *fix*, that an art form can be mastered. But who should want to master a word? Shouldn't we learn to live with it? To let it speak back to us? Even to be mastered by it, from time to time?

If the poem is an animal, knowledge is not fixed. (And that's a good thing.) It grows, evolves, as the writer struggles to hold it. Maybe the writer is like the parent who believes he has some control over his child, some grasp of his child's essence. The child is a poem, inarticulate and uncivilized, at first. Shaped by degrees of praise and discipline, and then sent out into the world. We hope we have given our dear animal everything it needs to survive. Endure. If we're successful, it leads a healthy life beyond your eyes. If we fail, it limps or runs back home crying.

The poem is an animal, a wild child despite our fullest attention, our best intentions. The poem is a beast, a monster. You are Dr. Frankenstein stitching it together to make it live. Except, it jumps from the table and tears through the wall of your laboratory, stomping through the countryside, mauling sheep, and terrorizing villagers. Alive with a dream of its own. A dream you could not have anticipated. (And this is a good thing.) The pursuit of something that cannot be caught or mastered can be a source of deep despair and frustration. But doesn't it keep you dancing on your toes? doesn't it keep you open and surprised?

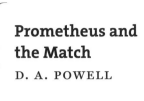

Prometheus and the Match

D. A. POWELL

The paradigm of *teaching* poetry is a flimsy place to begin, as many of my fellow writers have pointed out. But even though we know we can't cure diseases by dropping a few coins in the can at the 7–Eleven, no one wants to feel like an asshole. So here is my contribution on the subject of teaching.

Auden spoke of poetry as a kind of apprenticeship, though I fear that, too, is an inaccurate depiction of what happens between teacher and student. After all, it's not like a poet sits in the classroom making a poem, the way a blacksmith would stand at the forge and anvil, gradually allowing the younger writers to take a turn with the hammer, banging out a line or two.

Certainly poetry is not so much taught as it is modeled. But it's not modeled in any replicable way. A painter can demonstrate a brushstroke in real time. The making of a line of poetry, however, is not equally demonstrable. Or at least not in a way that will take the viewer through the thought process into the completion of a poem. No, if one conceives of each poem as an attempt to make the art itself new, the analogy of apprenticeship quickly falls apart.

Poetry requires Promethean energy if it is to make the leap from one reader to the next. Like its sister arts music and dance, poetry emanates in good part from the body. And so we are training our students not simply to write but to listen. That listening resides deeper than the cochlea of the ear and the neurons of the brain, it resides in the breath, the emotion, and the heart of the hearer. I know it's not fashionable to say "heart." But I don't mean it simply as a symbolic center of feeling. I mean it as the literal organ: a poem converges and diverges with the cadences of our physiognomy. Therefore to teach poetry, we have to ask of our students that they recite the poem, that they inhabit the poem, that they feel its pulse akin to or in discord with their own, that they wear it like a second skin.

It's a completely romantic notion to think that all fires within the human sphere were fed by some singular original spark: there were at least several original sparks, and certainly there were some that started independent of the others. So, too, with poetry and its multiple traditions, as well as its heretics and outsiders. Some students come to us fully encoded, clathrate with the sounds and rhythms of a poetic thread. Others come to us disquieted by the music of others, and their poems are made to shout down the noise, to disrupt it with their own outcry. And some sound their barbaric yawp because they have lived in silence and their music comes from a new place, a voice innovative and vital, unsanctioned, making its own permission.

From whatever source the blaze ignites, we can learn a little bit about how to handle it, and we can pass some of those tricks on: here's where the poem is burning out of control. Or: here's where you want to apply a bit of accelerant.

Fire has been around for centuries. Poetry, perhaps as long, though its earliest version was probably something akin to shouts and beats. As we've lived with it, we've managed it. We've never quite tamed it, thank God. If we did, it would fail to excite our imaginations. Therefore our charge as teachers: to give our students access to fuel and retardant. And to remind them that the most beautiful light comes from the most unrepentant flame. Anyone can strike a match. But who dares to light a bonfire in the streets? If we're at all invested in the potency of language, then we at times must support its annihilation of the old, rotten timbers which once represented progress. No city thrives unless it's willing to let itself be torched and rebuilt.

Oh, now it seems like I would abet arson. Language has such curious force, accruing meanings that lead us toward tricky disclosures. Arson in the *abstract* is what I should say. But I shouldn't even have to qualify it. Most people have clear heads; they understand the difference between the literal and the figurative. And if they don't, the problem doesn't lie with the poetry instructor. The true danger is that we might never cause a flash, either real or imagined.

The greatest peril of this age is the complacency of youth. They have fears and passions, but they often seem reticent to express them. And they might regard us with withering hesitation if we said, "I want you to shout," like the character of Howard Beale in *Network*. Plus, we're smart enough to know that mere shouting will just draw admonishing notes from our colleagues. The academy should excite young minds, but not excite them too much. And really, can our old hearts take the excitement of a full-blown riot? I doubt it.

And so our greatest pedagogical tool is our own writing. Because students are smart; they pick up on the disconnect, if there's any, between what we want them to read and what we ourselves write. We have to be present in our own work, livid, outrageous. Not for the sake of showmanship, although that's a good reason too, I suppose. But because we don't need either quietude or bull-pucky. We need poems that excite the imagination in a way that feels both innovative and earnest. The poetry teacher must be first and foremost a poet: taking risks and perhaps failing, but always willing to step forward and light the match. Perhaps only a few students will dare take the flame. But fire does spread. Sometimes it spreads so quickly and in so many directions, we can't say where it started. But that's okay. No one should ever want to take all the credit. Best to blame it on some mischievous character, while the furnaces glow with enterprise and ungodly power.

On Teaching Students How to Read Poetry

ERIC HAYOT

ONE

When you think the poem's no good, I tell them, don't ask what's wrong with the poem: what's wrong with you that you think the poem's no good? What I mean is: what in you resists the poem, doesn't like it, is disgusted by it, is afraid of or contemptuous of it? Do you feel better or smarter than the poem? Dumber than it? More worldly? More manly? More bored? More contemporary or ancient? More tasteful? The heart the poem's knife is pointed at is, finally, yours. Good readers of poems learn the shapes of many knives.

TWO

An experiment: teach William Carlos Williams's "The Red Wheelbarrow." Ask the students: what do you see? What color red is the wheelbarrow? Let them lay out their options, which will fall into two groups: Radio Flyer, and rusty. Polled, seven out of ten will choose the former. Then ask them what color are the chickens. Six out of ten will say, bright white; the others, focused on the rainwater, tell you that chickens in yards are dirty, muddy.

Where is the truth of the poem, you ask them. They elaborate their decisions. And you reply: the truth of the poem is that every time I teach it seven out of ten see it one way, the other three the other. If you want to be theoretical you can say that the poem is the dialectical arrangement of all the truths it makes visible, and that this particular dialectical arrangement puts us face to face with the great philosophical contest between the historical and the ideal, here spun out, alternatingly, on the poem's Buddhist wheel.

THREE

John Ashbery's pantoum: "Footprints eager for the past / The usual obtuse blanket." Obtuse? No kidding. But, start somewhere: How does it make you feel? Is it a happy poem? No. Sad? Kind of. Where are the words that make it sad? And so on. Start with your feelings; say what you can say. If you're patient there will be something, which is more than nothing.

Part of what you're teaching is patience, which is the patience of not knowing. They have to learn to be in the poem without having the answers; they have to learn that some poems are written to prevent them from having answers. This of course is a kind of answer: how does not knowing the answer make you feel? What would it mean for a poem to be about not having answers?

"And what is in store / For those dearest to the king?" Incontrovertible ache. Beyond that, effort, and silence.

GO!

Worst-case scenario: There has never been a human society without poetry. What would it take for you to be minimally responsible to that fact?

Mystery and Birds Five Ways to Practice Poetry

ADA LIMÓN

Because I work outside of the academic field, I don't get the opportunity to teach very often, but when I do, I'm surprised by how many people read poems as if they can have only one meaning. In my own experience, I find it nearly impossible to hear the beauty and meditative joy of a poem's lines, or the sensual sounds of a syllable, when I'm reading solely for narrative sense. So, I've come to think that one of the first things to learn about poetry is to simply relax in its mystery. We need to learn that a poem can have many meanings and that it can be enjoyed without a complete under-standing of the poet's intent.

On a good day a poem might bring you great joy; on a tough day, the same poem might reveal great agony, but the poem hasn't changed—it's what you have brought to the poem that has changed. The more you read a poem, the more time you spend with it, read it out loud to yourself or to others, the more it will open to you—start to wink and flirt and let you in. A poem is a complex living thing, its multiple edges and many colors are what makes this singular art form so difficult to define. There is an ancient Chinese proverb that says, "A bird sings not because he has an answer, but because he has a song." That is how I have come to think about poetry— that a poem isn't a problem to solve, rather it's a singular animal call that contains multiple layers of both mystery and joy.

It's that unique animal call that we have to carve out time for if we really want to do the work that poetry requires. Though I admit I struggle every day to find the right balance between my writing practice and the daily pressures of living, there are a few things that help me remain true to the work of poetry. Although these may not work for every writer, the follow-ing five points are what have kept me writing poetry with greater ease and discipline on a daily basis.

1. Write every day. It's easier than it sounds. Make time every day to write SOMETHING. Even if it's one line scribbled onto a napkin on the subway or the bus, or a whole precious early hour in the morning. This

practice lets the mind know that every day we must be observant, that we are paying attention, always.

2. Learn poems you love. Read whatever poems you can get your hands on. Not just the classics, but those poets who are writing today. Pick up journals, magazines, and anthologies; search for the poems that break you open. Read those poems over and over again until you have them memorized in your mouth. Don't worry about mimicking them, just accept them as your teachers and hold them close. Become an expert on the poems you adore.

3. Cultivate silence. Silence is essential in order to hear your own voice. Especially nowadays when we often have the television on, the radio on, or music playing all day long, it is essential to find some silence to listen to your own voice. Your own voice is the only thing your poetry needs.

4. Embrace revision. Revision might be the hardest thing that writers have to do, aside from battling our own internal demons, because it means admitting that we are wrong. Sometimes we are so wrong that we need to start all over again, and it's embarrassing. Sometimes we only need to change a comma, but listen, every poem needs revision and every poet needs to learn humility.

5. Practice gratitude. Cherish those friends and colleagues who care enough to read and comment on your work. If you truly pursue writing, you will come to realize how enormously important these people are to your writing life and therefore to your making of a *real* life. Make sure you read their work with the same care and closeness they offer you. And buy them coffee and cakes when they return a manuscript with pencil marks on every page. It is a true act of kindness that should be greeted with great gratitude. And be thankful that you want to write at all. What a powerful art to devote a life to, and how lucky we are to love such a wild untamable thing.

Different Language
BEN DOLLER

A.

Both my parents were teachers. One taught kids to paint. One taught shop. Together they taught me how to walk. Somewhere in the gap between expression and mechanism (but which discipline is which?) I find the subjects I choose to teach: to read and to write. A poem as a painting made of words or as a machine, etcetera?

To bring a student to language. To bring them to the brink. And back. How much can words do? Which words are the vocabulary? How can words do it? How do you read them? How do they read? Process and formal decision-making in the act of writing-as-making. That kind of brink.

The brink is the very edge. Sometimes of understanding. Sometimes of a new understanding. There are so many different kinds of words, ways.

B.

Together, my students and I investigate the notion of a text as a series of decisions that are made by both the author *and* the reader. Creative writing *is* construction, the creation of forms: forms of identity, forms of perception, forms of experience that begin in the assembly of words and end in making a reader read, think, and, hopefully, write on. When a student can articulate the variety of emotional responses and visions of a speaker which different translations of the same Sappho fragments elicit, that student has not only learned a literary lesson or gained an arrow for her own personal artistic quiver, but has had an experience with the possibility of language itself. And that student may turn from her book to the blank page with a renewed vision of her own.

A.

The most important part of teaching = to teach what it is to know.
—Simone Weil

What is it to know?

It is necessary to recognize the things words are.

And look what others have done with them. Reading is exactly 90 percent. Reading, writing, and arithmetic, too.

And we will sit together and we will have to listen to ourselves and others.

Each week my creative writing students write in a rigid form (including, but not limited to "Western" prosodic mimes) to feel the pushing against the wall.

Each week my creative writing students write in a free form to feel the pushing against the wall.

There really isn't anything wrong with the word "workshop."

B.

It is necessary for student writers to have a forum for their work and to participate in a creative community, one that ideally extends well beyond the few weeks we have together in each class. These communities, at their best, provide writers at all levels the opportunity to articulate and share considered responses to work-in-process—to own, expand, and even transform their thinking. This transformation is a fundamental goal of the education of our writers and citizens. In preparation for workshop, my students are asked to read their peers' work for discussion numerous times, at first *without* marking up the text, withholding criticism or comment. Then they are asked to return to the text, after a night's sleep, to mark the piece with annotations, and finally to compose a direct note to the author synthesizing their reactions and responses to the piece. This type of obligatory preparation makes students confident in their commentary and willing to discuss and share in an environment of mutual collaboration—which, in my experience, ultimately leads to workshop sessions that are as valuable for the entire class as they are for the author of the day.

A.

Teaching is the perpetual end and office of all things.
—Emerson

A Machine Made Of Paint. A free form is a rigid form. Therefore a rigid form is etcetera.

Teaching is talking with illustrations.

What and why is under the hood? What colors? Writing as a series of decisions.

B.

I also like to think of *workshop* in the sense of the sawdusty shop in which my father taught when I was a child: a place where each 2×4 had the potential for transformation—given a schematic, tools, and vision—a place where fascinating objects are made. Rather than rely solely on a vague *inspiration*, in my courses and workshops students are asked to engage literary traditions, to write in forms borrowed from a wide range of histories: sestinas, sonnets, homophonic translations, collaborations, journals, folk tales, and Oulipean experiments are all treated as equally valuable means to engender the next piece of work, and each challenge as an opportunity to learn what a writer has to offer. My students are encouraged to create their own forms as well, to see the world of literature as an active and malleable conversation to which each of them, regardless of background or experience, and regardless of genre, has the right to contribute.

A.

Poetry / Fiction / Creative Nonfiction / Drama / Documentary / Song.

There is no teaching until the pupil is brought into the same state or principle in which you are; a transfusion takes place; he is you, and you are he; then is a teaching; and by no unfriendly chance or bad company can he ever lose the benefit.
—Emerson

Though she may benefit equally from a separate state.

Together they taught me how to read.

I like to think I know how to read why it is the way it is. I'd like the students to know more.

WORKS CITED

Emerson, Ralph Waldo. *Emerson's Essays*. New York: Harper Perennial, 1981.

Emerson, Ralph Waldo. Sermon, quoted in Robert D. Richardson, Jr. *Emerson: The Mind on Fire*. Centennial Books. New York: University of California, 1996.

Weil, Simone. *The Notebooks of Simone Weil*. New York: Routledge, 2004.

What I Tell Them

JASWINDER BOLINA

I'd like to tell them there are too many poets. I'd like to tell them we don't need any more and don't need any more competition. Too many throbbing bodies, not enough room in the bed. I'd like to tell them, you should go to other departments. You should go to the other department and become exquisite bankers future in-laws will favor. You matter too little, and anyway there isn't any place for poetry. You know too little, what are you doing here?

I don't say these things, though I think sometimes I should. I don't say them because I've been shown photographs of Lascaux, so instead, I say, let me tell you about Lascaux and how you and art are irrepressible. I feel wise when I say this, though I'm only twelve or so years removed from where they are now, and I know too little. I tell them this too. I say, I'm only twelve or so years removed from where you are, and I know too little.

Then, there are other things, invented and borrowed, I go ahead and tell them, things I'd like to say in French or in Latin or very cryptically in English as though I'm under incredible strain: You don't matter; only the poem matters. Or, poems aren't made of ideas, they're made of words. Or, you don't have to be honest, but you gotta be sincere.

I don't say any of it in French or in Latin because I never learned much French or Latin. I don't render it cryptic. I say these things directly because I believe they're true. I worry I sound didactic or woefully earnest and have embarrassed myself, but then irony would be easier than earnestness, and anyway this isn't about me. Only the poems matter.

I tell them, you are rare people for whom poems matter but, even so, only so rare. After all, I tell them, everybody writes poetry. All of us, in our sentimental, self-important scrawl in hardback, blank journals bought from a rack next to the register in the bookstore. I have those journals too. They're in a box under the folding table I use for a desk. I take them out and, embarrassed, tear out a few pages every so often. Entire books eventually disappear. Everyone writes poetry, I tell them, which is why there's place for it, and you have these journals too, but you're rare people for ɔing public with this information.

I tell them, by going public with this information, you agree to the term and condition that your poetry is no longer your own. Sure, we talk to ourselves, and we write notes to ourselves, but no one writes poetry to himself, herself, oneself. You might write *for* yourself, but you write *to* somebody else. You should be nice to that person. That person is seated beside you. Say hello. But this person isn't enough. You want somebody else. I tell them, you want the somebody who will stroll into a library in Tucson or Greenwich on a Wednesday and find what you've written. You want that person to pull you down off a shelf and open you up and marvel. You want to be somebody's afternoon reading on the veranda, somebody's Xerox hung with a tack on the inspiring wall.

I tell them that much is possible, but what you write here won't appear in the *Norton*. No editor will call you. For that sort of thing to happen, you have to walk into a library, open a book of poems, and marvel. You have to do this several times a month—several times a week if you have time—over many years. You'll need to paper your wall.

What you write between treks to the library will disappear under the folding table, and you'll reach for it every so often and, embarrassed, discard a few pages until entire books disappear. Some of it, though, you'll keep, and some of it might find a way to a shelf and to somebody else. That much is possible, I tell them. Some of it will congeal and assemble.

I tell them the trick is entirely in language. Poems are made out of words, and these words need to be your own. Your words are what sincerity is made from, I tell them, and in this you have all you need for poetry. I tell them, use the words you remember from cartoons, words from your mother speaking of rutabaga, from your chemistry tutor and the redhead who at first ignored you, the words you think of when you think of the bodega on Granville and yourself later naked in the redhead's apartment. These words are yours, and your poems should be made out of them.

I give them examples. I tell them, "morning" is always "frigid" and "gray," our "clothing" was always "ragged and torn," and our "fingers" are always "stained with tobacco," the "fingers of smoke" "caressing the light bulb."

I tell them, your morning should be neurons and steam. You should arrive in a smock or in machinist's regalia. You needn't bother with smoking and fingers, we've had enough of cigarettes in poetry. Your words need to supplant our words so we can arrive at knowledge and also discover we know too little. It will be startling.

Your task is to arrange the words strangely in order to explain more clearly what happened. Your task is to help us understand what happened, I tell them, but what happened isn't always simply the facts. What happened isn't always a story. Sometimes, it's just some images. Sometimes, it's entirely sound.

To figure out which it is, I tell them, you'll need to let the poem overthrow you. It's made of words, and even if they're your words, they're part of language, and language is much bigger than you. Naturally, this will generate some conflict. The poem will sometimes need to be silent where you want to speak, or it'll need to be explicit where you turn to muttering. It will be confused about what you know for certain or certain about what confuses you. Sometimes, the poem will sputter and quit no matter how hard you admire or kick it. Sometimes, it neglects you completely, and this, I tell them, is okay.

You're here to relinquish, I tell them. You're here to sever a nerve.

Thirty-three Rules of Poetry for Poets Twenty-three and Under

KENT JOHNSON

AFTER NICANOR PARRA

1. Study grammar. Only by knowing grammar, knowing clearly the parts of speech and sensing their mysterious ways in sentence parts, will you be able to write interesting poetry. For poetry is all about grammar's interesting ways.

2. Don't suck up to other poets. Well, OK, you will do so, of course, like all poets do, but when you do, feel it in your bones. Take this self-knowledge and turn it into a weapon you wield without mercy.

3. Read the old Greeks and Romans in the original. Studying Greek or Latin is one of the best ways of becoming a man or woman of grammar. Well, duh, as they say here in Freeport at Tony's Oyster Bar.

4. Ask yourself constantly: What is the fashion? Once you answer, consider that noun, participial, infinitive, or prepositional phrase (the answer will mutate over time) your mortal enemy.

5. Ask yourself constantly: What is the worth of poetry? When you answer, "It is nothing," you have climbed the first step. Prepare, without presumption, to take the next one.

6. Don't drink and drive. Better yet, just don't drink.

7. At the second step, should you reach it, don't look down: You might get dizzy from the height and fall into an alcoholic heap. Trust me.

8. Read Constantine Cavafy's great poem "The First Step." Meditate upon it.

9. Don't worry if you have social anxiety at poetry events. Most everyone else will be as secretly anxious as you are.

10. Read Ed Dorn carefully, starting with *Abhorrences*, working your way back.

11. Remember that the greater part of it is merely show and acquired manners. Poets can be mean and they will try to kill you.

12. Ponder Bob Dylan's classic line: "I ain't gonna live on Maggie's farm no more."

13. After reading Roland Barthes's famous essay on it, watch professional

wrestling at least once a month. Reflect on how the spectacle corresponds, profoundly, to the poetry field.

14. Go on your nerve, and whenever you feel you shouldn't, do.

15. Don't smoke cigarettes, even if you think it makes you look cool to others (or to yourself).

16. Go by the musical phrase and not the metronome. But when convenient, or just because it's beautiful, go by the metronome.

17. Don't let anyone tell you MFA programs are bad. MFA programs are really great—you can get a stipend and live poor and happy for two or three years.

18. Make sure you act like an insufferable ass in your MFA program. Never suck up to other poets. Traditional or avant-garde . . .

19. If you don't know another language, make it your mission, as I suggested earlier, to learn one. Translation is the very soil of poetry. Its mystery.

20. The Web is a wonderful development. Don't make yourself a slave to its "cool" corporation of the moment.

21. Whenever you are in doubt about being a poet, instead of, say, being an architect or a physicist, or something of the superior sort, remind yourself of Leibniz's immortal question: "Why is there something rather than nothing?" (Keep this question in your pocket against your heart. Because no one can ever answer it, it is the key to your purpose.)

22. Write political poems. But remember: The politics you are likely protesting are present, structurally, inside poetry, its texts and institutions. Write political poems with a vengeance.

23. Read Wittgenstein. Don't ever feign you understand him. He didn't understand himself! Steal from his genius ammo dump.

24. When someone tells you there are two kinds of poetry, one of them bad, one of them good, chuckle gently.

25. Don't ever use a PowerPoint® at a Conference on Innovative Poetry. A PowerPoint makes you look like a tool!

26. Remember what I said (sorry to be so pedantic!) about grammar. If you can't confidently analyze a sentence, forget about poetry. Poetry is the art of language, right? Well, if poets cannot be the experts on grammar, then something is wrong. A generalized disregard of linguistics and grammar, by the way, is one of the main reasons the so-called *post-avant* is in crisis. I'm dead serious.

27. If you feel you have wasted your young life so far writing poetry, that writing poetry was a fool's, a loser's pursuit, and you sense despair and

absolute darkness before you, well, you are surely on the second step. There is no shame in turning back and leaving it all behind. Turn back without regret. On the other hand, if you are crazed and brave and you put your queer shoulder to the wheel, much wonder, blessedness, and inexpressible sorrow awaits.

28. Travel. Go to Asia, South America, Africa, Micronesia, North Dakota.

29. Read Eliot Weinberger, starting with both *What I Heard about Iraq* and *Karmic Traces*, working your way back.

30. Read Kenneth Rexroth's *One Hundred Poems from the Chinese* and *One Hundred More Poems from the Chinese*. If someone tells you there are two kinds of poetry, chuckle gently.

31. Look in the mirror and be honest. You are going to die. But right now you're alive . . . Look really hard. This is fucking astonishing. Why is there something rather than nothing?

32. Determine, as of now, that should you have children sometime, your devotion to poetry will somehow enrich their lives and not be a cause for their suffering. Listen to me and don't take this as melodramatic, middle-aged fluff. Quite a few kids have died for lack of what a poet found there.

33. On the third step, should you get there, its blank humming sound, realize this is almost surely the last step. Pump your legs up and down. Victory will be (as they used to say in the days of Deep Image and Language, back when poetry was innocent yet) dark, opaque, and strange.

Yakking Points

MARK YAKICH

for my students

Written language, especially poetry, is inherently a flawed translation of lived life. This sentence included.

Whenever you read a poem, read it out loud. Your ear will pick up more than your head will allow. That said, poetry had better be more than a medium for saying things in a pretty way. Poetry is more than ear candy.

To write what you know is fair advice. To write what you do not know but try to imagine may not be better advice, but it is more fun.

During war or economic downturn, poets will still write poems, and probably better ones than those made during periods of peace and prosperity. In either case, such a statement of truth is only made in hindsight.

The idea that a poem can be interpreted in an infinite number of ways is patently false. There may be a handful of ways, but that doesn't mean that examining a poem is a free-for-all.

There is no hidden meaning, only *meanings* you've not yet realized are right in front of you because you're not practiced in reading poems. Poetry is a convention like anything else. And you learn the rules of it like anything else—e.g., driving a car, baking a cake, fondling a lover.

Although many consider figurative language the essence of poetry, for the life of a poet metaphor will sooner or later become an illness.

Students often complain that by studying a poem ("picking it apart") you take all the fun out of it. They have not yet understood that unless you have written the poem yourself, studying the poem is the only fun to be had.

Literary theory is just another kind of literature.

Poetry depends on pattern and variation. Even nonlinear, non-narrative, anti-poetic poetry. The brain will try to make sense, by looking for patterns and variations, no matter what is presented before it. The words *apple*, *tadpole*, and *justice* have ostensibly nothing to do with each other, and yet the brain soon pieces them together simply because they are there.

Poetry is a form of prayer. Though most poets don't know to whom or for what they are praying.

The word *honest* in describing a poem is about as useful as a mop is to a dentist.

Fragmented poetry often purports to subvert the *normal* ways of daily discourse, worldview, or societal interaction, but as often it forgets that one's thoughts from moment to moment are fragmented. Thus, fragmented poetry becomes more mimetic and closer to verisimilitude than so-called conventional poetry.

When reading a poem, try to come to it on its terms not yours. Don't try to fit the poem into your life. Try to see what world the poem creates. Then, if you are lucky, its world will help you re-see your own.

Despite those who say that poetry makes nothing happen, humanity continues to be built on the literary device of the simile: Love thy neighbor as thyself.

You will gain a greater understanding of a poem by writing a single parody of it than by reading all the literary criticism of it.

There is no accounting for taste. What one reader admires, another disdains. You will develop your likes and dislikes over time. This is called aesthetics.

The idea of "finding your voice" is more hindrance than aid. As a poet, there is no reason to stick to one voice. And no matter what you do—even in trying the most random of writing exercises—you will not be able to escape your voice.

Do not fully discount what you dislike. From time to time, continue to read what you dislike because it will help you remember why you like what you like. And over a long period of time, some of your likes and dislikes will reverse. If they do not, your thoughts will stifle and your writing will be ruined.

Poetry's irrelevance is becoming and important.

If you're main claim to a poem is that you can relate to it, you aren't reading it sufficiently. Poems are not meant to be related to; they are meant to offer you something you didn't know, experience, or imagine before.

Do not think of revision as correction; think of it as opening up the possibilities of what's already on the page.

All poetry is political but not any more so than every single sentence in the English language is political. Consider the diction of our grammar: subject and object. Each sentence involves a power relationship, and politics, by definition, is a struggle for or management of power. For example, *I am that I am* is a battle for self-control.

Writing poems is about trial and error. In this way the writing of poems is like a science. In no other way is the writing of poems like a science.

Whitman and Dickinson. The two mothers of U.S. Poetry. The gay man of the streets and the virgin in the attic. Both barren by their own rights, and yet they are the two myths that bind us.

Mystery is more important than clarity in poetry. Or rather clarity is important but only when one doesn't at first recognize it as clarity. Dickinson more than Whitman embodies this. Her poems give us a clarity we didn't know before. Whitman's simply show us everything and dare us to look.

The more one reads Whitman the more one agrees with him but is less interested in him. In too much agreement there is boredom.

Emily Dickinson is allowed to leave her poems untitled. For every other poet, the lack of a title is either a missed opportunity or an admission that the poet himself doesn't care enough about the poem for anyone to bother with it.

An elderly painter once said the definition of the avant-garde is simply the people with the most energy. The same is true of poetry.

In lieu of reading the minds of others, there is poetry. If you agree, this is at once a true and false statement.

Your hope to become a great poet should never hang on an epigram.

Some Questions for the Threshold of Poetry

BRENDA IIJIMA

Try to exchange ideas of poetry with ideas of thinking.

Try to find out what limits and restrictions have been placed on poetry and understand for yourself if they are justified—conceptually, linguistically, socially, historically, aesthetically, philosophically, etc.

Search out the ideological constructs in your work, reflect on these, interrogate these . . .

Ask what makes spoken language different from written language. Use this knowledge in your poems.

What are the tensions in your work / work of others? Follow these fault lines to the molten core.

What poetry baffles, disturbs, confuses, irks, smarts, titillates, seduces, confers, causes wonder—come to terms with the ways poetry engages emotional registers. Construct an ethics from this knowledge.

What veils reality? Bring forth these pertinent observations.

What sounds originate outside of standard conceptions of music—engage these sounds, rhythms, tempos, resonances, dissonances, and vibrations in your work.

If you wrote your poems inhabiting a different body (race, gender, ethnicity, age, species) would meanings shift? How does identity shape your poetic process and social reception?

What are the relational terms of your writing, where are the connecting nodes? How does your poetry situate itself in the material biome? Do you write humancentrically? Do your subjects gaze at objects or have you rejected this modality?

How does your writing contend with environmental duress?

Seriously contemplate *thingness* and alternative ways of parsing reality that don't compartmentalize to extremes.

Time: what are the variables of time in your poem? Can there be multiple time zones in your poem? How is time perceived? Same goes for spatial considerations.

What texts does your work connect with or is it a freestanding entity—autonomous? Why, how, and are you sure?

Learn everything you can from other disciplines: science, economics, politics, religion, etc. Disparate subjects are really not disparate. Move outside of your own ego, empathize, open up.

Learn another language. This is the single easiest way to understand the dynamics of the English language and the built-in cultural system that it is. This could aid your poetry greatly and help ensure your work isn't insular.

How does the biological self affect writing, thinking, being? What are the nerve pathways of your poems? How does your body relate to language, utterance, expression?

What are your local, daily, experiential textures, gestural movements, weather formations, geological features, histories, morphing sociologies, politics of the near, etc.?

What are the action words in your work? These will reveal a lot about the tectonics at play.

Ask yourself and all your friends what you / they think art is and then think about your poems and your friend's poems and the poems of others you don't know. Have you consulted strangers, others outside your loop? Now's the time.

Don't Paraphrase

MATTHEW ZAPRUDER

I think as readers it is our task to try very hard, despite what seems natural or what we may have been taught to do when we read poetry, not to begin immediately to paraphrase or translate such poems to ourselves in order to *understand*. To truly experience poetry, we need to try just to be in the poem for a while. Maybe even having unfamiliarity, resistance, not understanding at times pass through us. Which is hard for me, at least, as it might be for you.

In such cases, it is often helpful for me to remember that the word *stanza* comes from the Greek word for room, and *verse* from the Greek word for turn. If I think of the poem as something I am actually physically moving my consciousness through, from one line down to the next, and from one room to another, it helps me stay there, within what is being said. Giving myself that task to do helps keep me from translating and explaining everything in the poem as I am going along.

Now we are there. And maybe also now thinking, this poem is doing its best to be as simple as possible. Which, maybe alas or not, is not always so simple. First of all, new experiences are by definition unfamiliar. And second, no one asks mathematicians or physicists to make very complex equations or theories simple and clear, if to do so would compromise their task of communicating the truth. So why should we expect always immediately to understand, and consider lack of understanding a failure on our part or on the part of a poem? Especially if we are reading a poem full of the complexities and contradictions of human life and feeling.

Some poems exist to clarify and distill the human conundrum. Of these, some powerful and great, others sentimentally reductive, I don't have much to say. They speak for themselves, and fortunately for them, by their nature already resist paraphrase.

Usually I dislike riddles. A riddle is something—usually a simple object—described in as complex a way as possible, in order to confuse, obfuscate, create a delay. Presumably for the purpose of *fun*. What has four wheels and flies? What walks on four feet in the morning, two during the day, and three in the evening? Garbage truck; man. I personally find them annoying.

Often we are taught to read poems as if they were a kind of literary sub-species of riddles, with a hidden meaning we must tease out by looking for what the poem is *actually saying*. Which of our teachers told us poetry has been deliberately hidden from the reader, by the poet, behind the words? Nothing could be further from poetry's true nature! Except in very rare situations (symbolism and political persecution), in poems words mean exactly what they always do. When I say table, I mean table. Flower means flower, and not beloved; if I wanted to say beloved I would, and nothing would stop me.

Yet why poetry, when it could all be gotten across so much more . . . simply? The poem must be saying something that cannot be said in any other way. Maybe it's not something grand, just ordinary. We all know recognition of the ordinary can be a blessing too. But if poetry is somehow in the way of the *true message*, it's all just one step up from a crossword puzzle.

I want poems to come as close to my life as possible. I want what I read and write to be important, both familiar and new, and to not be easily pushed away into a realm of beauty or artistic experience that is safely separated from our actual lives and those of people who surround us. The poems I love try to say, as clearly as possible, that which cannot in any other way be said.

We all know we are so much of the time in the middle of mixed emotions, that which seems for a moment to be clear but is not or vice versa. Moments of rare clarity and understanding succeeded by far more moments of mundane struggle, and so on, and so on. Wise people may know the point of all this, and live without such complexity. All I know is, when I read a poem that implies the speaker knows the answer to the unanswerable question of why we are alive, I feel poetry has fled.

Also, poems can be a process of unfolding, one that might welcome us, or maybe grudgingly allow us, to be inside it. Poems do not have to be all about the revelation, the learning at the end. They aren't necessarily goal-oriented. If anything they are more like a conversation with a friend. You start talking, you learn something, you double back, you get confused, you misunderstand, you laugh, you have some different feelings, you drift off, you come back, you know you have learned some things (though maybe you can't even say what) but most of all you know you know this person better. What's the goal? To be alive, and to experience. Which is more than enough, and a great pleasure.

Only poetry tries to take us together on a journey towards that which cannot be said, but which we are driven to understand. Old things that have always been there, waiting, on the tip of our collective tongue. Shelley in "Defence of Poetry" wrote of listening to a poem, that we are "moved and softened, yet know not whence or why." And the poem is where, as Wallace Stevens wrote, "out of the central mind / We make a dwelling in the evening air / In which being there together is enough."[1]

NOTE

1. Wallace Stevens. "Final Soliloquy of the Interior Paramour." *The Collected Poems of Wallace Stevens.* Vintage, 1990. 524.

Language Is the Site of Our Collective Infection

LARA GLENUM

1. An overgroomed poem is a hideous thing. Quit liposuctioning your poem! Quit waxing its ass! As long as you strive to make your poems supremely beautiful, you will be little more than a coffin-maker.

2. Poetry has nothing to do with beauty, other than that the norms of each are artificially constructed (and then naturalized).

3. There is no natural voice, no natural work of art. Everything is artifice, which is to say, everything is style. You are a maker, so make according to your own spasms and blindness.

4. Don't talk about *mastering* a form unless you want to enter into the social economy of slavery.

5. Poets who seek the *pure* and the *true*, who romanticize these terms, are kin to those who ask us to purify our race. The term *catharsis*, which lies at the heart of Western aesthetics, comes from the Greek verb "to purify," and women, non-whites, queers, and impoverished or disabled persons have historically been labeled as social contaminants, in need of suppression or excision.

6. Poetry has nothing to do with truth. If you want truth, inquire at your local dictator, who will certainly have a version to sell you.

7. Abject failure is a far better gift to the world than self-satisfied moderation, so dare to risk annihilation. Get mulish and outlandish. Cling belligerently to your unsightly protuberances and excesses. Take things too far. Shock yourself out of normative language.

8. The use of the lyric "I" does not confess a self, but rather a raucously messy nest of conflicting desires and proclivities that can be costumed this way or that. Don't try to resolve pesky disjunctions in your identity; savor them and tap them for their cultural power. Don't edit the noise out.

9. Cultivate a highly tactile sense of language. Perform experiments not *with language* but *on language*. Cook it, stuff it in a plastic bag filled with cupcakes and rodents, cram it into old dodo bones. See what happens.

10. Language is the site of our collective infection. Poems are medical waste. A lot of life-saving experiments and procedures can be performed with medical waste.

Open Door A Meditation
QURAYSH ALI LANSANA

By the time the young woman walked into my office to introduce herself I was annoyed. A colleague, her advisor, told me she was coming—an MFA student writer who'd spent a year and a half concentrating on prose then decided to craft her thesis in verse five months prior to graduation. I was dumbfounded and she was late. Our first session was sandpaper.

Upon initial review of her work in progress I was certain this, and her issues with punctuality, were damning. Not that the poems didn't reveal potential, gift in some ways, but that the aesthetic and contextual excavation would require heavy lifting. This young woman weighed two tons well before I read her work.

Then there's the issue of subject matter—the recent long illness and death of a parent. This would require psychology in addition to prosody. Dislodging and identifying myriad emotions while creating just enough distance to explore from both inside and outside those same emotions. How to enter the world of memory as both truth and "triggering town," as Hugo suggested.

A few years ago, during my first trip to Africa, I had the opportunity to make a pilgrimage to two of the most likely points of embarkation for my lineage: the Elmina and Cape Coast slave castles in Ghana. Both of these ominous forts possess a "door of no return," but the cell door at Elmina, with its narrow width and rusting steel bars, is the haunting image most associated with the Middle Passage. I curled in a fetal position in a corner and for thirty-six minutes wailed from a place so buried I may never fully comprehend.

I grabbed a rock from my bookshelf, a rock from the Dutch brick that secured the cannonball and steel whipping post for African women disinterested in the Captain, and placed it in my uncomfortable student's hand. She visibly shook and departed questioning her advisor's advice.

Surprisingly, she returned the following week, late, with new poems and new ideas. Thus began the exorcism, the undoing of a prose writer, the sculpting of sinew. It was never easy—we wrestled every meeting. She

immersed herself in dark regions and I pushed her to stay as long as possible before extraction. I introduced her to *Horizon Note*, a stunning book
by Robin Behn regarding her father's battle with Alzheimer's, as a study
guide. By April the manuscript was a textured array of feelings and aesthetics. We both grew in the process.

Sonnet Talk

C. S. GISCOMBE

I appreciate the articulate—"coherent verbal form"—but am not terribly interested by it. In university poetry classes I wish—instead?—to put my back into acknowledging the stuff around the poem (around and beyond the impulse and also the sources of impulse), the permissions usage grants us, what knowledge of poetry obligates us to do when we write (what knowledge of culture obligates us to do when we write), etc. And I want, in class (and alone at my desk as well), to be furiously caught up in language—the instabilities, the heft, the fringe elements.

I've recently been teaching two forms, the sonnet and the ghazal. I'll talk here about the former. I'm not terribly interested in sonnets (or ghazals) in terms of my own writing—that is I've never written a sonnet and probably never will write one. No hostility, no principled stand—I simply have other things to do. But I find the form interesting as a site, as a point of disembarkation for *talking* about that other stuff, for the ongoing work of investigation and experiment. Sonnets can be navigated but the point, in all my classes, is not to get it right but to see how it feels to get involved in it, that and to look at what the poem (or the essay or joke or speech) *does* and at the ways the world presses on it, and at how it presses *back* on the world.

We talk about Shakespeare and Donne and Michael Drayton and Shelley; we differentiate the Elizabethan sonnet from the obviously superior Italian sonnet. We consider responses to the form—Ted Berrigan, Edwin Denby, a twenty-four-line sexually explicit sonnet with commentary, both by Molly Peacock, sonnets-it-took-me-a-long-time-to-recognize-as-sonnets by James Wright and Robert Hayden—and I ask my students to look closely, finally, at two stands of sonnets that have been particularly important to me: Gwendolyn Brooks's "Gay Chaps at the Bar" sequence and Bernadette Mayer's book *Sonnets*. The point here being that both Brooks and Mayer tangle awkwardly and repeatedly with the form, with the received pattern of lines and syllables and turns, the daily order of arrival. Of course it's the wrestling that's important, the labor there, not the form so much. The form allows us to talk in class about the wrestling; it's a thing, a topic, a place or placeholder in the never-ending conversation. Like most such places it has application beyond itself, beyond sonnets and beyond poetry.

Bernadette Mayer said that the sonnets were "brief conclusive thought" and wondered, "If there are no conclusions why do we wish for them?"

But before we talk about Brooks and Mayer I start things by going to the board, chalk and eraser in hand, with thirty-five or forty minutes left before the end of class. It's a gimmick but I like doing it. I talk about iambic pentameter and point it out in Shakespeare or in Drayton's "Since There's No Hope Come Let Us Kiss and Part"; and I recite my two favorite iambic pentameter lines—"I hate to see that evening sun go down" (the beginning of W. C. Handy's "St. Louis Blues") and "I wish I was an Oscar Meyer wiener." The latter works as iambic pentameter but *wiener* must be slurred into a single stressed syllable, a worthwhile task for the voice. I come up with a first line (most recently, "My love was like a bat that fluttered by") and the class writes the sonnet—their choice of Italian or Elizabethan—in blab-school manner in the time remaining. Let it—the form—be an arbitrary occasion; let it come to life, monstrously, in the moment.

Gwendolyn Brooks wrote, in the first poem in "Gay Chaps," (her war series, her "souvenir for Staff Sergeant Raymond Brooks and every other soldier"),

> We knew how to order. Just the dash
> Necessary. The length of gaiety in good taste.
> Whether the raillery should be slightly iced
> And given green, or served up hot and lush.

Because of my life in the academy and my visibility beyond the university I know the complex trap of articulation, the easy praise we get for being *articulate*. The oratorical has its place yet I know that this—getting it right or *right*—is what's expected of me. That or to shake things up with surgically precise dance. I ask my students for less than that or more than that. For something other.

From my place at the blackboard though I insist on more or less complete sentences that spill over the precipices of rimed line-endings, which is to say I gnash and pontificate and cajole them when necessary into using the stuff they learnt in school and bending it. I pop a sweat and they sweat too. Much shouting in class, and laughter and more laughter as students argue verbs with one another. This is fieldwork, I don't know where it will end when we start. What we get to is something "that is not mine, but is a made place," and sentence and line we get it done before the end of class.

WORKS CITED

Brooks, Gwendolyn. *Blacks*. Chicago: David Company, 1989.

Duncan, Robert. *The Opening of the Field*. New York: New Directions, 1960.

Mayer, Bernadette. *Sonnets*. New York: Tender Buttons Books, 1989.

One evening, after my course on Asian North American literature, I struck up a conversation with two students. One of them asked what else I was teaching that term, and I responded that I was teaching contemporary poetry. This produced quite a divergent response:

"I would *never* take that class."

"I would *love* to take that class!"

"No way. I hate poetry."

"What's wrong with poetry?"

"I don't know. It doesn't interest me. It's just too difficult. I feel like I can't get a handle on it. It's harder to get what you need out of it."

"Really? I think it's easier. There's so many things you can talk about— tone, structure, imagery, style . . . What, are you interested in *plot*?"

"Yeah, I guess so."

Teachers of poetry will no doubt find this argument familiar. In Asian American literature, however, the student who dismisses poetry enjoys the backing of professional Asian American literary critics. Like my poetry-loathing student, Asian American critics have found it far easier to "get what they need"—autobiographical narratives of immigration, assimilation, and identity formation—from novels and memoirs, leaving poetry almost entirely out of the Asian American canon.

So the question of how to teach Asian American poetry is bound up with the question of how to make a case for poetry within the field of Asian American literary studies. It turns out that this isn't so hard to do. Any classroom account of how we came to be studying Asian American literature has to begin with an understanding of the Asian American movement of the 1970s, which helped establish Asian American studies as an academic discipline. The central genre of this period was not prose, but poetry. Early Asian American journals such as *Gidra* and *Bridge* included regular poetry features; the first Asian American literary magazine, *Aion*, was founded by two poets; and anthologies such as *Roots: An*

Asian American Reader included generous selections of poetry—and no fiction.

I find that there's no more engaging way to outline a history of the Asian American movement than to track its development through poetry. Lawson Fusao Inada's 1971 volume *Before the War* was the first major book of poetry published by a Japanese American writer. Inada's jazz-influenced rhythms show the influence of African American culture on Asian Americans at this crucial moment. But a poem like Inada's "Plucking out a Rhythm" also displays the anxiety attendant upon this influence. The poem unfolds in distinct stages that "build" a Japanese American figure from the ground up, then "disguise" him in the "turned-up shoes of Harlem,"[1] foregrounding the question of whether the jazz aesthetic can be a "natural" fit for the Asian American writer.

The work of Janice Mirikitani illustrates Asian American writing's deepening engagement with politics. Mirikitani's "Looking for America" lays out—more forcefully than any lecture—a catalog of the racist stereotypes that confront the Asian American. Mirikitani's directness is a jolt to students, and her framing of these issues through a poetic speaker opens up the question of how stereotypes shape the individual Asian American consciousness.

Students often respond more readily to these writers, whose rough surfaces show Asian American identity visibly under construction, than to more polished exemplars like David Mura or Li-Young Lee. There is an unfinished and even—dare I say it?—amateur quality to such works that in no way detracts from their power but that may grant access to students ordinarily intimidated by the impermeable surfaces of more professionalized work.

I'm certainly not suggesting that the poetry that works best in the classroom is that which is *easiest*. I have also seen students respond enthusiastically to work that is usually characterized as experimental or *difficult*. Students often name as their favorite texts not canonical novels but poetic and hybrid works like Theresa Hak Kyung Cha's *Dictée* and Fred Wah's *Diamond Grill*. These texts engage with the autobiographical strain that has dominated Asian American and Asian Canadian writing, but they also depart radically from conventional narrative treatments of these topics. *Dictée*'s mix of narrative, poetry, and images destabilizes historical and biographical narratives in favor of a concentration on the workings of language, and Wah's reminiscences are rendered as discrete prose poems that force readers to draw their own linguistic and thematic connections between them.

Why are texts like *Dictée* and *Diamond Grill* pedagogically successful? A work like *Diamond Grill* is, as Wah wryly puts it, "apparently, prose,"[2] allowing poetry-phobic students to lower their defenses long enough to give the text a chance. But I think students are also responding to the inventiveness and excitement of these texts, which take nothing for granted in their exploring and expanding of the very ground of Asian North American experience.

The bottom line, then, is that we should not shy away from giving poetry a central place in the Asian American literature classroom—and, indeed, that we should not shy away from giving Asian American poetry a central place in the way we teach literature more generally. Rather than adopting a defensive position in which we read a few token poems that do the same kind of narrative work that stories and novels do, we should expose students to the most exciting and exploratory work. Hybrid texts like *Dictée* and *Diamond Grill* may turn out to be even better candidates for inclusion in American and Canadian literature courses than usual suspects like *The Woman Warrior* or *Obasan*; the work of writers like Cha and Wah challenges any impulse toward tokenism through its poetic, critical approach to the terms under which *ethnic* stories are told. Finally, as it turns out, students just plain *like* these texts. One student recently scolded me for dropping *Dictée* from my syllabus in favor of a novel. And the two poetry-hating and poetry-loving students whose argument sparked my thinking here will soon be reading *Diamond Grill* as part of our course. We'll see if it's a text they can agree on.

NOTES

1. Lawson Fusao Inada. "Plucking out a Rhythm." *Before the War: Poems as They Happened.* New York: Morrow, 1971. 13.

2. Fred Wah. *Diamond Grill.* Edmonton: NeWest, 2006. 177.

{ Some Thoughts on
Teaching Poetry to
Spoken Word Artists
BARBARA JANE REYES

First, I must tell you, I don't teach for a living. I am one of those writers whom many of you would consider as holding a *day job*, when in fact, my *day job* in public health I consider my career. It's beneficial to the work of writing to have a life and perspective mostly outside of academic circles.

Second, I am interested in emerging API and especially Filipino American poets and readers of poetry, in having conversations with them, inspiring and encouraging them along the way. I am interested in their stories of being thwarted by poetry (not getting Shakespeare in high school, and being made to feel stupid because of this), and finding a way to come to poetry.

In the capacity of visiting artist or lecturer, my interactions with students are brief and jam-packed. I meet many emerging writers of color who consider themselves *spoken word artists*. I read their poetry, and I see them perform. In conversation, they tell me about word choice, about struggling to contain and convey political messages, utilizing metaphor, irony, striking the appropriate tone. They consider whether it's important for the poem appear on the page the way it sounds when they perform it. In other words, they articulate to me their poetics. So I tell them they are poets. Some respond with visible unease. I tell them poetry and spoken word are the same thing. They respond, "Really?" As if they have never heard this before: Spoken word is poetry.

Think about it: before reading and writing were widely practiced in any society, communities converged as tellers or listeners of talkstory, which served as both entertainment and education. Sestina and villanelle come from oral tradition; epic poems were once recited to listeners from memory. This is spoken word; it is not a new thing. These are not radical or complicated ideas that I am articulating here. Encountering resistance by spoken word artists to what I have just articulated here, I have taught poetic forms with strict rhyme and meter constraints, and which arise from non-Western, non-European oral traditions. These forms include ghazal, the Malay pantun (ancestor of the modern pantoum), the Philippine tanaga and balagtasan. In balagtasan, for example, the composition of the verse is as important as the composition of the political argument, which is as important as the extravagant and convincing delivery of the verse and the argument. Similar to poetry slam, the winner is decided by the audience. This is a good opportunity for an emerging poet to learn how to balance between considering the page and the stage.

I don't know where the belief that spoken word is not poetry was born, how it has been cultivated and propagated, but I do know that spoken word artists have been othered as the fictitious line has been drawn between them and the poets. When talking to students, I don't have the time to linger on where this cleaving began. Instead, let me refer to Juan Felipe Herrera's 2005 lecture, "A Natural History of Chicano Literature":

> Your friends, and your associates, and the people around you, and the environment that you live in, and the speakers around you . . . and the communicators around you, are the poetry makers. If your mother tells you stories, she is a poetry maker. If your father says stories, he is a poetry maker. If your grandma tells you stories, she is a poetry maker. And that's who forms our poetics.[1]

This is a fairly self-explanatory statement that I try my best to impart to them. Poetry is not meant to be locked up in inaccessible spaces. Poetry is about paying attention, not just to the stories all around us, but also and especially to how these stories are being told.

NOTE

1. Juan Felipe Herrera. "A Natural History of Chicano Literature." September 19, 2005. Online video clip. UCTV. Accessed on April 1, 2009. http://www.uctv.tv/search-details.asp?showID=11119.

{ **Politics and the
Porous Imagination**
ANTHONY HAWLEY

On January 19th, 2009, it occurred to me that I had never been a teacher
under any other administration than the Bush administration. Neither
had I been a published poet, artist, husband, or father in any other cli-
mate.

To say that I have fashioned my teaching practice around and against
this recent historical era would be a bit of an exaggeration. But the realization that the brevity of my *adult* life could until very recently be marked
by and contained within a singular and malevolent political culture utterly
foreign to my thinking was startling and instructive.

During the spring of 1999, I graduated college. During the fall of 2000,
I fumbled through my first semester of teaching while in graduate school
in New York City. During the first couple of weeks of my third semester teaching, 9/11 happened. During the fall of 2004 my first daughter
was born, the Red Sox won the World Series, and John Kerry did not become president. During the summer of 2005, I ended up spending two
weeks in an asphyxiating gated community in Colorado at a music festi-
val where my wife taught violin to high school students. This was a community where, at the same, the AEI World Forum was meeting and had
brought together some of the top conservative politicians from around the
world. During that week I found myself one morning drinking an outra-
geously priced coffee and reading *Tender Buttons* at a Hyatt Hotel dining
room when Newt Gingrich and two assistants sat down at a table next to
me and Newt posed the following rhetorical question: "How can we define
ourselves as a country as long as our borders remain open?"

This is all true; I swear. So what?

What I want is a porous poem; a poem whose borders leak; a poem whose
borders remain malleable; a poem whose borders might be infiltrated.
In teaching, I encourage students to find openings in their poems points
of entry that keep the poem's edges permeable and absorbent. Ways out.

Exits. Portals. Apertures. Doorways. Gaps. Holes. Make a fugitive
Make a peripatetic space. Allow foreign agents in.

refusing inertia, the truly porous poem builds holes into itself. This
ration is somewhat akin to Gordon Matta-Clark's "building cuts"—
aking holes to alter habitats and their surroundings. Make space work
less. Make more passage. This way air passes through and makes the poem
vibrate. The reader should be able to hear that air as much as he or she
does the words on the page.

When teaching any age group, I want students to think about how a
poem might become this kind of space. What keeps it pulsing on the page,
what keeps the poem moving on and off the page, and most importantly,
what keeps the poem in contact with the outside. Too often, popular culture tends to prioritize what's *air tight* or *rock solid*. Let in the outside. Let
weather in. Let voices in. Keep borders porous. How can we enlarge the
country of the poem as long as its borders are closed?

Utilizing Distraction

KRISTI MAXWELL

Traction is in distraction, and traction as a concept can be, which is to say, traction in one's own thinking can happen through distraction. Obstacles placed in the scuffed-up court of concentration do several things. Dis / traction as a preliminary writing technique (as opposed to a revision technique) prepares one for the future inevitability of non-constructed (i.e., uncontrollable) distractions that might otherwise stifle; it encourages spontaneity in selection, rather than inhibition in selection due to dwelling too long in *what now* and *which*; it facilitates cultivation of flexibility; it etceteras and parentheses.

Dis / traction as a revision technique is another employment of dis / traction. It says "no" to the racking of a brain (a racking we must remember associates itself with an archaic torture device), a racking which may in turn rack, or, at the least, wreck, a poem.

To practice dis / traction, one must create an atmosphere of disorientation. An atmosphere to write *through* rather than (the more passive) *in*. One might have another one read (and not softly) beside her, toward her ear. The ear will tow in things as the mind toys with a line. This mission here, then, is to simultaneously seep and avoid. Bypass and admit. A poem is a palimpsest always. Being a palimpsest, being both here and there, having both here and there in the poem's here, the poem is implicitly distracted.

However, a distracted writing process and a distracted piece of writing should not be conflated. One would for no reason necessarily describe a poem as distracted because its making incorporated / admitted / invited distraction. Both a distracted writing process and a distracted piece of writing exist; the former does not necessarily have a hand in the latter; both may have merit or neither may. A thing will work, or it won't. Flaws may illuminate the laws a poem is limited or charged by. Using dis / traction as a writing technique differs from writing carelessly. Dis / traction as a writing technique ideally helps us to be humble readers. Readers compelled to return, this time with better attention or with attention on a thing it wasn't initially. Attentiveness benefits from the tension of distraction. One must cultivate cognizance of her own distractedness so she'll sense a corrective urgency, a stilling that might require stealing away.

Distraction exists. Welcome dis / traction in writing rather than wait for a welcome distraction (from writing? from thinking about writing? from tinkering so that writing feels little like writing at all?). Loiter less in a *right* time and *right* place for writing. Displace instead. Dis place is for writing.

Why

RICHARD SIKEN

Because poetry is the language of the imagination and you need a larger imagination. Because you need more than a gun and a jug of water. Because you have explicable and inexplicable needs and the world is full of things and you want some of them and to get them you need to be able to say them and think them. Because the loss of the imagination is the loss of the human. Because undigested biography is boring. Because what we call sincerity is an oversimplification. Because sometimes desire in a poem sounds like whining. Because nostalgia is always creepy and it makes you seem helpless. Because you can evoke instead of recount. Because you can trace the path of the mind as well as the way the body drags through the mud. Because we're savvy and media drenched and you can leave out the parts of the story we already know. Because knowing where to put the commas is boring and subject-verb-object is boring but knowing how to break a line to push against the sentence, make a friction, spin against the way you drive, find the place to breathe, is interesting. Because what it does is more interesting than what it is about. Because you have a rich inner life, or want one, and everyone looks good smoking a cigarette in a café with a notebook and a faraway look. Because notebook. Because the page. Because paper is cheap and no one really gets hurt. Because language existed before you. Because you rise up into language for only so many hours before falling back down into silence and you might as well do something useful while you're here. Because you're susceptible, elastic, thin-skinned, moody. Because landmark. Because amnesia. Because you will not remember this moment with accuracy. Because language belongs to those who use it and some things develop sideways. Because the landlord will let himself in without notice. Because your supervisor will change your schedule without notice. Because hot pants. Because parataxis. Because we need more than a clunky extrapolation. Because we are waiting for you to make sense of it for us. Because poetry can move the fulcrum of the mind just enough so that the world, this same world, becomes electrified and bewildering. Because poetry is mysterious and criticism is not.

Because craft can be taught but vision can't, which is problematic, since you need both. Because a consistent way of seeing is a philosophy. Because when you mess with syntax, you're messing with morality. Hot pants, because some things are worth repeating. Hot pants, because image is the coal you shovel into the poem to fuel its little engines. Because there are more ways of getting there than just plot. Because the sound of a singular human voice. Because they will not lay down in the streets and give you the keys to the city until you give them what they want and what you want to say and what they want to hear will overlap anyway so why not give it to them, love, love, it's not like there's only so much, it's not like it's gonna run out, so give it to them, give it to them. Because you can go ahead and make it happen, finish the thought, say the dream was real and the wall imaginary, raise the dead, heal the sick, cast out demons, and levitate. Because readers are greedy and great literature is about its readers not its writers. Because participation. Because witness. Because history. Because, in spite of it all, it's between you and the page. Because, in spite of it all, it's just words on a page. Because sometimes, in spite of it all, it's still in your head and not on the page and you have to do it all over again. Because you want to be heard, or overheard, or you don't and you need to invent a coded language to get the message underneath the radar. Because you want to write it down and slide it under the door and run away or you want the words to outlast you or at least do their job while you are sleeping. Because even when intent and urgency push past dexterity into blather and deceit you have still accomplished something. Because sometimes the places you'd like to smooth over are the places where you have betrayed yourself and you should take a minute to really think about that. Because you don't need to be brave but it helps to be unashamed. Because we are all always moving forward in time, word by word, and you can trust us to follow you into the future. Because we are going to spend the rest of our lives in the future. Because black square, white square, goes the linoleum.

The Roster

SABRINA ORAH MARK

I should never have accepted the gig at Shadow College. I was young, though. Foolish. When I received the offer I was teaching literature and poetry as an adjunct at a large university. I was underpaid, the permanent faculty despised me, and even the English Department secretary had started refusing me letterhead. My students had disappeared, as had the chair in my office. My evaluations were blank at best. Occasionally an associate professor would give me the finger in the mailroom. Even the director of creative writing who loved everybody could not love me.

So I took the gig.

Shadow was a small, private college. I was told there was a forest nearby, and a good bookstore in town. My teaching load would be light. My salary would quadruple. I'd be on tenure track, and could look forward to sabbaticals and health benefits (even dental). I was thrilled, as I'd had a terrible toothache for years. The students were described as "nontraditional," which I took as older. Older is good, I thought. The older the better.

I was given only one class to teach the first semester so that I had enough time, as the dean put it, "to find my bearings." He brushed some dust off his bow tie, and touched me on the arm. "We don't," he insisted, "want your creative work to wither away due to the demands of the coffin." "Don't you mean," I asked, "the classroom?" "Yes," he said. "That's what I said," he said. "The demands of the classroom." He blushed. "God forbid," he said, "we should be the fly in your ointment." He pointed me in the direction of my classroom and gave me a little push. "Consider us the ointment in your ointment," he said. "As a matter of fact," he continued, "consider our college a flyswatter of sorts. A surplus of ointment." Never for a moment did it seem this dean believed he had taken the idiom too far. Never in my life did I respect a man more.

I felt idealistic for the first time in years. And with this feeling I entered the classroom. The students were already seated. Their heads already were bent over their notebooks. This would be, I thought, a slice of very terrific cake. Based on my experience, the fact that they even were present was astonishing. I introduced myself and handed out the syllabus. Because this was an advanced creative writing workshop, I emphasized the success of the class depended on the students. I was merely there, I promised, as a guide who would abandon them at the most beautiful and terrifying point of their journey. I asked them to go around the room and introduce themselves.

Emily was first. She held her notebook over her face. Only her eyes showed. She was barely audible. I caught something about God and punctuation. She spoke as if there was a dash permanently lodged in her throat. I was relieved when the notebook slipped from her tiny, white hands and with great clarity and longing she began to speak of a master who I took for her muse. This is good, I thought. This one's got passion. Bruno was next. In lieu of introducing himself he stood up, walked over to the light switch, and began flicking on and off the lights. "Bruno," I said, "please sit down." He sat down. He was very frail. He spoke in Polish. He slowly peeled a hard-boiled egg, and as he peeled I knew somewhere deep in my heart he wrote of attics, and fathers, and birds. Walter was next. He was round and sad. He put his arm around Bruno and generously volunteered to be his translator. It would be a burden, he admitted, but a necessary task. Unfortunately, he could not stay. He'd be back next week, he promised. He wrung his hands. He apologized. He had lost a briefcase that contained his writing. He was nervous. He hoped it would be returned to him. "Eternally," he added. He loped out the door, mumbling something about a collector and angels. Samuel could not go on. "You must go on," I said. "We are going around the room." Samuel agreed he must go on. But he could not go on. Gertrude was next. There was something about her hair that suggested she dwelled in a continuous present. She spoke in imperatives, and as she spoke she drew tiny boxes in her notebook. Although nothing like the others, she seemed to belong to them inexplicably. And finally came Franz. He confided to us he'd awoken that morning to find himself sitting in the classroom. He apparently had no idea how he'd gotten there. He was clearly shaken. He asked that we not bring apples to class. He was terrified of apples.

To say these students seemed familiar would be a vast understatement. The smell of old books drifted off them and combined to make what I can only describe as a tiny maelstrom in the middle of the classroom. They seemed *underlined*. If a face could be the face of a person stared at too long, this is how their faces appeared.

I loved them. I loved them fiercely. The fact that we met only once a week quickly became unbearable. I could not get them out of my head. In class they barely noticed me. "Benjamin," Emily would say, "tell Schulz to capitalize the horse." "Which one?" asked Walter. "The one that becomes very small like a wooden toy." "And while you're at it," bellowed Gertrude, "tell Schulz to stop drawing pictures of my feet." "Drop it, Stein," warned Walter. I loved how they were as tender as they were harsh with one another. Many times I tried to speak, but my mouth filled up with stones. They carried on as if I wasn't there. "What," I once heard Franz whisper to Emily, "is Beckett waiting for?" Samuel often stared out the window as if someone was coming soon to pick him up. "Hey Kafka," said Samuel, "I heard you." They wrestled for a few minutes, and then broke into the strangest laughter I've ever had the pleasure of hearing. "Dickinson," said Gertrude ignoring the boys, "maybe you should consider turning these poems into prose poems." "In your dreams," said Emily.

I would see them moving down the halls of the English Department in deep discussion and I'd say, "hi guys," but they never saw me. Never heard me. I became feverish with longing. I stopped sleeping, stopped eating, stopped bathing. Sometimes in class I would lie down in the middle of the floor and hope they would pile on top of me. Smother me. I wanted to be the coats they wore. I wanted to be the scarves around their necks.

I began following them home. One by one. Once I even pressed my lips on Samuel's window and left behind a slightly shaken, mushy lipstick mark. I carved my name into a tree in Gertrude's yard. I rummaged through Emily's trash. I left a box of macaroons on Bruno's porch with a note that read *forever yours*. I collected train schedules for Franz and stuffed them in his mailbox. And because Walter never did find his briefcase I bought him over a dozen of them; expensive, leather briefcases that cost me three months of my salary. I left them on his doorstep, knocked, and ran away.

Like most stories of obsession this one doesn't end with scandal or murder or permanent ruin. One day, in the middle of the semester, I just packed up my bags and took the bus to my mother's. I was at the end of my rope, and it was either the void or I'd have to shinny back up. Retrace my steps. Get out of there quick. Go back to the beginning. No one, to my knowledge, ever realized I was gone. What mark could my absence possibly make? I was obsolete from the very beginning. Except for that one beautiful moment when I asked Bruno to please sit down and he sat down, did those students ever hear one word that came out of my mouth. "And that time," my mother reminds me, "when you told Samuel he must go on but he could not go on." She says this to console me. "Yes," I say. "That was fantastic."

After my short stay at Shadow College I quit teaching. I work in a post office now. I like stamping packages the best. I'm incredibly fond of the postmark.

Mailing the Black Box

G. C. WALDREP

So I'm at the post office standing in line for what seems like a very long time with it heavy in my arms and then finally I'm at the counter and the clerk is manhandling some forms and wants to know what's inside. "It's a black box," I say. "I can see that," he says, "but what's inside?" I think for a minute. "Nothing," I say. "It's not that kind of black box." The clerk crosses his arms. "Well, something's got to be inside," he says, "and I need to know what it is, so that I can fill out these forms." He gestures at three slips of paper on the counter in front of him. One's red, one's blue, and one's a sort of sickly green. "Sir, I can't let you mail that parcel unless you tell me what's inside the box." I sigh. We are in a predicament. I understand the man is just doing his job; it's not like he's being rude or anything. "I don't know," I finally say. "You don't know?" he repeats. "That's right," I say. "I don't know, because nothing's happened yet." The clerk thinks about this for a long minute, staring hard at me, and then begins writing on one of the forms. I can hear his pen, an old-style fountain pen, scratching against the paper. "*Nothing's happened yet*," I make out in his tidy, upside-down script. He fills in the address, pauses, then enters a zero in the valuation column. I pay for the postage and thank him. It occurs to me as I walk back out into the busy afternoon that the post office must have black boxes of its own, somewhere in the bowels of the buildings, in each of the sorting centers. So that after something happens, someone else can come along and open the box. So that somebody can tell the story.

Contributors

Kazim Ali's most recent books are a volume of poetry, *The Fortieth Day*, a novel, *The Disappearance of Seth*, and a collection of lyric essays, *Bright Felon: autobiography and cities*. He teaches at Oberlin College and in the Stonecoast MFA program of the University of Southern Maine.

Rae Armantrout's latest book of poems, *Versed*, came out in January of 2009. *The New York Times* listed her previous book, *Next Life*, as one of the 100 Notable Books of 2007.

Hadara Bar-Nadav is the author of a book of poetry *A Glass of Milk to Kiss Goodnight* and a chapbook *The Soft Arcade*, forthcoming in 2010. She is an assistant professor of English at the University of Missouri–Kansas City.

Dan Beachy-Quick is the author of several books, most recently *A Whaler's Dictionary* and *This Nest, Swift Passerine*. He teaches in the MFA program at Colorado State University.

Bruce Beasley is a professor of English at Western Washington University and author of six collections of poems, most recently *Lord Brain* (winner of the University of Georgia Press Contemporary Poetry Series competition) and *The Corpse Flower: New and Selected Poems*.

Claire Becker lives in Oakland and teaches in the high school mainstream program at the California School for the Blind. Her first book, *Where We Think It Should Go*, will be published in 2010.

Jaswinder Bolina is the author of *Carrier Wave*, winner of the 2006 Colorado Prize for Poetry. He teaches at Ohio University where he is completing a PhD in Creative Writing.

Jenny Boully's latest book is *not merely because of the unknown that was stalking toward them*, and her previous books include *The Body: An Essay*, *[one love affair]**, *The Book of Beginnings and Endings*, and *Moveable Types*. She teaches poetry and nonfiction at Columbia College Chicago.

Joel Brouwer is the author of three books of poems: *Exactly What Happened*, *Centuries*, and *And So*. He teaches at the University of Alabama.

Lily Brown holds a degree in Women's Studies from Harvard College and an MFA in poetry from Saint Mary's College of California. Her first book, *Rust or Go Missing*, will be published in 2010.

Laynie Browne is the author of seven collections of poetry, most recently *The Scented Fox*, 2007 National Poetry Series selection.

Stephen Burt is an associate professor of English at Harvard. His book of essays on contemporary poetry, *Close Calls with Nonsense*, will appear in 2009.

Julie Carr is the author of *Mead: An Epithalamion, Equivocal, 100 Notes on Violence* (winner of the Sawtooth Poetry Prize), and *Sarah—Of Fragments and Lines* (National Poetry Series). She is also the co-publisher, with Tim Roberts, of Counterpath Press, lives in Denver, and teaches at the University of Colorado at Boulder.

Joshua Clover is a poet, scholar, and critic, sometimes in a university system. His books include *The Totality for Kids* and *1989: Bob Dylan Didn't Have This To Sing About*.

Matthew Cooperman is the author of *DaZE* and *A Sacrificial Zinc*, among other books. He teaches poetry at Colorado State University, where he also co-poetry edits *Colorado Review*.

Oliver de la Paz is the author of *Names Above Houses* and *Furious Lullaby*. He teaches at Western Washington University.

Linh Dinh is the author of four books of poems, two collections of stories, and a just-released novel, *Love Like Hate*. Often translated, he has also published widely in Vietnamese.

Ben Doller is the author of *Radio, Radio*, and *FAQ:*. He has taught in West Virginia, Iowa, Ohio, Idaho, and California. He lives with his wife, the poet Sandra Doller, and their dogs, Ronald Johnson and Kiki Smith.

Sandra Doller (née Miller) has a new name. Her first book, *Oriflamme*, was published in 2005, and her second collection *Chora* is forthcoming in 2010.

Julie Doxsee is the author of two books: *Undersleep* and *Objects for a Fog Death*. She lives in Istanbul, Turkey.

Lisa Fishman's fourth book, *F L O W E R C A R T*, is forthcoming; she is also the author of *The Happiness Experiment* and the recent chapbook *Lining*. She lives in Madison and Orfordville, Wisconsin, and directs the MFA Poetry Program at Columbia College Chicago.

Graham Foust lives in California. He once sold Carol Burnett a pair of shoes.

John Gallaher is the author of three books of poems, most recently, *Map of the Folded World* and *The Little Book of Guesses*. He lives in rural Missouri where he coedits *The Laurel Review*.

Forrest Gander's recent books include the novel *As a Friend*, the book of poems *Eye Against Eye*, and the translation *Firefly Under the Tongue: Selected Poems of Coral Bracho*. He is a professor of English and comparative literature at Brown University.

C. S. Giscombe teaches English at UC Berkeley. His recent poetry books are *Prairie Style* and *Giscome Road*.

Peter Gizzi is the author of *The Outernationale, Some Values of Landscape and Weather, Artificial Heart*, and *Periplum and other Poems*. He serves as the poetry editor for *The Nation*.

Lara Glenum is the author of two books of poetry: *The Hounds of No* and *Maximum Gaga*. She is also the coeditor, with Arielle Greenberg, of *Gurlesque*, an anthology of contemporary women's poetry and visual art.

Kenneth Goldsmith is the author of ten books of poetry and founding editor of the online archive UbuWeb (ubu.com). He teaches writing at the University of Pennsylvania, where he is a senior editor of PennSound.

Johannes Göransson has written several books of poetry and translated several Swedish and Finnish poets, including Aase Berg, Ann Jäderlund, and Henry Parland.

Noah Eli Gordon is the author of several collections, including *Novel Pictorial Noise*, which was selected by John Ashbery for the National Poetry Series, and subsequently chosen for the San Francisco State University Poetry Center Book Award. He is an assistant professor at the University of Colorado–Boulder.

Arielle Greenberg has taught at summer camps, community centers, libraries, low-residency programs, Syracuse University and Bentley College, and is an associate professor in the Creative Writing Program at Columbia College Chicago. She's the author of two poetry collections, editor of a college composition reader on youth subcultures, coeditor of three poetry anthologies, and is currently at work on two nonfiction projects: one on the new back-to-the-land movement and another on birthing with midwives.

Richard Greenfield is the author of *A Carnage in the Lovetrees* and *Tracer*.

Sarah Gridley is the author of two books of poetry: *Weather Eye Open* and *Green is the Orator*. Her poems have appeared in various journals, including *Crazyhorse, Denver Quarterly, Gulf Coast, jubilat,* and *New American Poetry*. A recent recipient of an Individual Excellence Award from the Ohio Arts Council, she is an assistant professor of creative writing at Case Western Reserve University in Cleveland.

Anthony Hawley is a poet and visual artist.

Terrance Hayes's most recent poetry collection is *Wind in a Box*. He teaches at Carnegie Mellon University in Pittsburgh, Pennsylvania.

Eric Hayot is an associate professor of comparative literature and director of Asian studies at Pennsylvania State University. He is the author of *Chinese Dreams: Pound, Brecht, Tel quel* and *The Hypothetical Mandarin: Sympathy, Modernity, and Chinese Pain*.

Brian Henry has published five books of poetry: *Astronaut, American Incident, Graft, Quarantine,* and *The Stripping Point*. His translation of Tomaž Šalamun's *Woods and Chalices* appeared in 2008.

Brenda Hillman has published eight collections of poetry, the most recent of which are *Cascadia*, *Pieces of Air in the Epic*, and *Practical Water*. She has also edited Emily Dickinson's poetry for Shambhala Publications, and, with Patricia Dienstfrey, coedited *The Grand Permisson: New Writings on Poetics and Motherhood*. Hillman serves on the faculty of Saint Mary's College in Moraga, California, where she is Olivia C. Filippi Professor of Poetry; she also works as an activist with CodePink.

Jen Hofer is a poet, translator, interpreter, urban cyclist, knitter, bookmaker, and teacher. Her poems, prose, and translations are primarily published by small autonomous presses.

Paul Hoover's newest poetry book is *Sonnet 56*. He is editor of the anthology *Postmodern American Poetry* and, with Maxine Chernoff, the annual literary magazine *New American Writing*.

Christine Hume is the author of several books, most recently *Shot*, a bilingual *Selected Poems*, and a chapbook *Lullaby: Speculations on the First Active Sense*. She directs and teaches in the interdisciplinary Creative Writing Program at Eastern Michigan University.

Brenda Iijima is the author of *Animate, Inanimate Aims* and *Around Sea*. Forthcoming works include *revv. you'll—ution* and *If Not Metamorphic*.

Lisa Jarnot is the author of four collections of poetry including *Night Scenes*.

Kent Johnson's latest book is *Homage to the Last Avant-Garde*. In 2005, he was named "State Teacher of the Year" by the Illinois Community College Board of Trustees.

Bhanu Kapil teaches during the year at the Jack Kerouac School of Disembodied Poetics in Boulder, Colorado. She writes and thinks about chimps, schizophrenics, immigrants, wolf-girls, and monsters in a genre that could be loosely described as Indian Writing in English.

Karla Kelsey is the author of *Knowledge, Forms, the Aviary* and *Iteration Nets*. She teaches poetry at Susquehanna University.

Aaron Kunin is the author of a collection of small poems about shame, *Folding Ruler Star*, and a novel, *The Mandarin*. He lives in Los Angeles and teaches early modern literature and poetics at Pomona College.

Quraysh Ali Lansana is the author of two collections of poetry, a children's book, and the editor of several books, including *Role Call: A Generational Anthology of Social and Political Black Literature and Art*. He is director of the Gwendolyn Brooks Center for Black Literature and Creative Writing at Chicago State University, where he is also an associate professor of English and creative writing.

Dorothea Lasky is the author of *AWE* and *Black Life*. Currently, she researches creativity and education at the University of Pennsylvania.

Sueyeun Juliette Lee is pursuing her PhD in English Literature at Temple

University. She edits *Corollary Press*, a small chapbook series devoted to new work by writers of color. Her publications include *That Gorgeous Feeling*, *Mental Commitment Robots*, *Perfect Villagers*, and *Trespass Slightly In.*

Ada Limón's third book of poems, *Sharks in the Rivers*, is forthcoming. She serves as the creative director of *Travel + Leisure* and teaches an occasional master's class at Columbia University.

Timothy Liu is the author of eight books of poems, most recently *Polytheogamy* and *Bending the Mind Around the Dream's Blown Fuse*. He lives in Manhattan.

Sabrina Orah Mark is the author of *The Babies* and *Tsim Tsum*. Her chapbook *Walter B.'s Extraordinary Cousin Arrives for a Visit & Other Tales* was published in 2006.

Dawn Lundy Martin's debut collection of poems, *A Gathering of Matter / A Matter of Gathering*, won the 2006 Cave Canem Poetry Prize. Dawn is a member of the Black Took Collective, the winner of the 2008 Academy of Arts and Sciences May Sarton Poetry Prize, and an assistant professor at the University of Pittsburgh.

Kristi Maxwell is the author of *Hush Sessions*, *Realm Sixty-four*, and the chapbook *Elsewhere & Wise*.

Joyelle McSweeney is the author of two books of poetry and two genre novels. With Johannes Göransson, she coedits Action Books and, with John Woods, the online journal *Action, Yes*.

Christina Mengert is the author of *As We Are Sung* and coeditor, along with Joshua Marie Wilkinson, of *12x12: Conversations in Poetry and Poetics*. She teaches creative writing at the University of Colorado–Boulder and for UCLA's Writers' Extension Program.

Albert Mobilio's books of poetry include *Bendable Siege*, *The Geographics*, and *Me with Animal Towering*. He teaches at the New School's Eugene Lang College and is an editor of *Bookforum*.

K. Silem Mohammad teaches creative writing at Southern Oregon University in Ashland. He is the author of *Breathalyzer*, *A Thousand Devils*, and *Deer Head Nation*, and he edits the poetry magazine *Abraham Lincoln*.

Fred Moten teaches at Duke University.

Jennifer Moxley is a poet who teaches at the University of Maine.

Laura Mullen is the author of five books and teaches at Louisiana State University. Her work has been widely anthologized, most recently in *American Hybrid*.

Sawako Nakayasu's most recent book is a translation of Takashi Hiraide's *For the Fighting Spirit of the Walnut*, and new books include *Hurry Home Honey* and *Texture Notes*.

Aimee Nezhukumatathil is the author of *At the Drive-In Volcano* and *Miracle Fruit*; and honors for her poetry include an NEA fellowship and the Pushcart

Prize. She is associate professor of English at SUNY–Fredonia where she was awarded a Chancellor's Medal. She lives in Western New York with her husband and son.

Hoa Nguyen is the author of *Your ancient see through*, *Red Juice*, and *Hecate Lochia*. She lives in Austin, Texas.

Jena Osman's books of poetry include *An Essay in Asterisks* and *The Character*. She coedits the ChainLinks book series with Juliana Spahr and teaches in the Creative Writing Program at Temple University.

D. A. Powell's books include *Tea*, *Lunch*, *Cocktails*, and *Chronic*. With David Trinidad, he is the coauthor of *By Myself: An Autobiography*.

Kristin Prevallet is the author of *I, Afterlife: Essay in Mourning Time* as well as *Shadow Evidence Intelligence*. She edited and introduced *A Helen Adam Reader*, and she teaches in the Institute for Writing Studies at St. John's University in Queens, New York.

Bin Ramke's tenth book of poems, *Theory of Mind: New and Selected Poems*, appeared in 2009. He is the editor of the *Denver Quarterly* at the University of Denver where he holds the Phipps Chair in English and has taught in the graduate program in creative writing since 1985. He also teaches on occasion at the School of the Art Institute of Chicago.

Jed Rasula is the author of the poetry titles *Tabula Rasula* and *Hot Wax*, and several scholarly works: *The American Poetry Wax Museum*, *This Compost*, *Syncopations*, and *Modernism and Poetic Inspiration*. He coedited *Imagining Language* with Steve McCaffery, and is working with Tim Conley on an anthology of metropolitan modernism, *Burning City*. He teaches at the University of Georgia.

Srikanth Reddy is the author of *Facts for Visitors*, which received the 2005 Asian American Literary Award for Poetry, and a book-length poem titled *Voyager*, forthcoming in 2011. A graduate of the Iowa Writers' Workshop and the doctoral program in English at Harvard University, Reddy is currently an assistant professor at the University of Chicago.

Barbara Jane Reyes is the author of *Gravities of Center*, *Poeta en San Francisco*, which received the James Laughlin Award of the Academy of American Poets, and the forthcoming *Diwata*.

Boyer Rickel's publications include *remanence*, *Taboo* (essays), *arreboles*, and two poetry chapbooks, *reliquary* and *Surrender Ode*. Recipient of poetry fellowships from the NEA and Arizona Commission on the Arts, he has taught in the University of Arizona Creative Writing Program since 1991.

Elizabeth Robinson has been recognized as a National Poetry Series Winner and a Foundation for Contemporary Arts 2008 Grants to Artists recipient. She is the author of ten books of poetry, most recently *The Orphan & its Relations*.

Martha Ronk is the author of eight books of poetry, most recently *Vertigo*, a National Poetry Series selection published in 2008. Her book of fiction, *Glass Grapes and other stories*, was published in 2008. She is a professor of English at Occidental College in Los Angeles.

Emily Rosko is the author of *Raw Goods Inventory*. She has received the Stegner, Ruth Lilly, and Javits fellowships.

Prageeta Sharma is the author of three books of poetry, *Bliss to Fill*, *The Opening Question*, and *Infamous Landscapes*. Sharma is an associate professor of English and the director of creative writing at the University of Montana in Missoula.

Evie Shockley is the author of *a half-red sea* (2006) and two chapbooks, and a coeditor of the poetry journal *jubilat*. She teaches African American literature and creative writing at Rutgers University, New Brunswick.

Eleni Sikelianos is the author of eight books, including, most recently, *Body Clock*. She teaches in and currently directs the Creative Writing Program at the University of Denver.

Richard Siken lives in Tucson.

Poet and critic Ron Silliman has published more than thirty books, most recently *The Age of Huts (compleat)* and *The Alphabet*. He is a member of the *Grand Piano* collective.

Tracy K. Smith is the author of *Duende*, winner of the 2006 James Laughlin Award of the Academy of American Poets, and *The Body's Question*, which won the 2002 Cave Canem Poetry Prize. She teaches at Princeton University.

Juliana Spahr's most recent book is *The Transformation*.

Sasha Steensen is the author of *A Magic Book*, *The Method*, *correspondence* (with Gordon Hadfield), and *The Future of an Illusion*. She edits Bonfire Press and serves as a poetry editor for *Colorado Review*; she teaches creative writing and literature courses as well as bookmaking and letterpress printing at Colorado State University.

Peter Streckfus's first book, *The Cuckoo*, was published in 2004. He is on the faculty of the Program in Creative Writing at the University of Alabama.

Cole Swensen is the author of twelve volumes of poetry; the most recent is *Ours*. She teaches at the Iowa Writers' Workshop and is a coeditor of the anthology *American Hybrid*.

Michael Theune edited *Structure & Surprise: Engaging Poetic Turns*. He teaches English at Illinois Wesleyan University in Bloomington, Illinois.

Tony Trigilio's recent publications include the poetry collection *The Lama's English Lessons* and the chapbook *With the Memory, Which is Enormous*. He teaches in the Creative Writing-Poetry Program at Columbia College Chicago, where he also coedits the poetry journal *Court Green*.

Spring Ulmer grew up off the grid in the backwoods of Vermont. She's the author of *Benjamin's Spectacles*, winner of the Kore Press First Book Award, and *The Age of Virtual Reproduction*, forthcoming.

Karen Volkman's books of poetry are *Nomina, Spar*, and *Crash's Law*. She teaches in the MFA program at the University of Montana.

Catherine Wagner is the author of *My New Job, Macular Hole*, and *Miss America*. Recent chapbooks include *Bornt, Articulate How*, and *Hole in the Ground*.

G. C. Waldrep's collections of poems are *Goldbeater's Skin, Disclamor*, and *Archicembalo*. He teaches at Bucknell University and lives in Lewisburg, Pennsylvania.

Mark Wallace is the author and editor of a number of books and chapbooks of poetry, fiction, and criticism, including most recently *Felonies of Illusion*. He teaches creative writing at Cal State San Marcos.

Tyrone Williams is the author of three collections of poetry: *c.c., On Spec*, and *The Hero Project of the Century*. He teaches literature and literary theory at Xavier University in Cincinnati, Ohio.

Mark Yakich's latest poetry collection is *The Importance of Peeling Potatoes in Ukraine*. He lives in New Orleans.

Jake Adam York is the author of two books of poems, *Murder Ballads* and *A Murmuration of Starlings*. Currently an associate professor of English and director of creative writing at the University of Colorado–Denver, he produces *Copper Nickel* with his students.

Stephanie Young lives and works in Oakland. Her books of poetry are *Picture Palace* and *Telling the Future Off*. She edited *Bay Poetics* and current editorial work includes Deep Oakland (www.deepoakland.org).

Timothy Yu is the author of *Journey to the West* and *Race and the Avant-Garde: Experimental and Asian American Poetry since 1965*. He lives in Madison, where he teaches at the University of Wisconsin.

Matthew Zapruder is the author of two collections of poetry: *American Linden* and *The Pajamaist*, as well as co-translator from Romanian, along with historian Radu Ioanid, of *Secret Weapon: Selected Late Poems of Eugen Jebeleanu*. He lives in San Francisco, works as an editor for Wave Books, and teaches in the low-residency MFA program at UC Riverside–Palm Desert. His third full-length collection of poems, *Come On All You Ghosts*, is forthcoming in 2010.

Andrew Zawacki is the author of *By Reason of Breakings, Anabranch*, and *Petals of Zero Petals of One*. He teaches at the University of Georgia.

Rachel Zucker is the author of four books of poetry, most recently *Museum of Accidents*, and coeditor, with Arielle Greenberg, of two anthologies. For more information, please visit: www.rachelzucker.net.

Index